Housing Markets in the United States and Japan

A National Bureau
of Economic Research
Conference Report

Housing Markets in the United States and Japan

Edited by Yukio Noguchi and
James M. Poterba

The University of Chicago Press

Chicago and London

YUKIO NOGUCHI is professor of economics at Hitotsubashi University. JAMES M. POTERBA is professor of economics at the Massachusetts Institute of Technology and director of the Public Economics Research Program at the National Bureau of Economic Research.

The University of Chicago Press, Chicago 60637
The University of Chicago Press, Ltd., London
© 1994 by the National Bureau of Economic Research
All rights reserved. Published 1994
Printed in the United States of America
03 02 01 00 99 98 97 96 95 94   1 2 3 4 5
ISBN: 0-226-59015-1 (cloth)

Library of Congress Cataloging-in Publication Data

Housing markets in the United States and Japan / edited by Yukio Noguchi and James M. Poterba.
    p.   cm. — (A National Bureau of Economic Research conference report)
    "The research papers collected in this volume were presented at a joint Japan Center for Economic Research (JCER)–National Bureau of Economic Research (NBER) conference in January 1991"— Acknowledgments.
    Includes bibliographical references and indexes.
    1. Housing—United States—Congresses.   2. Housing—Japan— Congresses.   I. Noguchi, Yukio, 1940–.   II. Poterba, James M.   III. Series: Conference report (National Bureau of Economic Research)
    HD7293.H68   1994
    381'.4569'080952—dc20   93–48441
                                                                     CIP

Contents

Acknowledgments

The research papers collected in this volume were presented at a joint Japan Center for Economic Research (JCER)–National Bureau of Economic Research (NBER) conference in January 1991. We are grateful to Yutaka Kosai, president of JCER, and Martin Feldstein, president of NBER, for laying the groundwork for such joint meetings. They also provided important guidance in shaping the agenda for this conference.

Organizing a conference with participants from two continents is not a simple task, and the staff at JCER and NBER provided outstanding logistical support for our meeting. We are particularly grateful to Ilana Hardesty of NBER, who attended the conference and served as conference coordinator, and to Hiromichi Mutoh and Professor Seiritsu Ogura of JCER for very able assistance. We also wish to thank Kirsten Davis, director of the NBER Conference Department, for ongoing help in planning and organizing the meeting.

After a conference, the real work of publishing the proceedings begins. We wish to thank Deborah Kiernan and Jane Konkel of the NBER and Kumiko Mizutani of the JCER for their help in preparing this volume for publication.

Introduction

Yukio Noguchi and James M. Poterba

The economics literature is replete with comparisons between various aspects of the Japanese and U.S. economies. Previous studies have analyzed their saving rates, their industrial structures, and their productivity growth rates. Until very recently, however, the housing markets in the two nations have escaped systematic comparison or contrast, perhaps reflecting a naive view that the housing market does not affect international trade or manufacturing productivity growth. Recent emphasis on the differences in personal saving between the two nations, however, has drawn attention to the role of the housing market in affecting wealth accumulation and the flow of saving available for corporate investment. The comparison between house price to income ratios in Japan and the United States is sometimes invoked as a key factor explaining the higher saving rate among young Japanese than among young U.S. households. More generally, because investment in housing capital comes at least in part at the expense of investment in other physical assets, such as plant and equipment, there is a growing realization that incentives for housing consumption and investment may be central factors in determining business investment and productivity growth.

Housing markets in both Japan and the United States have also attracted more attention, independently, in the five years. The rapid rise in Japanese land and housing prices in the late 1980s was an important factor in explaining the increase in share prices. The decline in real estate values, along with falling stock prices, in the early 1990s has led to concern over the fragility of some Japanese financial institutions. In the United States, the decline in nominal house prices in some major cities in the late 1980s triggered concern about the

Yukio Noguchi is professor of economics at Hitotsubashi University. James M. Poterba is professor of economics at the Massachusetts Institute of Technology and director of the Public Economics Research Program at the National Bureau of Economic Research.

possibility of a long-run house price collapse. Recent financial innovations such as the rise of home equity loans have made housing wealth more liquid, and are often cited as contributory factors in the decline of the U.S. personal saving rate.

Housing also plays a key role in comparisons between living standards in the United States and Japan. Since housing is a large component of the consumption bundle in both the United States and Japan, real wage comparisons using a price index of imported goods suggest that Japanese workers receive higher wages than their U.S. counterparts. When the comparison uses comparable consumption baskets including nontraded goods, however, the real wage of U.S. workers is higher because the cost of housing services is significantly lower in the United States than in Japan.

This volume brings together ten studies of the housing markets in Japan and the United States. There are two papers, one by a Japanese author and one by an American, on each of five major issues—house prices, the link between financial markets and housing markets, housing and the journey to work, housing and saving, and public policies toward housing. The papers provide a wealth of statistical information about the similarities and differences in housing markets in the two countries.

This brief introduction has three parts. The first provides an overview of the housing markets in Japan and the United States. It presents summary statistics comparing housing conditions, and the role of housing in the economy, for both nations. The second section summarizes the topic papers that make up the remainder of the volume. A brief conclusion suggests further directions for research.

Overview: Housing in Japan and the United States

Housing conditions are systematically better in the United States than in Japan. Table 1 reports several measures of housing quality for Japan, the United States, and three other developed nations. It shows that the average number of persons per room is substantially larger (0.71) in Japan than in the United States (0.50), and that the average living space in U.S. houses is more than 50 percent greater than in Japanese houses. Many Japanese homes still lack basic amenities. While only 2.4 percent of U.S. housing units lack access to a flush toilet, 41.8 percent of Japanese units lack such plumbing.[1] The 1988 *Survey on the Demand for Housing,* conducted by the Japanese Ministry of Construction, finds that 51.5 percent of households are dissatisfied with their housing conditions. More than one-third of homeowners want to enlarge or improve their current homes, and another third wish to switch to another house.

Current Japanese housing conditions are the results of a decades-long shortage of housing. Much of the urban housing stock was destroyed during World

---

1. Japanese Ministry of Construction, *Nihon no Juta ku Jijo,* rev. (Tokyo: Gyosei), 1993.

Table 1   **International Comparison of Housing Conditions**

	Japan	United States	Germany	France	United Kingdom
Rooms per house	4.7	5.1	4.5	3.7	5.0
Persons per room	.71	.50	.60	.75	.50
Area per house (m²)	81	135	94	85	N.A.
Home-ownership rate (%)	62	65	40	51	63
Average new house price/average household income	7.4	3.4	4.6	N.A.	4.4

Source: Chochiku Keizai Kenkyu Center, *Yearbook of Individual Financing* (1989) for all entries except last row, which is from Housing Industry Newspaper Company, *Housing Economy Databook.*

War II, and the shortage was compounded by rapid migration from rural to urban areas in the 1950s and 1960s. Industrial development was a national priority during this period, and housing investment was discouraged. Housing loans were not available from private financial institutions. As a result, the number of households sometimes exceed the number of houses in Japan.[2] In part because Japan has less housing per person or as a share in GNP than does the United States, the ratio of residential investment to GNP has been substantially higher in Japan than in the United States for most of the last two decades.

The United States has not experienced comparable periods of housing shortage. The volume of new housing built in a given year is subject to substantial variation, and a doubling in the level of new construction between a trough and a peak of the construction cycle is not unusual. Nevertheless the overall level of construction has been adequate to provide more than enough housing units for the stock of households. In the U.S. rental market in the late 1980s, the vacancy rate for housing units was sometimes above 10 percent.

Housing conditions in both the United States and Japan have improved over time. In Japan, the total floor space per dwelling rose 22 percent between 1968 and 1988, and the area per person rose even more quickly, by 71 percent.[3] This reflects a reduction in the number of individuals per housing unit, as well as an increase in housing unit size. In the United States, the median dwelling increased from 5.0 rooms in 1970 to 5.3 rooms in 1990. For new homes, the increase in apparent quality is even more dramatic. The average new single-family home completed in the United States in 1970 contained 1,500 square

2. The household-to-housing unit ratio was 0.96 in 1958, 1.01 in 1968, 1.08 in 1978, and 1.11 in 1988 (Japanese Statistics Bureau, *Housing Survey of Japan,* various issues).
   3. Ibid.

Table 2   Home ownership Rates, Japan and the United States, 1960–90 (%)

Year	Japan	United States
1950	N.A.	55.0
1960	68.4	61.9
1970	59.6	62.9
1980	61.2	65.6
1990	61.4[a]	64.1

Sources: Japan: Statistics Bureau, *Housing Survey of Japan.* Entries are interpolated as necessary from surveys conducted in years ending in 8 and 3. United States: 1950–70 from U.S. Bureau of the Census as reported in U.S. League of Savings Associations, *Savings and Loan Fact Book* 1979. More recent entries from Harvard University Joint Center for Housing Studies, *The State of the Nation's Housing 1991.*
[a]From 1988 survey.

feet of living area; this increased to 2,080 square feet by 1990. In 1970, 32 percent of all units completed had one bathroom, while only 48 percent had two or more. By 1990, 87 percent of new houses had two or more baths.[4]

Although the characteristics of housing units differ between the United States and Japan, the tenure mix—the fraction of households who own their own homes—is similar in the two nations. The current home-ownership rate is near 65 percent in both countries, although this reflects the convergence of two quite different trends. Table 2 presents time series on home-ownership rates in the two countries. In the United States, the home-ownership rate rose between the end of World War II and the mid-1980s. It has been stable, or possibly declined, since then. The Japanese home-ownership rate, however, declined in the two decades after World War II. This reflects the population migration from rural areas, where home-ownership rates are high, to urban areas, where renting is more common. The Japanese home-ownership rate has not changed substantially since 1970.

Overview of Subsequent Studies

The comparison of housing markets in Japan and the United States is an enormous undertaking. To structure and limit the subsequent analysis, we chose to focus on five issues that are central to understanding the housing markets in both countries. Our choice of topics necessarily excludes some that are of great importance in one nation but not in the other, such as the decay of central city housing in the United States or the policy-induced distortion between agricultural and residential land use in Japan. The remainder of this section presents a brief overview of the issues considered in the subsequent chapters, and introduces their research findings.

4. U.S. Bureau of the Census, *Construction Reports C-25: Characteristics of New Housing* (various issues).

Land and House Prices

Both the United States and Japan have experienced rising real house prices during the last twenty years. In Japan the most rapid price increase took place in the late 1980s, and it was attributable largely to rising land prices. In the months since our conference was held, land prices have stabilized, and in many areas, they have declined. For the nation as a whole, prices fell just over 5 percent between 1991 and early 1992, while in Tokyo and some other urban areas, the price decline was more than 15 percent.[5] In the United States, the 1970s were the period of most rapid price appreciation, and the 1980s were a period of stable real house prices. The U.S. real price increase of the 1970s was much smaller, however, than the Japanese price increase of the late 1980s.

Table 3 presents summary information on real house prices in both countries. It shows the 30 percent real price increase in the United States during the 1970s, and the 45 percent increase in Japan a decade later. The table also reports the ratio of the price of an average house to average household annual income. This ratio is higher in Japan, often by a factor of two, than in the United States for the entire sample period. In addition, this crude measure of housing affordability shows that housing became less affordable in Japan during the mid- and late 1980s. At the end of the 1980s, an average house in the greater Tokyo metropolitan area cost 7.4 times the average worker's pretax income. As the data in table 1 suggest, this ratio is higher than that of any other major developed country.

The principal source of rising house prices in Japan was rising land prices. The Japanese paper on house prices, by Yukio Noguchi, is therefore directed toward understanding the causes and consequences of the recent price run-up. The paper argues that it is difficult to reconcile the time series on Japanese land prices in the 1980s with an "efficient markets" view in which land price changes are driven by fundamentals involving the supply of or demand for land. Rather, the paper concludes that the land price appreciation was due in part to a "speculative bubble." The paper also considers the long-term differences between house prices in Japan and other nations. It concludes that high prices in Japan are largely the result of government policies that distort land use, rather than an absolute land shortage.

The companion paper, on house prices in the United States, is by Karl E. Case. He summarizes the available time-series data on real house price movements in the United States. The paper focuses on the period since 1960, although it also provides some longer-term historical data. Case emphasizes the important differences in the house price experiences in different regions of the United States, and notes that one area may experience rapidly rising house prices while another region faces falling prices. This paper also addresses the

---

5. Report of the National Land Agency as summarized in the *New York Times,* 28 March 1992, 37.

Table 3   **House Prices and Annual Household Income**

Year	Index of Real House Prices		Average House Price/ Average Annual Income	
	Japan	United States	Japan	United States
1970	—	101.4	5.4	2.6
1975	2101	109.2	6.4	3.0
1980	3051	132.9	6.2	3.5
1985	3537	123.1	5.6	3.2
1989	5371	125.0	7.4	3.2

Sources: Japan: 1970 entry is from Takatoshi Ito, *The Japanese Economy* (Cambridge: MIT Press, 1991), 412. Subsequent data are from Housing Industry Newspaper Company, *Housing Economy Databook.* Real house price is the ratio of the nominal price of new units divided by the consumer price index, deflated to 1987 prices. United States: House price index is the price of a constant-quality house (1987 quality, thousands of dollars) divided by the personal consumption deflator. The ratio of house price to income is constructed as the median price of an *existing* home sold in a given year, divided by median household income. Both data series are drawn from the *Statistical Abstract of the United States.*

extent to which house prices should be viewed as set in a rational asset market. Case observes that there is downward nominal rigidity in changing prices to meet market conditions.

Housing and Financial Markets

Financial policies and credit market conditions can exert profound influences on the level of new construction and the demand for housing. In the United States, housing investment has historically been subsidized through a variety of credit market institutions, such as savings and loans. Policy has been quite different in Japan, with strict limits on the availability of housing finance and consequent restriction on the supply of new homes.

The paper on housing finance in Japan, by Miki Seko, provides detailed information on the structure of financial arrangements that are used by home buyers in Japan. The paper explores the role of the Japan Housing Loan Corporation, which is responsible for one-third of the mortgage originations in Japan, in affecting housing demand. It provides important information on typical mortgage loan characteristics, such as the down-payment ratio of approximately 30 percent. The paper closes with a discussion of options for increasing the flow of financial capital to the Japanese housing market.

The companion paper by Patric Hendershott tracks the rapid changes in the links between credit markets and housing markets during the 1980s. In the three decades after World War II, most mortgage loans were originated by savings institutions, such as thrifts and savings and loans. These institutions attracted a large inflow of saving deposits in part because they were legally sheltered from competition from commercial banks and other financial intermediaries. The thrift institutions were also covered by various government deposit insurance programs. The prominence of these institutions in housing finance resulted in occasional "credit crunches" when deposit inflow was inadequate to cover the demand for new home purchases, but on balance provided a subsidy to housing.

Beginning in the late 1970s, mortgage markets in the United States became better integrated with other credit markets. The market for mortgage-backed securities, bundles of individual home mortgages that were traded as financial commodities, became one of the largest fixed-income security markets, and the inflow of funds to thrift institutions ceased to be an important factor in housing finance. The increasing sophistication of investors in mortgage securities, however, led to a wave of increasingly complicated mortgage products, such as adjustable-rate mortgages and insured mortgages. Hendershott explains how these changes have affected the cost of borrowing for house purchase, and what effects they will have on housing markets in the future.

Housing Markets and the Journey to Work

The third pair of papers tackles an issue that is central to understanding the local structure and housing markets and metropolitan areas. How do housing market conditions interact with commuting decisions? The Japanese paper, prepared by Tatsuo Hatta and Toru Ohkawara, begins by describing the lengthy commutes faced by many Japanese workers. They focus on the Tokyo metropolitan area and argue that, because Tokyo is the largest metropolitan area in the world and housing is scarce in the central city, workers have little alternative but to commute long distances.

The Hatta/Ohkawara paper begins with a careful comparison of Tokyo and New York, as a means to provide insight on the structure of large cities in Japan and the United States. The paper then considers two public policies that affect commuting distances in Japan. The first is the income tax provision allowing employers to deduct their costs of reimbursing employees' commuting expenses. The authors demonstrate that this provision raises land prices near Tokyo, because it reduces the amount commuters must pay to reach the center city. The second policy concerns land use. The paper shows that the provisions that encourage agriculture relatively close to large cities and inhibit skyscrapers in downtown Tokyo lead to less concentrated employment in Tokyo than in New York. The paper concludes that these policies have distorted the allocation of jobs and the length of journeys to work and that removing these distortions would result in efficiency gains.

The companion paper by Michelle White highlights the differences between journeys to work in the United States and Japan. White presents descriptive information on commuting patterns and shows that most commuting in the United States involves trips in private cars rather than the use of public transit, as in Japan. White also argues that the traditional focus on a central business district where jobs are located and a periphery of residential suburbs is an increasingly inaccurate description of urban structure in the United States.

The ongoing shift of jobs to sectors that do not require access to harbors, rail lines, or other features of central cities has resulted in job migration to the perimeter of many urban areas. This has led to shorter commuting times for many workers, but also has induced a set of long-range problems for U.S. cities, which are faced with shrinking employment bases, declining housing stocks, and rising tax burdens.

Housing and Saving

One of the key factors inducing recent interest in the housing markets of Japan and the United States is the possibility that differential rates of saving for house purchase explain part of the disparity in personal saving rates in the two countries. The paper by Toshiaki Tachibanaki provides a wealth of valuable information on the interaction between housing market conditions and household saving. It documents the striking decline over time in the fraction of Japanese households who claim their saving is primarily for house purchase, and argues that this is primarily due to renter households in Tokyo and other metropolitan areas *giving up* on the hope of ever being able to afford a home. The rapid rise in land and house prices in the 1980s has apparently led to a group of "discouraged renters" who are not saving to purchase a house as they might have two decades ago. In spite of this trend, saving for housing is still an important factor in Japanese personal saving. The study documents the key role of forced saving through mortgage principal repayment and notes that its importance has increased through time. Finally, Tachibanaki observes that intergenerational wealth transfers play a key role in housing acquisition. Nearly one-third of Japanese homeowners obtained their house as a result of bequest or inheritance.

Jonathan Skinner presents a companion paper on housing and saving in the United States. After describing the important role of housing in the net worth of U.S. households and pointing out that for many low- and middle-income households their home is their principal asset, his paper focuses on the effect of rising house prices on household saving. The 30 percent increase in real house prices during the 1970s could affect the household saving rate in various ways. It could lead to increased spending by current homeowners, who receive a windfall when their house price rises. It could lead to increased saving by current renters, who plan to purchase a home in the future. It could also lead to reduced saving by some renters, if the "discouraged renter" model that applies to some Japanese households applies in the United States. Skinner notes that the existing empirical evidence suggests that some homeowners increased their spending as a result of the house price increase, while there is not much evidence for the "discouraged renter" view.

Public Policies toward Housing Markets

The final two papers examine the impact of public policies on housing markets in the United States and Japan. This is a very broad topic, and each paper narrows the subject area in various ways. Takatoshi Ito describes the Japanese policy environment, focusing primarily on tax policies. While credit policies are another important public policy instrument affecting housing markets in Japan, this subject was examined in an earlier chapter. Ito argues that several tax policies have dramatic effects on the structure of Japanese housing markets. First, the relatively light property tax burden on land in agricultural uses distorts land use patterns and precludes converting agricultural land near cities to housing or commercial development that would be more profitable in the absence of tax incentives for farming. Second, the favorable bequest tax treatment of real estate induces "lock-in" effects, with elderly households choosing not to sell their homes and move to alternative accommodations, because they would forgo substantial tax benefits by doing so. Finally, the paper outlines a range of tax incentives for company-provided and government-provided housing that arguably reduce the quality of housing in the owner-occupied and rental housing markets.

The last paper, a companion paper on public policy and housing in the United States by James Poterba, also focuses on tax policy issues. In the United States, tax subsidies to both owner-occupied and rental housing are substantial. The magnitude of these subsidies has varied over time, and while historically there were credit market subsidies to housing investment, these subsidies have largely vanished. Poterba describes the changes through time in the level of housing market subsidy, explaining the very substantial tax incentives for home ownership in the late 1970s, when high inflation rates combined with high marginal tax rates and interest deductibility to result in very low user costs of owner-occupied housing. The paper also explains the important changes in the tax treatment of rental housing in both the 1981 and 1986 tax reforms. The 1981 reform substantially expanded tax subsidies to rental properties, while the 1986 reform countermanded this policy and eliminated these incentives. The paper provides an overview of the various other public policies that affect housing in the United States, including a range of instruments designed to encourage the provision of housing for low-income families.

Future Directions

The papers in this volume only begin the vast task of comparing the housing markets in Japan and the United States. They highlight the institutional differences between the two nations and suggest the need for further empirical research to quantify their effects. The issues they raise are of interest both for understanding how the efficiency of the domestic economy might be improved and for considering the link between housing markets and international economic linkages.

1 Land Prices and House Prices in Japan

Yukio Noguchi

1.1 Introduction

Japan has had a serious housing problem throughout most of the postwar period. Although the problem of absolute scarcity of dwellings no longer exists, housing conditions remain extremely unsatisfactory today although Japan has become one of the world's largest economic powers. Spaces are narrow, locations are inconvenient, and related social infrastructures are insufficient. Above all, houses are extremely expensive.

One may propose a number of reasons why the housing problem remains serious in Japan. But no one would deny that the single most important reason is land prices, which are significantly higher than in other countries and have continued to rise almost every year during the postwar period. The sharp rise in land prices during the latter half of the 1980s has aggravated the problem. It is widely recognized that the land price problem is not only the heart of the housing problem but also one of the most serious social and economic problems of present-day Japan.

In this paper, I discuss major issues related to the land problem in Japan, focusing on the land price issue. In section 1.2, I present several facts and data. I point out that the housing problem in large cities in Japan is almost synonymous with the land price problem, because most of the housing cost consists of land purchase cost. I also point out that the extraordinary land price inflation during the 1980s in the Tokyo and Osaka areas has considerably lowered the house-purchasing power of wage income. Section 1.3 is the discussion of the cause of the recent land price inflation. The focus of the discussion is bubble versus fundamentals. My conclusion is that the land price inflation during the 1980s cannot be explained unless the bubble element is introduced. This is

Yukio Noguchi is professor of economics at Hitotsubashi University.

demonstrated in two ways: first, by showing a difference between present discounted value of rents and the actual land price, and second, by showing the deviation of the actual price from the price obtained from a land price equation. Section 1.4 is an examination of structural factors underlying the chronically high land price in Japan. I argue that the essential cause for high land prices is not the absolute shortage of land but various social and economic factors that enhance the value of land as a type of marketable asset. Particularly important are distortions brought about by the tax system and the Land Lease Law. Finally, in section 1.5, I review recent trends in government land policies and discuss their implications.

1.2   The Housing Problem and the Land Price Problem

1.2.1   Share of Land Purchase Cost in Housing Cost

In order to evaluate the relative weight of the land price problem in the housing problem, I calculate the share of land purchase cost in housing cost for model cases in several Japanese cities.[1] The figures shown in table 1.1 indicate a large regional difference in the nature of the problem. In local cities, the share is less than one-half. In small local cities, it is somewhere around 30–40 percent. This ratio is about the same as that in other countries. Thus, in these cities, the land problem is not the major obstacle to improving housing conditions.

The situation is considerably different in large cities, however, where the land purchase cost is over 60 percent of housing costs. In the Tokyo and Osaka areas, it is nearly 90 percent even in suburban sites. The ratio becomes as high as 98.5 percent in the central district of Tokyo. In these regions, therefore, the housing problem is almost synonymous with the land problem or land price problem.

At this point, one may wonder why Japanese people stick to buying a house with land rather than renting a house or buying a house with leased land. One reason is the supply-side condition. As discussed in section 1.4, the new supply of leased land is virtually nil due to the excessive protection of the lessee's right provided by the Land Lease Law. It is true that there are new supplies of rented houses, but most of them are for students, single persons, or couples without children who will not occupy the house for a very long period. This is due to the protection of tenants provided by the Building Lease Law. It follows that one is forced to buy land at a certain stage of one's life cycle if one wishes to live in a decent house. This is true not only for a detached house but also for a condominium, because land purchase cost is included in the condomin-

1. In this calculation, a detached house of a standard size (site 167 square meters, house 89 square meters) is assumed. The land price used in this calculation is local government benchmark price (Kijun Chika, July 1989).

Table 1.1   **Share of Land Cost in Housing Cost for Model Cases**

	Land Price per Square Meter[a]	Land Cost (a)	Construction Cost (b)	Total Cost (c)	Ratio (a/c)
Tokyo					
Minato	580	138,371	2,047	140,418	0.985
Suginami	106	25,289	2,047	27,336	0.925
Machida	39	9,304	2,047	11,351	0.820
Other big cities					
Osaka	60	10,020	1,469	11,489	0.872
Nagoya	26	4,342	1,469	5,811	0.747
Hiroshima	17	2,839	1,469	4,308	0.659
Fukuoka	14	2,338	1,469	3,807	0.614
Local cities					
Otaru	4	668	1,469	2,137	0.313
Akita	5	835	1,469	2,304	0.362
Toyama	8	1,336	1,469	2,805	0.476
Kurashiki	6	1,002	1,469	2,471	0.406
Miyazaki	6	1,002	1,469	2,471	0.406

Notes: Prices are 10,000 yen. Assumptions are: (1) site, 167 square meters; house, 89 square meters. (2) Housing construction cost per square meter: 230,000 yen in Tokyo, and 165,000 yen in other cities.

[a]Land price is local government benchmark price (Kijun Chika), National Land Agency (July 1989).

ium price. The demand-side reason is that people regard a house as an asset that produces capital gain. In fact, it is said that people buy a house in order to own rather than to live.

It follows that, as far as the housing problem in large cities is concerned, the land price problem is the most important element. I will therefore confine my argument in this paper to the land price issue.

1.2.2   Level of Land Price

As is well known, land prices in Japan are extremely high compared to those in other countries. Since systematic data are difficult to obtain in other countries, a comparison is made here only with U.K. data.[2] Residential sites that command the highest prices in the United Kingdom are located in the inner city of London, and the price of land was about £4 million per hectare, or £100,000 per square meter, in 1986. According to table 1.2, which shows the government benchmark prices (Koji Chika) of residential sites in Japan, one square meter of land at locations in Tokyo comparable to the above site in London costs £4 million, or forty times that in London.[3] Needless to say, inter-

2. Valuation Office, Property Market Report no. 46, Autumn 1986. Comparison with the United Kingdom is meaningful because its natural conditions are similar to that of Japan.
3. There are several land price indices: (1) government benchmark price (GBMP, Koji Chika): about 70 percent of market price; (2) local government benchmark price (Kijun Chika): same level

Table 1.2   **Residential Land Price Index (1983 = 100)**

	1984	1985	1986	1987	1988	1989	1990	1991
Greater Tokyo	102.2	103.9	107.0	130.1	219.3	220.2	234.7	250.2
Tokyo	102.9	105.9	112.7	169.6	283.2	265.3	264.5	264.8
Special								
wards	103.2	107.2	117.9	208.5	300.5	284.9	286.0	286.9
Kanagawa	102.0	103.6	106.0	118.8	220.7	203.9	205.3	211.3
Saitama	101.5	102.0	102.3	104.7	167.3	181.5	202.0	226.4
Chiba	101.8	102.6	103.4	109.8	179.3	210.3	261.6	312.6
Greater Osaka	103.6	106.7	109.5	113.2	134.3	178.2	278.1	296.2
Osaka	103.5	106.9	110.4	115.2	138.9	188.2	298.5	304.8
Kyoto	103.9	107.1	110.5	114.3	124.5	164.1	274.2	315.1
Hyogo	103.6	106.0	107.1	109.7	140.1	182.6	269.3	292.2
Nara	103.2	105.8	107.7	109.5	112.7	143.0	214.8	235.2
Greater Nagoya	102.4	104.0	105.5	107.2	115.0	139.9	160.9	191.1
Aichi	102.2	103.7	105.1	106.7	115.1	135.6	163.9	192.7
Mie	103.7	106.0	108.1	109.9	112.2	118.0	136.0	173.8

Source: National Land Agency, Koji Chika (benchmark land price), published yearly.

Notes: Government benchmark price (Koji Chika). The indices are those of January 1 of each year indicated. For example, land price in Greater Tokyo has increased by 234.7/220.2 in 1989.

national comparison of land prices must be done with caution, because the underlying legal system as well as the nature of land price in statistics may be different in different countries. Even considering these conditions, the above data would be sufficient to demonstrate the abnormal level of land prices in Japan.

There is an important caveat to this fact, however. If we compare the cost of using space as represented by office rental, we find no significant difference between the two countries. The cost of renting one square meter of office space at Marunouchi, a business district of Tokyo, is around £200,000 per year including guarantee deposits. In London, it costs £100,000 at locations comparable to Marunouchi, meaning that office rental at Marunouchi is only twice as high as that in London. Thus, space utilization cost as measured by the office rental costs in Japan, surprisingly, is not so high as the land price would lead us to believe. This poses a puzzle: if land price is the discounted present value of rents, why is land price in Japan so high?[4]

---

as the GBMP; (3) assessed price for the inheritance tax (Rosenka): about 70 percent of the GBMP; (4) assessed price for the property tax: ratio to the GBMP is lower than the Rosenka. The ratios are different in different locations. The GBMPs are calculated for about twenty thousand standard points on January 1 every year. Price of each point is evaluated by two official appraisers. The Evaluation Committee of the National Land Agency reviews the reports by the appraisers and makes final judgments. The prices are presumed to capture the "normal prices." Thus both discounted present value of rentals and actual transaction prices at similar locations are taken into consideration. Local government benchmark prices are calculated in a similar way.

4. Structural factors discussed in section 1.4 provide partial answers. In addition, the difference in expected future growth in rentals is an important factor. While rentals reflect present use of

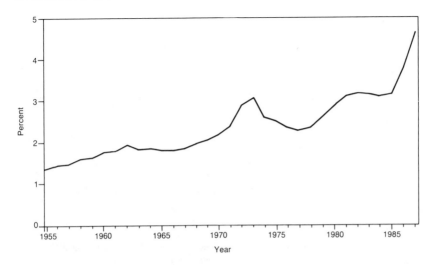

Fig. 1.1   Ratio of land asset to GDP

Note: Land asset is total private land value in the National Account Statistics.
Source: Economic Planning Agency, *Kokumin Keizai Keisan Tokei Nenpo (Yearbook of National Account Statistics),* issued yearly.

1.2.3   Rate of Increase of Land Price

Figure 1.1 shows the long-run trend of nationwide land value in terms of the ratio to GDP. The ratio has a long-run upward trend. This reflects a long-run increase in land productivity brought about by the land use conversion from agricultural to urban use and by the accumulation of capital. The average annual growth rate is about 2 percent for the period 1955 through 1985. Increases of this magnitude seem to be reasonable. Thus, as far as the trend in the national average until the mid-1980s is concerned, land price increase cannot be regarded as extraordinary.[5]

The ratio shows short-run fluctuations from time to time, however. The deviation from the trend first occurred in the early 1960s, and then in the early 1970s. The deviation during the second half of the 1980s is the third burst in the postwar period. This kind of fluctuation, rather than the long-run trend of land price increase, should be regarded as problematic.

Table 1.2 shows the trend of land prices in the three major urban areas in Japan during recent years. In Tokyo, land prices almost tripled during 1986 and 1987. During this period, income increased approximately 10 percent. Thus, house-purchasing power of wage income decreased to less than one-half of what it was two years earlier.

---

land, in many cases there are possibilities of converting land into more productive use in the future. Such possibilities may be reflected in land price.

5. Regression analysis in section 1.3 supports the hypothesis that the ratio of land value to GDP has been constant since 1977.

Table 1.3   **Ratio of Average Condominium Price to Annual Income**

	1984	1985	1986	1987	1988	1989
Greater Tokyo	5.64	5.62	5.36	6.48	8.14	8.62
0–9 km area	6.93	6.95	7.10	10.89	15.62	15.31
10–19 km area	6.15	5.78	5.93	7.93	10.43	10.68
20–30 km area	5.20	5.12	4.94	5.86	7.25	8.18
Greater Osaka	4.44	4.36	4.13	4.34	4.94	6.27
Greater Nagoya	3.53	3.54	3.45	3.51	3.89	4.27

Source: Toshi Kaihatsu Kyokai, *Jutaku Kakaku to Sarariman Syotoku tono Kairi Zesei no ta meni (For the reduction of the discrepancy between housing prices and workers' income),* issued yearly.
Notes: Average annual salary is 6.4 million yen. (The same figure is used for all areas.) Average space of a condominium is 75 square meters.

Table 1.3 shows this fact in a more concrete way. It is usually said that the most expensive house that can be purchased by an ordinary worker is about five times the annual salary. If the price of a house is within this limit, interest payments would be less that one-seventh of annual salary in cases where half of the purchase cost is financed by a loan and the interest rate is 5 percent. In 1984, the average price of a standard condominium in Tokyo was roughly within this limit. But the average ratio of condominium price to annual income rose to 8.6 in 1989. This means that the share of interest payments to annual income would be 22 percent with the same assumptions. If we consider the repayment of principal, the total payment would be somewhere around one-half of annual income. This means that it has become impossible for an average worker to purchase a house in Tokyo, based solely on wage income.

1.3   An Analysis of the Recent Land Price Inflation

1.3.1   Is Concentration in Tokyo the Major Cause?

In this section, I analyze the extraordinary land price increase during the latter half of the 1980s. The most important issue in this discussion is whether the major cause was changes in the fundamentals, especially changes in the economic structure, or speculative bubbles. "Fundamental price" of land is the discounted present value of future rentals. "Bubble" is the difference between the actual price and the fundamental price.[6]

If land price increases are caused by changes in economic structure, the increases result from a rise in land productivity. Hence, policies that directly aim at reducing land prices should not (or cannot) be taken. Land price reduc-

6. There are of course many difficulties in calculating the fundamental price. For example, "future rentals" means expected future rentals, which are unobserved variables. Additional difficulties are discussed in section 1.3.3.

Table 1.4   **Trends in Land Price and Office Rentals (indices: 1980 - 100)**

Year	Land Price, Commercial Districts		Office Rental		GNP
	Tokyo	Osaka	Tokyo	Osaka	
1980	100.0	100.0	100.0	100.0	100.0
1985	150.6	132.0	128.1	123.3	131.1
1989	413.9	297.4	231.0	152.0	161.7
1990	421.7	435.1	258.6	186.4	170.2

Sources: Land price: National Land Agency, Koji Chika (benchmark land price), issued yearly. Office rental: Japan Building Association, *Biru Jittai Chosa no ta meni (Summary of Building Survey),* issued yearly. GNP: Economic Planning Agency, *Kokumin Keizai Keisan Tokei Nenpo (Yearbook of National Account Statistics),* issued yearly.

tion can be expected only as a result of policies such as increases in the supply or urban land or diversification of economic activities to local cities. On the other hand, if a bubble is the major element, land prices can and should be the direct target of land policy, because land prices cannot be regarded as a proper signal for allocating the land resource.

Some people argue that land price inflation during the 1980s was caused by structural changes in the Japanese economy, especially the concentration of new economic activities in Tokyo.[7] The importance of Tokyo as an international city has undoubtedly increased, and new trends such as the internationalization of financial activities have increased the demand for offices, which has worsened the shortage of land in the central business district of Tokyo.

This is reflected in the trend of office rentals. As shown in table 1.4, the rate of increase in office rental costs in Tokyo was about the same as that of GNP until the mid-1980s and became greater during the late 1980s. It must be noted, however, that the rate of land price increase was greater than that of office rent. This means that the land price inflation in Tokyo cannot be explained only by the concentration of economic activities in Tokyo. Moreover, the increase of land prices was not isolated in the Tokyo area but diffused to other areas. The figures in table 1.2 indicate that, while rises in land price in the Tokyo area have subsided, the upward pressure on land prices spilled into the Osaka area, and then to Nagoya and other regional cities. If the concentration in Tokyo were the main cause, land prices in other cities would not have been affected. As shown in table 1.4, land prices in Osaka increased remarkably, while office rental costs grew at about the same rate as that of GNP.

7. Miyao (1988) argues that land price movement can be completely explained by changes in industrial and urban structure and changes in the interest rate.

1.3.2 Easy Money Policy

Let us next look at the relations between land price inflation in the 1980s and monetary policy during this period.

In an effort to curb the sharp appreciation of the yen following the Plaza Accord of September 1985, the Bank of Japan relaxed monetary conditions considerably. The official discount rate, which was 5 percent until January 1986, was lowered in several steps to a historic low postwar level of 2.5 percent in February 1987. Long-term interest rates also fell from 6.6 percent in October 1985 to 5.0 percent in February 1987, and further to 3.8 percent in May 1987.

It is generally believed that this provided the major impetus for land prices to soar. In fact, this period coincides exactly with the period in which land prices began to rise, especially in the central district of Tokyo. (As seen in table 1.2, residential land prices in the Special Wards of Tokyo increased by 78 percent in 1986.) Thus, there is no denying that the easy money policy was one of the major causes of the sharp increase in land prices during the 1980s.

Let us examine this point further. As shown in table 1.5, net purchases of land by the nonfinancial corporate sector increased dramatically during the latter half of the 1980s. Cumulative purchases during 1985–89 amounted to about 28 trillion yen. This exceeds the amount during the preceding five years by as much as 25 trillion yen. The difference can be interpreted as "speculative purchase." This amounts to 4.4 percent of the total holding of land by that sector, which was 567 trillion yen at the end of 1989.

On the other hand, lending from banks to real estate businesses increased by about 22 trillion yen during the same period. Besides, there was lending from "nonbanks" (lending institutions having no deposits). The increase dur-

Table 1.5	Net Purchase of Land (billion yen)	
Fiscal Year	Nonfinancial Corporate Sector	Household Sector
1975	676	−1,911
1980	1,130	−3,764
1981	1,336	−4,062
1982	142	−2,864
1983	530	−3,316
1984	415	−3,170
1985	3,841	−6,781
1986	3,278	−6,308
1987	4,602	−8,288
1988	6,480	−10,926
1989	10,076	−14,475

Source: Economic Planning Agency, *Kokumin Keizai Keisan Tokei Nenpo (Yearbook of National Account Statistics),* 1990.

ing this period is estimated at about 18 trillion yen. On the other hand, business fixed investment by real estate companies during this period was 12 trillion yen. This implies that about 28 trillion yen was spent for purchasing land.

To be precise, the net land purchase figure and the lending figure cannot be compared directly because the former does not include transactions within the sector and the latter refers only to the real estate business. However, these differences are not so great, since most of the purchases by the corporate sector consist of those made by the real estate companies and most of the sales are from the household sector. We can thus conclude that most of the speculative purchases of land were financed by lending from the financial institutions.

1.3.3   Calculations of the Discounted Present Value of Rents

I have argued above that the concentration of business in Tokyo and the easy money policy may have contributed to the land price inflation, especially in Tokyo. However, this does not mean that land price inflation can be completely explained by the fundamentals. Let us therefore examine how much of the actual land price increase can be explained by the above factors.

One way to do this is to calculate the theoretical price of land, which is represented by the discounted present value of rent, and compare it with the actual land price. This is not straightforward calculation, since the actual rent is far below the economically reasonable level, due to the Land Lease Law. Therefore, I use the data on rental costs of office buildings.[8] Needless to say, the result of this practice depends heavily on assumptions concerning the capitalization rate and the expected growth of rentals.[9] Here I chose these parameters so that the calculated land value in the central business district of Tokyo (Otemachi) becomes equal to the actual land value.[10] Because of this procedure, results obtained here are only the relative, rather than the absolute, level of the theoretical price.

The results are shown in the "theoretical price" column of table 1.6. In most of the locations in Tokyo, the market price of land is twice as high as the theoretical price. The difference is still larger in Fukoka and Sapporo. The

8. Theoretical land price was calculated by

$$(L + nB)r = anR - tL - snB,$$

where L = land price, n = ratio of the total floor space to site area (number of stories of building when 100 percent of site is used), B = construction cost, a = rentable space ratio, R = rental, t = property tax rate on land, s = property tax rate on building, and, r = required rate of return. Assumptions used for the calculation are n = 8, b = (10,000 yen per square meter) = 24, a = 0.7, r = 0.0411, t = 0.005, and s = 0.014. In the case of a residential house, B = 18, n = 1. (The value of B is slightly lower than what was assumed in table 1.1. This is due to the rise in construction cost.)

9. In the regression analysis reported in section 1.3.4, we find that capitalization rate is more stable than the actual interest rate. This does not, however, reveal what the appropriate capitalization rate is.

10. I chose Otemachi as the basis because it is a well-developed area, so that there would relatively little speculative element in land price. Since the assumed volumetric ratio is different from the actual value, the theoretical price is not exactly equal to the actual price.

same calculation was done for residential land using the data of apartment rentals, and the results are shown as theoretical prices in table 1.7. Again, the actual price is about twice as high as the theoretical price.

From these findings, we can conclude that land is valued considerably above its theoretical value. The difference between the theoretical and the market prices can be interpreted only as arising from excessive expectations for capital gains, namely, a speculative bubble.

1.3.4   Estimation of the Bubble Using a Regression Model

Another way to examine the existence and the magnitude of the bubble is to estimate a land price equation and to regard the difference between the estimated and the actual price as the bubble.

For this purpose, I consider a model in which land rent is a fixed proportion of product and land price is determined as its discounted present value. More specifically, I estimate the following equation:

Table 1.6   **Prices of Selected Office Sites in Japan**

	Current Market Price ($¥10,000/m^2$)[a]	Annual Office Rental Cost ($¥10,000/m^2$)[b]	Theoretical Price ($¥10,000/m^2$)[c]
Otemachi, Chiyoda-ku	2,500 (1,650)	19.1	2,149
Ginza, Chuo-ku	2,300 (1,600)	11.5	1,203
Shimbashi, Minato-ku	2,850 (2,050)	12.9	1,377
Akasaka, Minato-ku	2,080 (1,300)	10.0	1,016
Nishi-shinjuku, Shinjuku-ku	2,860 (1,600)	11.6	1,216
Yokohama city	1,140 (635)	4.2	295
Umeda, Osaka	1,820 (1,210)	6.6	593
Fukuoka city	820 (600)	2.9	133
Nagoya city	940 (630)	4.2	295
Sapporo city	653 (430)	3.4	195

[a]Current market prices are based on the GBMPs reported in 1987. Those in parentheses are for 1986.

[b]Rents are based on a survey reported in the February 23, 1987 issue of *Nihon Keizai Shinbun*.

[c]Method for calculating theoretical price is described in footnote 8.

Table 1.7   **Prices of Selected Residential Sites in Japan**

Location	Market Price ($¥10,000/m^2$)[a]	Rental Cost ($¥10,000/m^2$ year)[b]	Theoretical Price ($¥10,000/m^2$)
Areas bordering on the Chuo Line			
Yotsuya	445	7.9	153
Nakano	110	4.2	71
Ogikubo	105	3.3	51
Kichijoji	93	3.1	46
Musashi-Koganei	48	2.6	36
Areas bordering on the Toyoko Line			
Shoto	545	6.9	131
Nakameguro	150	3.9	64
Jiyugaoka	170	4.3	73
Hiyoshi	54	3.2	49

[a]Market price represents GBMPs reported in 1987 (residential land within the radius of one kilometer from the nearby railway stations).

[b]Estimated rents for apartments are based on advertisements carried by *Shukan Jutaku Joho* (Weekly housing news), September 1987 (those units located within a distance of fifteen minutes' walk from nearby stations).

$$\log PLAND = a + b \log GDPLND + c \log INTRST + d\ GROWTH + \\ e\ ISLAND + f \log NEBDEN + g \log SECOND + \\ h \log TERTIA,$$

where $PLAND$ = real urban land price by prefecture, calculated as land value divided by urban area (100 yen per square meter); $GDPLND$ = real prefecture GDP per unit of urban land (100 yen per square meter); $INTRST$ = long-term real interest rate (yield of government bonds, annual percentage rate); $GROWTH$ = population growth rate (annual percentage rate); $ISLAND$ = dummy variable equal to one if prefecture is not on Honshu; $NEBDEN$ = population density in neighboring prefectures (number of people per square kilometer); $SECOND$ = share of the secondary industry in prefecture GDP (percentage); and, $TERTIA$ = share of the tertiary industry in prefecture GDP (percentage).

If the above theory of land price determination is correct, and if the long-term interest rate is the appropriate capitalization rate, then the coefficients b and c should be equal to one and minus one, respectively. The $GROWTH$ variable is used as a proxy for the expected growth of rents.[11] The $ISLAND$ and

11. I also tried the rate of growth of prefecture GDP. The coefficients of other variables are not significantly affected. Since the use of population growth produces a better result in terms of the standard error and the coefficient of determination, this result is reported here.

the *NEBDEN* variables have been used to capture spillover effects of economic activity. The former should have a negative sign and the latter a positive sign. The *SECOND* and the *TERTIA* variables are intended to represent possible differences in production technologies in different industries. All nominal variables were deflated by the GDP deflator.

The above equation was estimated using the forty-seven prefectures' data during the period 1977–87. The result is shown in table 1.8. The equation fits well with a fairly high coefficient of determination. All variables except for the log *SECOND* have significant coefficients with the right signs.

That the estimated value of b is close to unity supports the above theory of land price determination. On the other hand, the absolute value of the estimated coefficient of the log *INTRST* variable is significantly smaller than one. This seems to imply that the true discount rate used for capitalizing land rent is more stable than the observed long-term interest rate. In view of the fact that land does not depreciate so that rent can be obtained for infinitely long periods, this seems to be a reasonable result.

From the above analysis, we can conclude that the overall land price movement can be explained fairly well by the fundamentals. In fact, land prices calculated from this equation fit the actual price fairly well for regions other than the Tokyo and Osaka areas. This implies that land prices in these areas do not contain bubbles. Even for the Tokyo and Osaka areas, this equation explains actual land prices fairly well until the mid-1980s. Considering the relation between housing prices and income mentioned earlier, it can be said that land prices during this period were approximately the long-run equilibrium price.

For the latter half of the 1980s, however, actual land prices in the Tokyo and Osaka areas deviate considerably from the calculated value. Figure 1.2 shows this for Tokyo. This difference cannot be explained by factors such as land productivity and financial factors, and therefore is regarded as a bubble caused by excessive expectations for future capital gains. In Tokyo, the magnitude of the bubble was 54 percent of the actual land price in 1987.

Table 1.8   **Land Price Equation**

	Coefficient	Standard Error
Constant	−2.159	0.103
log *GDPLND*	1.097	0.038
log *INTRST*	−0.137	0.043
GROWTH	0.091	0.011
ISLAND	−0.161	0.013
log *NEBDEN*	0.085	0.023
log *SECOND*	0.110	0.130
log *TERTIA*	1.125	0.242
Coefficient of determination	0.839	

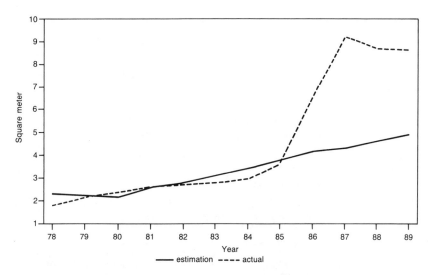

Fig. 1.2   Land price in Tokyo (100,000 yen per square meter)
Note: Estimated from the land price equation reported in table 1.8.

1.4   Structural Factors Underlying the Land Price Problem

1.4.1   Is Land Absolutely Scarce?

Section 1.3 discusses the extraordinary land price inflation during the recent years. As mentioned in section 1.2, another aspect of the land problem is chronically high land prices. This implies the existence of structural factors. In this section, I examine these factors.

Let us first see if physical constraints are important. Many people argue that the scarcity of land is the major cause of high land prices in Japan. It is true that the area of land of this country is small compared with other countries of similar population and that a large portion of it is covered by mountains. But if we compare the area of land devoted to urban uses, Japan is not worse off than those countries. In fact, the area of urban land accounts for only a tiny fraction of the national landmass—2 to 3 percent, depending upon the definition of urbanized area. This is small even in comparison with the habitable area, which is about one-third of the total amount of national land. The amount of total land available in Japan has thus little if anything to do with the land problem we face today.

Even in the urbanized areas, plenty of land is still underused or left idle. According to a survey by the Ministry of Construction, 65,000 hectares (approximately 160,000 acres) of land within the Greater Tokyo area could be developed into housing tracts.[12] This is equal to the area of the twenty-three

12. The available land consists of 36,000 hectares (89,000 acres) of farmland, 23,000 hectares (56,800 acres) of underused land (vacant lots and parking lots), and 6,000 hectares (14,800 acres)

wards of Tokyo. Moreover, most of the buildings do not use all the legally allowed capacity. To casual observers, urban land in this country may appear very densely used. In fact, the opposite is true. The volumetric ratio (the ratio of the floor space to the site area) authorized by the building code stands on the average at 242 percent, but only 40 percent of the authorized ratio is actually used.

The above fact can also be confirmed by international comparisons of rents. As we have seen, space utilization cost in Japan is not much different from that of the United Kingdom. This implies that the supply of space for urban use is not particularly low as compared to other countries.

To summarize, Japan, contrary to widespread belief, still has a surplus of land. This suggests that if the degree of land utilization is raised, many, if not all, of the problems associated with land will evaporate.

1.4.2   Distortions in the Tax System

The above argument suggests that what matters are social and economic factors rather than physical or natural factors. The most important is that people regard land as an asset. In fact, the puzzle in section 1.2.2 cannot be solved unless we understand that land in Japan is priced as an asset rather than as a factor of production.

One problem lies with the property tax.[13] The statutory standard property tax rate stands at 1.4 percent. The valuation of land for the property tax rate is very low, and the valuation is further lowered to one-quarter in the case of small residential sites. This makes the effective property tax rate much lower than the statutory rate.

In the early 1980s, the effective property tax stood at about 0.1 percent of the market price of land. As the local governments did not raise valuations in accordance with the rising market price in recent years, the effective tax rate in the Greater Tokyo area has dropped to about 0.06 percent. Thus, the tax liability for owning land has been reduced to a negligible amount. This is a major factor that encourages people to treat land as an asset. If it were costly to own land, not many people would leave their land vacant or in an inefficient use.[14] Another bias exists in the inheritance tax. Inherited land is valued at

---

of vacated factory sites, publicly held idle land and idle land belonging to the now defunct Japan National Railways.

13. It is often said that there are other tax advantages. For example, interest payment can be deducted, and losses incurred in the transaction can be offset for other income. But these provisions are not restricted to land. They are admitted to other types of assets as well.

14. It is generally believed that "the Japanese are deeply attached to the land they own." This is no more true than the contention that "Japan is short of land." This can be verified by the story about *nawanobi*—the difference between the area of farmland officially registered with the government and its actual size. In its early years, the Meiji government (1868–1912) tried to survey the nation's farmland to use the data for assessing the land tax, which was a fairly heavy tax. Since the resistance of farmers was so strong, it surveyed a few samples where possible at different locations and accepted voluntary reports filed by farmers. As a result, the bulk of the nation's

about 70 percent of the GBMP, which itself is about 70 percent of the market price. Hence, inherited land is valued at about half the market price for taxation purposes. Moreover, for small residential sites, the assessed value is further reduced by one-half. Although assessed prices have been raised to reflect recent rises in market prices, they were raised at lower rates, with the result that inherited land is valued at less than one-half of the market price in the Tokyo and Osaka areas. On the other hand, financial assets are assessed at the market value. This bias encourages people to hold inheritable assets in the form of land.

Furthermore, if one purchases land by borrowing money, one can reduce tax liabilities because borrowing can be deducted from the asset.[15] Consider a person whose asset is valued at x yen for the inheritance tax. If he borrows $2x$ yen and purchases land, his tax liability is reduced to zero. By doing so, he can save tx yen of inheritance tax, where t is the average tax rate. It follows that, for this person, effective valuation of land is $2x + tx$ rather than the market value $2x$.[16] Thus, the bias introduced by the inheritance tax has the effect of increasing the market price of land.

1.4.3   The Land Lease Law

Another problem lies in the Land Lease Law and the Building Lease Law, particularly the former. The Land Lease Law was strengthened during World War II as social legislation with the aim of strengthening the right of the lessee by bending the principle of freedom of contract provided in the Civil Code. During the war, a large number of families were faced with the danger of being evicted from their leased land or houses while their heads were called away for military duty, and this caused a serious social problem. With a view to protecting the right of the lessee and tenant, the government strengthened these laws. Under the strengthened provisions, a land lease contract is automatically renewed when the term expires, unless the landlord makes a formal objection without delay. The new contract is assumed to continue for the period of thirty years where there is a solid structure and twenty years for other cases. The objection of a landlord is admitted only in cases when he can show a personal

---

farmland was underreported. One may argue that farmers of the Meiji period underreported to reduce their tax liabilities because the smaller size they officially registered would not matter, for they had no intention of selling it on the market. If the tax rate were as low as the current property tax rate, they must have reported the full size of their farmland to protect its commercial value. Today, people hold on to their land in anticipation of higher prices because their exposure to property tax is at a minimum—serving to underscore that the tax rate, not the attachment to land, has profoundly swayed their attitude to landownership.

15. Since abuses of this provision became so apparent, the government has changed the valuation procedures. Under the new rule, if land is purchased within three years before death, it is evaluated at the purchase cost. The previous valuation rule still applies, however, for land purchases before that.

16. The tax rate t depends on the magnitude of the asset and the number of heirs. For typical cases, it is around 20–40 percent.

need to use the land or other "just causes," which are interpreted very strictly in the court.

The rents can of course be negotiated between the lessor and the lessee. If they fail to reach an agreement, they can request the court to determine the "fair and reasonable rent." Until the judgment is made, however, the lessee can continue to use the land by depositing the amount he personally deems reasonable to the court. Thus, the landlords have little negotiating leverage, and tenants have little incentive to accept increases in rents. As a result, the actual rents are left at irrationally low levels, and the rental market does not function properly. (Similar conditions exist for building leases. In actual practice, however, the revision of rents are more frequent than in the case of land lease, because the length of lease is in general shorter for rents.)

These two laws played a role in protecting the interest of the underclass during the years following their enactment. Now, however, they have outlived their relevance to the changed market reality, because they have in effect dissuaded landowners from leasing their holdings. To landowners, leasing is tantamount to selling land at a deep discount, whereas they stand to make huge capital gains by simply holding on to land, without incurring too much property tax liability.

Under such conditions, utilization of land actually penalizes its owner; the wisest way to manage land is to keep it idle or use it for a temporary purpose such as a parking lot until such time as he can make big capital gains on it. This is why there are so many vacant lots and underused parcels of land at unlikely places in urban areas.

1.5 Land Policies

In this section, I review the recent trend of government land policies and discuss necessary directions based on the analyses above.

1.5.1 Monetary Policy

The Bank of Japan changed its tight money policy in May 1989, when the official discount rate was raised from 2.5 to 3.25 percent. It was raised in several steps, and by the fifth step in August 1990, it became 6.0 percent. Long-term interest rates (yield of government bonds) rose from a low of 4.7 percent (April-June 1988) to 7.8 percent in August 1990.

It must be noted, however, that real interest rates did not rise as much as the nominal rate, since the rate of inflation rose during this period. (The annual rate of increase of the CPI, which was 0.1 percent in 1987, rose to 2.3 percent in 1989). In fact, the movement in nominal interest rates was not the same as that in land prices: land prices in Tokyo stopped rising in 1988, and in Osaka they continued to rise during 1989 (see table 1.2).

In addition to the general tightening of monetary conditions, the Ministry of Finance imposed a zero-growth restriction on the total amount of bank lending to real estate companies in April 1990. As a result of this restriction, bank lending to real estate companies declined during 1990. This had a strong impact on land transactions and land prices. In fact, land prices in some districts in Osaka dropped significantly during the latter half of 1990.

1.5.2 Strengthening Landholding Taxes

In order to discourage speculative holding of land, landholding cost has to be raised. Strengthening the property tax would be the most powerful method to achieve this objective.

There is, however, strong opposition to this policy. Since more than half of all households possess land in some form or other, anti-property-tax feeling is strong. Thus, all political parties, including the Communist party, officially oppose any increase in the property tax. Confronted with this political condition, almost all local governments are reluctant to raise assessments in accordance with the rise in the market price of land. As a result, effective rates of property tax on land continue to fall even as land prices rise.

In spite of this situation, the national government has significantly changed its attitude toward land taxes. The Basic Land Law, which passed the Diet in December 1989, recognizes the importance of land tax, though in an abstract expression. The Subcommittee of Land Tax, which was established in the Tax Council in April 1990, released a report in October 1990, recommending the introduction of a new landholding tax. The new national tax is imposed on relatively large landholdings. If this tax were successfully introduced, land use patterns in Japan would change significantly. Unfortunately, however, the new tax was weakened significantly by the Liberal Democratic Party (LPD).

1.5.3 Liberalization of the Land Lease Law

In view of the fact that the Land Lease and Building Lease Laws are major causes of the land problem, choking the new supply of land and houses for lease, it is necessary to relax the restrictions imposed by them or to completely abolish these laws.

The Legislative Council of the Ministry of Justice has been studying options for amending these laws. It released a draft amendment in February 1989 and submitted it to the Diet in 1991. The amendment proposed a new type of leasehold called a "fixed-term leasehold," which was a step forward. Under this arrangement, the lessee must return the land to the landlord when the contract expires. The amendment, however, did not pass the Diet, due to objections by the opposition parties.

In principle, liberalization of contracts hurts neither the lessor nor the lessee. Unfortunately, this vital point is not recognized by the public, and the present laws are still regarded as necessary protection for the underclass.

1.5.4 Securitization of Land

Leasing of land means that its owner keeps economic benefits from ownership while the land is used by others. As mentioned before, however, few Japanese landowners are willing to lease land because of the disadvantage arising under the existing Land Lease Law. Under such circumstances, securitization is an effective tool for separating ownership from the utilization right.

One possible method is for the government to issue government bonds whose value appreciates in step with a rise in the market price of land. This bond could be called a "land-price-indexed bond." [17] It in effect creates "paper land." The government would be able to use this bond to purchase land, especially land held solely for the purpose of obtaining capital gains. If the owners of idle land agree to securitize their ownership, their land can be used by the government or by other public bodies. In this way, the separation of ownership and the right to use the land would be realized.

A number of obstacles must be overcome before the land-price-indexed bond can be issued, such as the restrictions imposed by the Securities and Exchange Law and technicalities of taxation. These notwithstanding, to the extent that the land problem in Japan is rooted in the widespread attitude that land should be treated as a type of marketable asset, securitization of land could become one of the most powerful tools of land policy.

References

Economic Planning Agency. 1989. *Hesei Gannendo Keizai Hakusho (The 1989 economic White Paper)*. Tokyo: The Government Printing Agency. (English translation available).

Miyao, Takahiro. 1988. *Toshi to Kezai no New Trend (New trends in cities and economy)*. Tokyo: Nihon Hyoronsha.

National Land Agency. 1985–1989. *Tochi Hakusho (The White Paper on land)*. Tokyo: Government Printing Agency.

Nishimura, Kiyohiko. 1990. Nihon no Chikakettei Mechanism (The mechanism of land price determination in Japan). In Kiyohiko Nishimura and Yoshiro Minowa, eds., *Nihon no Kabuka Chika (Stock price and land price in Japan)*. Tokyo: Tokyo University Press.

Noguchi, Yukio. 1989. *Tochi no keizaigaku (Economics of land)*. Tokyo: Nihon Keizai Shinbunsha.

17. This idea was first proposed by me in 1979.

2 Land Prices and House Prices in the United States

Karl E. Case

2.1 Introduction

The behavior of single-family home prices in the United States has become a topic of increasing interest during the past two decades. Prior to 1970, house prices moved slowly at about the rate of inflation or slightly below, and regional differences, while they existed, were relatively modest by current standards. During the 1970s, however, house prices nationwide grew significantly faster than the rate of inflation, and homeowners earned tax-sheltered imputed rents and tax-sheltered capital gains on their leveraged assets, producing dramatic rates of return and low user costs throughout the decade. The decade of the 1980s produced much lower returns overall, but brought with it sharp differences in price behavior across regions and significantly increased volatility.

This paper reviews the behavior of house prices in the United States. First, the paper takes a national perspective, piecing together a description of what we know about house prices since 1950 but focusing on the past two decades. Second, it describes differences in price behavior across regions of the country, especially since the first California boom between 1976 and 1980. Third, it reviews what we know and do not know about the causes of house price movements. A final section looks at the impact of increasing regional disparities on mobility and regional growth.

Karl E. Case is professor of economics at Wellesley College and a visiting scholar at the Federal Reserve Bank of Boston.

The author wishes to thank Brooke Frewing for research assistance and James Poterba and Robert Shiller for helpful comments.

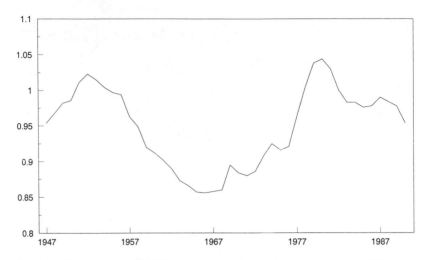

Fig. 2.1   House prices, 1947–90. Residential investment component of GNP deflector relative to GNP deflector

Sources: 1947–87 Data Resources, database (Lexington, Mass.: McGraw-Hill, *U.S. Prices Data Bank;* U.S. Department of Commerce, *1988–90 Survey of Current Business* (Washington, D.C.: Government Printing Office, August 1990–May 1991).

2.2   Housing Prices since 1950: National Trends

The most significant problem in studying the movement of home prices is the lack of consistent data. The two most commonly cited time series used as proxies for home appreciation are the residential investment component of the GNP deflator (see Mankiw and Weil [1989], Hendershott and Hu [1981], and others), and the census's Constant Quality Home Price Index (see Apgar et al. [1990], Hendershott and Hu [1981], and others), which is available only since 1963. While neither is ideal, they are as good as any available national data series on prices prior to 1970.[1] Since 1970, Case and Shiller (1988) have constructed very precise appreciation indices for four cities, but the national data are still weak.

Figure 2.1 shows the pattern of real home prices since 1947 as represented by the residential investment component of the GNP deflator. According to the index, prices dropped from a peak in 1952 to a low in 1966, and then rose until the early 1980s. Table 2.1 looks at the change in the index by decade, relative to two measures of income and construction costs.

Between 1950 and 1960, house prices dropped an average of 0.78 percent per year in real terms, while real per capita income rose 1.90 percent per year

---

1. The possible exception is a series from the Federal Home Loan Bank Board, which is available since 1960 and is discussed below. Home Loan Bank officials have cautioned against relying on those numbers.

and real median family income rose even faster at 3.2 percent. A similar pattern, with rapid income growth and slightly declining real home prices, recurs in the 1960s. During the 1970s, however, the pattern reverses itself. Income growth in the 1970s, particularly family income, dropped sharply while house prices rose more rapidly.

Rising house prices, of course, make homeowners better off, as their equity grows. On the other hand, when house prices outpace income, housing becomes less affordable to those who do not own. Thus, during the 1950s and 1960s, the return on owning a house was low, but housing became more affordable. During the 1970s, rates of return to owners were dramatic, but housing became less affordable.

This pattern is borne out by the census figures presented in table 2.2. The table gives the ratio of median reported house price to median household income in five metropolitan areas for census years 1950, 1960, 1970, and 1980. In all five cities, the ratio drops significantly from 1950 to 1960 and from 1960 to 1970. The ratio rises during the 1970s.

Both Hendershott and Hu (1981) and Case and Shiller (1990) calculate excess rates of return to home ownership for different periods between 1950 and 1989. While the return measures in the two papers are slightly different, both include estimates of imputed rent, capital gains, property taxes, maintenance, and depreciation and include changes in tax treatment and interest rates. Hendershott and Hu find returns of about -6.5 percent for most owners and -14.5 percent for more leveraged owners in upper-income brackets during the 1956–63 period. Both papers find very high excess returns during the 1970s.

Apgar et al. (1990) construct a data set that shows the impact of changing

Table 2.1   **House Prices, Construction Costs, and Income, 1950–88 (average real annual percentage increase)**

	House Price (Series 1)[a]	House Price (Series 2)[b]	Construction Cost[c]	Per Capita GNP[d]	Median Family Income[e]
1950–60	—	−0.78	+0.56	+1.90	+3.20
1960–70	0.0	−0.33	+1.33	+3.10	+2.96
1970–80	+2.77	+1.66	+0.74	+1.33	+0.03
1980–88	−0.31	−0.74	−0.13	+1.65	+0.81

[a]U.S. Bureau of the Census, *Constant Quality Home Price Index, Construction Reports,* series C-27 (Washington, D.C.: Government Printing Office), since 1963 only.

[b]Residential investment component of the GNP deflator relative to the GNP deflator. Data Resources, database (Lexington, Mass.: McGraw-Hill). See figure 2.1.

[c]E. H. Boeckh Construction Cost Index, small residential structures, composite; U.S. Bureau of the Census, *Historical Statistics of the United States: Colonial Times to 1970,* series N-121 (Washington, D.C.: Government Printing Office), U.S. Bureau of the Census, *Statistical Abstract of the United States, 1990* (Washington, D.C.: Government Printing Office).

[d]*Historical Statistics,* series F-2, 224; *Statistical Abstract, 1990.*

[e]*Historical Statistics,* series G-179, 296; *Statistical Abstract, 1990.*

Table 2.2   Family Income and House Prices: Selected Cities, 1950–80

	Price/Income Ratio			
	1950	1960	1970	1980
New York	3.02	2.30	2.04	3.40
Boston	3.02	2.19	1.80	2.57
Los Angeles	2.68	2.12	1.94	4.16
Chicago	2.95	2.35	1.81	2.68
Dallas	2.17	1.69	1.50	2.15

Source: U.S. Bureau of the Census, *Housing Characteristics of the Population* (Washington, D.C.: Government Printing Office, 1950, 1960, 1970, 1980). Figures are the ratio of median reported home value to median household income.

prices on both owners and potential owners between 1967 and 1989. Table 2.3 reproduces a table from the Apgar study. The house price variable is constructed using the census constant quality index applied to the 1977 median value of house purchased by a first-time buyer. The table shows that unanticipated inflation in house prices reduced the total burden of owning for a first-time buyer to less than 10 percent of income in the late 1970s, while the cash burden climbed to 40 percent of income in 1980. The early 1980s saw dramatic increases in interest rates and much slower appreciation. The combination pushed up cash costs to a high of 44.5 percent of income and the total burden to a high of 37.2 percent of income in 1982.

2.2.1   Regional Differences in Price Behavior

While nationally house prices lagged inflation in the 1950s, 1960s, and 1980s and rose more rapidly than prices in general during the 1970s, there were marked differences across regions. To illustrate these differences, this section presents data on four metropolitan areas between 1970 and 1986. The data presented are from Case and Shiller (1987). They constructed weighted repeat sales (WRS) indices of appreciation based on forty thousand multiple sales of the same property drawn from a large sample of sales in the four cities.[2] Tables 2.4 and 2.5 summarize the data.

While substantial variance in performance can be seen across the four cities, all saw house prices at least keep pace with inflation as measured by the CPI. In Atlanta and Chicago, existing house prices remained remarkably constant in real terms over the sixty-five quarters of the sample period. While nominal prices nearly tripled, so did consumer prices in general. Real increases in Atlanta and Chicago averaged less than 1 percent per year.

The increases recorded in Dallas and San Francisco stand in marked con-

2. The Case and Shiller methodology is very similar to one proposed by Bailey, Muth, and Norse (1963). The raw data are from Atlanta, Chicago, Dallas, and San Francisco. The San Francisco data are from Alameda County.

Table 2.3   Income and Housing Costs, U.S. Totals, 1967–89 (1989 dollars)

Year	First-Time Buyer's Income	House Price	Mortgage Rate (%)	Mortgage Payment	Other Costs	Owner Costs Before-Tax Cash	Tax Savings	After-Tax Cash	Expected Appreciation	Total Cost	Cost as % of Income, First-Time Buyers Cash Burden	Total Burden
1967	27,016	55,822	6.40	3,351	2,701	6,052	317	5,735	1,645	4,673	21.2	17.3
1968	27,134	56,883	6.90	3,595	2,714	6,308	396	5,913	2,257	4,344	21.8	16.0
1969	26,816	58,380	7.68	3,987	2,716	6,703	508	6,195	3,201	3,863	23.1	14.4
1970	28,241	57,208	8.20	4,107	2,749	6,856	586	6,270	2,517	4,572	22.2	16.2
1971	28,213	57,818	7.54	3,897	2,831	6,728	410	6,318	2,612	4,307	22.4	15.3
1972	28,764	59,770	7.38	3,966	2,930	6,896	424	6,473	3,031	4,078	22.5	14.2
1973	27,860	61,161	7.82	4,235	2,913	7,148	385	6,764	4,047	3,661	24.3	13.1
1974	28,142	60,735	8.78	4,599	2,916	7,515	444	7,071	4,594	3,514	25.1	12.5
1975	26,885	62,145	8.97	4,787	2,934	7,721	520	7,201	5,286	2,802	26.8	10.4
1976	26,025	63,755	8.90	4,881	2,968	7,849	558	7,291	5,163	2,935	28.0	11.3
1977	25,828	67,579	8.83	5,139	3,044	8,183	160	8,023	6,285	2,622	31.1	10.2
1978	26,187	72,271	9.40	5,783	3,044	8,827	394	8,433	7,614	2,076	32.2	7.9
1979	25,211	75,787	10.63	6,726	2,944	9,670	592	9,078	8,754	1,980	36.0	7.9
1980	24,313	75,215	12.53	7,723	2,955	10,678	921	9,757	7,716	3,922	40.1	16.1
1981	24,112	74,190	14.51	8,727	3,003	11,730	1,233	10,497	6,250	6,502	43.5	27.0
1982	23,626	71,674	14.78	8,579	3,069	11,649	1,138	10,510	3,612	8,796	44.5	37.2
1983	24,130	71,118	12.29	7,175	3,101	10,276	887	9,389	2,245	8,666	38.9	35.9
1984	24,582	71,218	12.00	7,033	3,132	10,615	853	9,312	2,305	8,717	37.9	35.5
1985	24,772	70,167	11.18	6,507	3,101	9,608	750	8,858	1,924	8,298	35.8	33.5

(continued)

Table 2.3 (continued)

Year	First-Time Buyer's Income	House Price	Mortgage Rate (%)	Owner Costs							Cost as % of Income, First-Time Buyers	
				Mortgage Payment	Other Costs	Before-Tax Cash	Tax Savings	After-Tax Cash	Expected Appreciation	Total Cost	Cash Burden	Total Burden
1986	25,212	72,117	9.80	5,974	3,046	9,019	630	8,389	2,564	6,921	33.3	27.5
1987	24,978	73,715	8.94	5,664	2,976	8,639	445	8,194	3,340	6,003	32.8	24.0
1988	25,783	73,386	9.01	5,674	2,932	8,606	253	8,352	3,106	6,499	32.4	25.2
1989	26,000	72,628	9.81	6,021	2,900	8,921	322	8,599	2,750	7,208	33.1	27.7

Source: Apgar et al. 1990.

Notes: Annual income of families and primary individuals: 1970 from the *1970 Census of the Population*; 1967 to 1969 from the *Panel Survey of Income Dynamics*; 1971 and 1972 interpolated from the *Panel Survey of Income Dynamics* and *1970 Census of the Population*; 1973 to 1983 from the *American Housing Survey*; 1983 to 1989 from the *American Housing Survey* adjusted by the *Current Population Survey*. "First-time buyers" defined as married-couple renters aged 25 to 29. All dollar amounts expressed in 1989 constant dollars using the Bureau of Labor Statistics consumer price index (CPI-UX) for all items. CPI-UX deflator slightly revised from that used in previous *State of the Nation's Housing Reports.*

House price is *American Housing Survey* median value of house purchased by first-time home buyers aged 25 to 29 in 1977, indexed by U.S. Bureau of the Census, *Constant Quality Home Price Index: Construction Reports*, series C-27, which was recently revised to incorporate improved methodology for estimating the price of a home of constant quality; hence the index differs somewhat from that used in previous *State of the Nation's Housing Reports.* Mortgage rates equal Federal Home Loan Bank Board contract mortgage rate. Mortgage payments assume a thirty-year mortgage with 20 percent down. Other costs include property tax, insurance, fuel and utilities, and maintenance. After-tax cash cost equals mortgage payment plus other costs, less tax savings of home ownership. Tax savings is based on the excess of housing (mortgage interest and real estate taxes) plus nonhousing deductions over the standard deduction. Nonhousing deductions are set at 5 percent of income through 1986. With tax reform, they decrease to 4.25 percent in 1987 and 3.5 percent from 1988 on. Total cost equals after-tax cash cost plus opportunity cost of down payment, amortization of fees, and closing costs, less expected equity buildup. Expected equity buildup is estimated as a weighted average of increases in house prices in the previous three years. (Weights are one-half for the previous year, one-third for the second year, and one-sixth for the third year.) *American Housing Survey* data indexed by Bureau of Labor Statistics consumer price indices for various components of housing cost.

Table 2.4   **Changes in Prices of Existing Single-Family Homes Computed Using the WRS Method (%)**

	Nominal Change		Real Change	
	Total	Average Annual Rate	Total	Average Annual Rate
1970:1–1986:2				
Atlanta	+196.1	+6.9	+3.4	+0.2
Chicago	+200.2	+7.0	+4.9	+0.3
Dallas	+309.3	+9.1	+43.0	+2.2
San Francisco	+496.6	+11.3	+99.0	+4.3
CPI-U[a]	+186.2	+6.7	—	—
1970:1–1975:1				
Atlanta	+40.8	+7.1	+2.0	+0.4
Chicago	+46.4	+7.9	+6.0	+1.2
Dallas	+39.2	+6.8	+0.8	+0.2
San Francisco	+53.8	+9.0	+11.4	+2.2
CPI-U[a]	+38.0	+6.7	—	—
1975:1–1981:1				
Atlanta	+55.9	+7.7	−6.8	−1.1
Chicago	+71.3	+9.4	+2.4	+0.4
Dallas	+124.5	+14.4	+34.2	+5.0
San Francisco	+187.0	+19.2	+71.6	+9.4
CPI-U[a]	+67.2	+8.9	—	—

[a]All items, all urban consumers.

Table 2.5   **Changes in WRS Indices and Changes in Median Prices of Existing Single-Family Homes in Four Cities, 1981–86**

	Change in Nominal Prices				Change in Real Prices			
	National Assn. Realtors		Weighted Repeat Sales		National Assn. Realtors		Weighted Repeat Sales	
	Total	Average Annual Rate	Total	Average Annual Rate	Total	Average Annual Rate	Total	Average Annual Rate
Atlanta[a]	+44.6	+8.5	+28.2	+5.7	+17.7	+3.7	+4.5	+1.0
Chicago[b]	+19.3	+3.4	+19.8	+3.4	−4.0	−0.8	−3.4	−0.7
Dallas[b]	+48.4	+7.8	+31.0	+5.3	+19.1	+3.4	+5.6	+1.0
San Francisco[c]	+45.4	+7.0	+25.8	+4.3	+16.2	+2.8	+0.9	+0.2
CPI-U[d]	+25.1	+4.1						

[a]1981:1 to 1985:3.
[b]1981:1 to 1986:2.
[c]1981:1 to 1986:3.
[d]All items, all consumers.

trast. Property values in Dallas rose an average of 2.2 percentage points per year faster than the CPI, while real increases in San Francisco averaged 4.3 percent per year. Such high and sustained real appreciation rates are remarkable. Real house prices in Dallas increased by nearly 43 percent. In San Francisco, they nearly doubled.

The second and third parts of table 2.4 look at two shorter periods of time. The first corresponds to the inflation/recession cycle of 1971–75. The second runs from the bottom of the 1974–75 recession to the period of very high interest rates in early 1981.

Between 1970 and 1975, house price increases were modest and fairly uniform. In all four cities, price increases totaled between 39 and 54 percent over the five years, while prices in general rose 38 percent. San Francisco led the pack with real increases of 2.2 percent per year.

The period from 1975:1 to 1981:1 shows anything but uniform house price increases across the cities. The first California boom (to be discussed below) is evident. Over the six years, annual appreciation of homes in the San Francisco sample averaged 9.4 percent in real terms. Meanwhile, real prices in Atlanta dropped nearly 7 percent for an average decline of 1.1 percent per year.

While house prices in Chicago increased at about the same rate as consumer prices in general, Dallas was experiencing a miniboom of its own. Homes in Dallas appreciated 34.2 percent, or an average of 5.0 percent in real terms.

Between 1981 and 1986, relative calm returned to all four of these markets, although other parts of the country, particularly the Northeast, boomed. Table 2.5 presents the National Association of Realtors (NAR) median price of an existing single-family home and WRS indices for the period. In no case did the real WRS index grow more than 1 percent per year. In Chicago, it fell 0.7 percent per year.

The same pattern is reflected in excess returns estimated in Case and Shiller (1990). Table 2.6 presents a summary of the nonleveraged excess returns estimated for the same three periods since 1970. Once again performance is fairly similar across the cities during the first half of the 1970s, while Dallas and San Francisco moved sharply ahead during the last half. The 1980s brought negative excess returns to Chicago and San Francisco, while Atlanta and Dallas had small positive excess returns.

Table 2.6	Excess Returns to Investment in Single-Family Owner-Occupied Housing, 1970–86 (%)		
City	1971:1–1975:1	1975:1–1981:1	1981:1–1986:2
Atlanta	7.7	4.0	0.5
Chicago	5.6	6.0	−4.2
Dallas	7.5	11.9	1.5
San Francisco	9.2	15.1	−1.7

Source: Case and Shiller (1990).

Table 2.7   Recent Housing Price Booms in the United States (%)

Location	Period	Total Nominal Change in Median	Average Annual Nominal Change	Average Annual Real Change
California[a]	1976–80	106.9	19.9	9.3
Boston	1983–87	114.5	21.0	17.7
New York– New Jersey	1983–87	108.4	20.2	16.9
Washington, DC	1986–88	30.4	14.2	10.2
California[b]	1987–89	53.2	23.8	19.1
Honolulu	1987–90	101.6	26.3	21.2
Seattle	1988–90	63.3	27.7	22.3

Sources: National Association of Realtors, Home Sales (Washington, D.C.: NAR), monthly; CPI, Data Resources, database (Lexington, Mass.: McGraw-Hill).
[a]Figures based on San Francisco mean price. Unpublished data from the NAR.
[b]Based on figures for San Francisco, although similar price increases were recorded in Los Angeles and Orange Country.

2.2.2 Increased Volatility: The Booms

Perhaps the most important phenomenon in recent years has been the increased volatility evident in several cities. Table 2.7 describes seven booms that have occurred since the late 1970s. While the first California boom of 1976–80 was a dramatic event, in real terms it was just a hint of what was to follow.

The Boston and New York booms were similar to each other in magnitude, with real prices rising at 18 percent and 17 percent, respectively, over a four-year period. At peak in both cities, prices were rising at nearly 40 percent per year (see Case [1986] for the Boston pattern over the period based on repeat sales).

The second California boom was shorter lived, but perhaps more dramatic near the peak. The Wall Street Journal carried a front-page article on June 1, 1988, with the headline "Buyers' Panic Sweeps California's Big Market in One-Family Homes." Realtors reported multiple offers and prices rising at 4 percent per month, or over 50 percent per year, at the peak.

The most recent booms have been in Honolulu and Seattle. In Honolulu, the median price jumped from $186,000 in 1987 to $375,000 in the third quarter of 1990. In Seattle, the median was up from $88,700 in 1988 to $144,800 in the third quarter of 1990.

The downside of a boom is a bust. While booms have been dramatic and frequent, prices appear to be less volatile on the downside. The most dramatic decline in the NAR median home price was a 28.5 percent real drop recorded between 1985 and 1988 in the Houston metropolitan area. Since 1988, the median price in Boston has dropped 12 percent in real terms. The declines

Table 2.8   Median Price of Existing Single-Family Homes, 1982 and 1989

Metropolitan Area	1982	1989	Change (%)
Atlanta	53,300	84,000	51.9
Boston	80,200	182,800	127.9
Chicago	73,000	107,000	46.6
Dallas/Fort Worth	74,000	92,300	24.7
Denver	76,200	85,500	12.2
Detroit	47,500	73,700	55.1
Houston	77,200	66,700	−13.6
Kansas City	58,100	71,600	23.2
Los Angeles	113,400	215,500	90.0
Minneapolis	72,400	87,200	20.4
New York	70,500	183,400	160.1
Philadelphia	58,100	108,900	87.4
St. Louis	57,000	76,900	34.9
San Diego	98,600	175,200	77.7
San Francisco	124,900	260,600	108.6
Washington, DC	87,200	144,400	65.6
Coefficient of variation	.277	.475	—

Source: National Association of Realtors, *Home Sales Yearbook: 1989* (Washington, D.C.: NAR). Cities are the largest U.S. metropolitan areas (by population) for which the NAR has data back to 1982.

currently in Boston and New York appear from anecdotal evidence to be significantly greater than the declines in the median would suggest. Some areas have seen nominal declines of up to 25 percent. Nonetheless, there appears to be significant stickiness and resistance to sharp downward movements even where fundamental factors would suggest a collapse.

2.3   Regional Differences in House Price Levels

Differences in price performance across regions and increased volatility have led to differences in price levels across regions that are substantial and larger than they were in earlier years. Table 2.8 presents the median price of existing single-family homes in 1982 and 1989 in the largest sixteen U.S. metropolitan areas for which the data are available from the NAR. In 1982, the highest-priced city (San Francisco) had a median price that was 2.6 times the median price in the lowest-priced city (Detroit). In 1989, the highest city was 3.9 times higher than the lowest. Table 2.8 shows that the coefficient of variation across these sixteen cities grew from .277 in 1982 to .475 in 1989.

The only consistent series of metropolitan area–specific median home prices for years prior to 1981 is the Mortgage Interest Rate Survey, conducted annually since 1963 by the Federal Home Loan Bank Board.[3] The survey is con-

3. See Federal Home Loan Bank Board, Office of Thrift Supervision, "Rates and Terms on Conventional Home Mortgages, Annual Summary, 1989" (Washington, D.C.: Government Print-

ducted in thirty-two metropolitan areas. Based on this larger sample of cities, a coefficient of dispersion (CD) was calculated for each year between 1973 and 1989. While the level of the coefficient is lower in the larger sample, the pattern is the same. The CD stood at .164 in 1973, rising slowly to .188 by 1979. From 1979 to 1983, it jumped sharply from .188 to .245 and continued to climb to .272 by 1989.

Looking at similar homes in specific areas of the country reveals dramatic differences that cannot be seen in the aggregate data. For example, a three-bedroom, one-and-a-half-bath home on ten thousand square feet of land in a good neighborhood is currently worth $120,000 in a number of Midwest cities, $240,000 in the Northeast, and as much as $700,000 in parts of California.

While a great deal of attention has been paid to house prices in the United States, economists have devoted very little time to the study of land prices. In fact, there are virtually no generally available data on land prices in the United States.

It's not clear why this is so. Part of the reason is that most land is sold in combination with capital, and the task of separating the land from the capital value is difficult. Since nearly all property taxes in the United States are levied on the combined value of land and capital, there is no compelling reason for tax administrators to undertake to disentangle the two. Nonetheless, it remains a puzzle why so little academic attention has been focused on land prices.

It is a virtual certainty that the increase in volatility across regions is the result of differentials in land values. There is evidence that construction costs explain only a small fraction of the price increases recorded in several of the boom areas.[4] Table 2.1 shows that only a small part of the increase in house prices nationally between 1970 and 1980 was due to increased construction costs.

Figure 2.2 presents data from Boston based on over ten thousand individual sales of raw land, obtained from Middlesex County deed records. The figure shows the average price per square foot expressed in 1967 dollars for each year between 1915 and 1988. While no formal analysis of these data have been accomplished, it is easy to see a dramatic increase precisely during the boom years of 1985–87.

2.4   The Causes of Price Changes

This section of the paper briefly reviews some of what is known about why house prices have behaved the way they do. This is not an exhaustive review of the existing literature, but rather an abbreviated discussion of several recent issues.

---

ing Office, 1989). In 1989 the responsibility for the survey was transferred to the Federal Housing Finance Board.

4. See Case (1986) and Case and Shiller (1990).

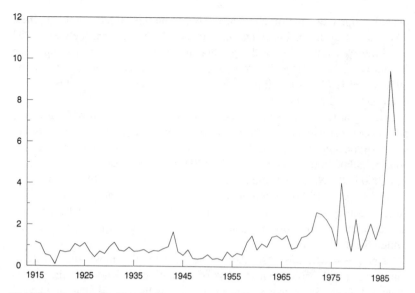

Fig. 2.2   Real median land prices in Middlesex County, Massachusetts, 1915–88, price per square foot (1982 dollars)

2.4   Demographics

The most often cited paper on house prices in recent years was written by Mankiw and Weil (1989, hereafter M&W). The focus of the M&W paper is the baby boom. Demographic data show that there was a jump in the birth rate in the United States between 1946 and 1964, resulting in a population bulge that has been working its way up the age distribution. The size of the bulge is quite dramatic. In 1960, 24.0 million people, or 13.3 percent of the population, were between the ages of twenty and thirty. By 1980, the number had grown to 44.6 million. That bulge began to enter the housing market during the 1970s, precisely at the time when house prices were booming.

To test for the effects of the baby boom, M&W construct a demand variable based on the relationship between the quantity of housing consumed and age in the 1970 census. After estimating the quantity of housing demanded by each age group, the population was "aged" to construct an estimate of demand over time as the size of each age cohort changes in predictable ways. The M&W measure of demand declines into the mid-1960s and then begins to climb through the 1970s, falling again in the 1980s.

As a measure of price change, M&W use the residential construction component of the GNP deflator relative to the deflator itself. This ratio is shown in figure 2.1, and it moves closely with the M&W measure of demand. Thus, when simple correlations are run, they show a powerful relationship.

The paper in part was designed to test a model suggested by Poterba (1984).

They use a simple version of the Poterba model to simulate the likely effects of the baby boom on prices. The model predicts that, since the age distribution of the population in the 1970s is known with certainty in the 1950s and 1960s, if demographics had a price effect, it should have been anticipated. Thus, both the upturn in the late 1960s and the downturn in the 1980s should have happened *before* the demand growth actually occurred. In essence, they conclude that the "naive" model, without forward-looking agents, seems to predict better.

The conclusion that caused a great deal of concern in the press and among housing-market participants, is that "if the historical relation between housing demand and prices continues into the future, real housing prices will fall substantially over the next two decades" (M&W, 235).

The response to the M&W article has been dramatic. The National Association of Home Builders, for example, published a twelve-page response, complete with color photographs, and had a national media conference to refute the conclusion. Mankiw was on national television several times, describing and defending the study.

Popular criticism focuses on one basic point. Although an interest rate variable is included, M&W estimate a model of price formation based essentially on a single demand-side variable. Previous work has shown the effect of employment growth, tax rates, interest rates, income growth, rent levels, and so forth on the demand side, and housing production and costs on the supply side.[5] Of critical importance, it is argued, are construction costs. If prices fall to the point where construction is no longer profitable, there will be exit from the home building industry, and housing starts will fall. If starts fall below the level of household formation, prices will stabilize. Since household formation remains positive over the next few decades, what is really important is the relationship between household formation and production.

One interesting fact that poses a puzzle for the M&W position is the relationship between population growth and house price movement in a cross-section of U.S. cities. Table 2.9 presents data on cities for whom the NAR has been publishing data since 1982. The simple correlation coefficient between 1970–80 population growth and nominal median house price change between 1980 and 1989 is −.506. The simple correlation coefficient between 1980–87 population growth and median house price change, again 1980–89, is −.355.

A casual glance down the columns reveals that the most rapidly growing cities were in the Southwest, an area that experienced a serious economic decline during the 1980s, while the slowest-growing areas were in the Northeast, where the economic environment was strong. In addition, housing production was very rapid in the Southwest and relatively slow to respond in the increase in demand in the Northeast. Thus, the explanation for the seeming paradox of a negative relation between demographics and house price growth in a cross-

5. See Case (1986), Case and Shiller (1990), and others.

Table 2.9   Population Growth and House Prices, 1982–89 (%)

City	Change in Population, 1970–80	Change in Population, 1980–87	Average Annual Change in Median House Price, 1982–89
Phoenix	4.4	3.6	0.7
Miami	3.4	1.5	2.1
Orange County, CA	3.1	1.9	8.7
Albuquerque	2.8	2.0	2.4
Denver	2.7	1.9	1.8
Atlanta	2.4	3.0	5.9
Dallas	2.2	3.3	3.0
Portland	1.9	0.8	2.7
Oklahoma City	1.8	1.7	−0.1
Los Angeles	1.4	2.4	9.0
Charlotte	1.4	1.6	5.5
San Francisco	1.2	1.4	10.4
Minneapolis	0.8	1.2	3.2
Columbus	0.8	0.8	4.0
Baltimore	0.5	0.6	6.2
Indianapolis	0.5	0.7	4.9
Kansas City	0.4	1.0	2.7
Albany	0.3	0.2	11.1
Chicago	0.2	0.4	5.5
Toledo	0.2	−0.1	2.4
Providence	0.2	0.4	14.5
Boston	−0.3	0.2	11.4
New York	−0.4	4.0	12.6
Buffalo	−0.8	−0.8	7.2

Sources: Median prices, National Association of Realtors, *Home Sales* (Washington, D.C.: NAR), monthly. Population growth, U.S. Bureau of the Census, *Statistical Abstract of the United States, 1990* (Washington, D.C.: Government Printing Office).

Note: For Albuquerque, Charlotte, and Toledo, data have been available only since 1983; for Phoenix and Miami, data have been available only since 1984.

section requires an analysis of supply and a number of other demand-side variables.

The academic response to M&W is just now beginning to emerge in the literature. Hendershott (1990) shows that the M&W equation in fact fits the data only from the 1950s and 1960s, and a forecast of the 1970–87 period is actually off by a factor of four. In addition, Hendershott estimates an expanded model that includes the real after-tax interest rate (entered as both a level and change) and real income growth (to capture the impact of increased labor force participation). Both interest-rate variables and the income growth variable are significant with the correct sign. The income variable indicates an elasticity of real prices with respect to real income of .3.

Hendershott's expanded equation predicts a cumulative real decline of 9–12 percent by the year 2007 if interest rates remain high relative to their historic norms and an *increase* of 4–7 percent if the real after-tax interest rate drops back to its 1947–87 mean.

2.4.2   The Efficiency of the Housing Market: Inertia in House Prices

In Case (1986), the suggestion is made that the upward volatility evident since the late 1970s is at least partially the result of speculative behavior. That is, the booms recorded above may at least in part be speculative bubbles.

Three papers of Case and Shiller have brought evidence to bear on the assertion. First, Case and Shiller (1989) find evidence of positive serial correlation in real house prices in four cities: Atlanta, Chicago, Dallas, and San Francisco. A change in price observed over one year tends to be followed by a change the following year in the same direction and between 25 percent and 50 percent as large. In addition, the paper finds evidence of inertia in a measure of excess returns estimated for the same four cities.

Second, Case and Shiller (1988) present the results of a survey of two thousand people who bought homes in May 1988 in Orange County (California), San Francisco, Boston, and Milwaukee. The results provide strong evidence that buyers are influenced heavily by an investment motive, that they have strong expectations of future price increases in housing, and that they perceive little risk. Responses to a number of questions suggest that emotion plays a significant role in housing purchase decisions. In addition, buyers do not agree about the causes of recent price movements.

Finally, Case and Shiller (1990) use time-series cross-section regressions to test for the forecastability of prices and excess returns using a number of independent variables. They find that the ratio of construction costs to price, changes in the adult population, and increases in real per capita income are all positively related to house prices and excess returns. The results add weight to the argument that the market for single-family homes is inefficient.

M&W also provide some support for the proposition that the housing market is an inefficient asset market when they fail to find a significant relationship between the rent price ratio and capital gains.

2.4.3   Downward Stickiness

An important stylized fact about the housing market in the United States that has not been well explored in the literature is that house prices are sticky downward. That is, when an excess supply occurs, prices do not immediately fall to clear the market. Rather, sellers have reservation prices below which they tend not to sell.

After the first California housing boom ran into a 21 percent prime and a 17 percent mortgage rate in July 1981, the number of sales fell sharply. The inventory of unsold properties on the market went to all-time high levels. At the same time, new construction dropped to record low levels. Nominal prices stopped rising in 1981, but fell only slightly despite a huge excess supply.

Boston and New York/New Jersey/Connecticut have experienced an excess supply and low demand since the fall of 1986. Prices stopped rising in nominal terms, as a large excess supply built up. But nominal prices stayed virtually flat through the spring of 1989, when they began to fall.

Significant reasons exist to predict such rigidity. First, there is no panic selling since the housing market is very different than the stock market. In the stock market, people can exit their equity positions quickly and without cost. The analog of a Treasury bill in the housing market is moving to a rental unit. For those with considerable equity that would mean paying a large capital gains tax (otherwise deferrable) and a 6 percent brokerage fee, as well as putting up with the aggravation of a move. The transactions costs are very high.

Many of the households that responded to the questionnaire in Case and Shiller (1988) were recent sellers as well as buyers. When asked what they would have done if their house had not sold for the price that they wanted to get, only a small fraction said that they would lower the price until the property sold. Most indicated that they had a reservation price below which they would not go.

If the market is downwardly rigid in nominal terms (at least in normal times), one could argue that the housing market is a "quantity clearing" rather than a "price clearing" market. That is, when an excess supply develops either from overbuilding or from a drop in demand, nominal prices stick while real prices drop slowly. At the same time, new production drops sharply, and sellers of existing homes resist downward movement by not selling. Thus, sales and starts would be expected to move with the cycle, while prices would remain fairly rigid.

Figure 2.3 presents a plot of existing house prices and sales, which seem to support the notion that the housing market is a quantity clearing market.

The best evidence of downward stickiness would be persistently high inventory. Unfortunately, no consistent source of data on inventories exists. While multiple-listing-service inventories might be tracked, properties are often listed when sellers are actively searching for buyers. Many stop listing after their house has been on the market for a long time. This produces a "discouraged seller" effect, similar to the discouraged worker effect, that can lead to a decline in formal listings when properties remain overpriced.

A Boston data service called Market Intelligence has produced a fairly good series on inventories, including bank-owned properties, properties under construction, and informal listings. The data show the number of properties implicitly or explicitly on the market, divided by the number of sales in the last year by location and type of property. During the fourth quarter of 1990, the inventory of unsold single-family homes in the Boston metropolitan area was approximately one year, while the inventory of unsold condominiums was closer to eighteen months. Many individual properties have been in the inventory for over two years. While there is no norm for such inventory numbers, the consensus among real estate professionals is that less than six months is

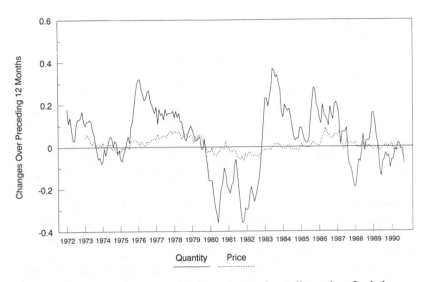

Fig. 2.3   Existing house sales and prices, changes in median price of existing single-family homes (constant dollars)
Source: National Association of Realtors, *Home Sales* (Washington, D.C.: NAR), monthly.

healthy. The behavior of inventories across regions is a potentially fruitful area for further research.

It is very important to note that prices "tend" to stick in the downward direction, as do wages. But there is certainly plenty of evidence that, when excess supplies exist for a long time as the economy worsens, prices begin to fall more sharply. This happened in the Southwest as an overbuilt market ran into a depression economy, and it has happened to some extent in New England and New York, where the evidence suggests substantial nominal declines depending on the specific area.

If house prices in the Northeast and in California were to break sharply downward, the banking problems currently being experienced in the United States would surely worsen. Consider for example the Boston metropolitan area. In the five eastern counties of Massachusetts, approximately 700,000 households own the housing unit that they occupy. The average nominal appreciation that occurred during the boom years of 1984–87 was $135,000. That implies an aggregate increase in value of $94.5 billion. Certainly a good part of that value was leveraged, as the volume of mortgage credit outstanding in New England exploded between 1984 and 1987. The corresponding figure for the New York metropolitan area (1983–87) is close to $400 billion. Estimating the impact of a 30 percent drop in single-family home equity on bank capital is beyond the scope of this paper. Given the magnitude of the assets created by the booms, however, there can be no doubt that the effect would be significant.

2.5 Consequences of Regional Differentials: Out-Migration and Slow Growth

There is ample evidence that regional differentials in home prices have increased during the 1980s. There is little evidence, however, about the effects of these differentials. Drier et al. (1988) provide anecdotal evidence that high house prices made it difficult for firms to attract workers to the region after prices boomed in 1985 and 1986. Clearly, if house prices lead to interregional migration, they can have an impact on employment growth. Case (1992) provides some evidence that high house prices retarded labor-force growth in New England between 1985 and 1987 and contributed to the labor shortage experienced in the region in 1987 and to a significant increase in wages in the region.

The most significant evidence of the impact of house prices on migration is in a recent paper by Gabriel, Shack-Marquez, and Wascher (1991). Gabriel develops a place-to-place migration model in which household moves depend on the relative housing costs and labor market opportunities in the origin and destination regions, as well as moving costs and other population characteristics. Estimates of a logistic model show that house prices are a significant determinant of regional migration patterns in the United States.

References

Apgar, W. C., D. DiPasquale, J. Cummings, and N. McArdle. 1990. *The State of the Nation's Housing 1990.* Cambridge, Mass.: Harvard University, Joint Center for Housing Studies.

Bailey, M. J., R. F. Muth, and H. O. Nourse. 1963. A Regression Method for Real Estate Price Index Construction. *Journal of the American Statistical Association* 58 (December): 933–42.

Case, K. E. 1986. The Market for Single Family Homes in Boston. *New England Economic Review* (May–June): 38–48.

———. 1992. The Real Estate Cycle and the Economy: Consequences of the Massachusetts Boom of 1984–1987. *Urban Studies* 29 (2): 171–83.

Case, K. E., and R. J. Shiller. 1987. Prices of Single Family Homes since 1970: New Indexes for Four Cities. *New England Economic Review* (September-October): 45–56.

———. 1988. The Behavior of Home Buyers in Boom and Postboom Markets. *New England Economic Review* (November–December): 29–46.

———. 1989. "The Efficiency of the Market for Single Family Homes," *American Economic Review* 79(1): 125–37.

———. 1990. Forecasting Prices and Excess Returns in the Housing Market. *Journal of the American Real Estate and Urban Economics Association* 18:253–73.

Drier, P., D. C. Schwartz, and A. Greiner. 1988. What Every Business Can Do about Housing. *Harvard Business Review* (September/October): 52–61.

Gabriel, S. A., J. Shack-Marquez, and W. L. Wascher. 1991. Regional House Price Dispersion and Interregional Migration. Department of Finance and Business Economics, School of Business Administration, University of California, Working Paper no. 90–14.

Hendershott, P. H. 1990. Are Real House Prices Likely to Decline by 47 Percent? Paper presented at the midyear American Real Estate and Urban Economics Association meetings, May.

Hendershott, P. H., and S. C. Hu. 1981. Inflation and Extraordinary Returns on Owner Occupied Housing: Some Implications for Capital Allocation and Productivity Growth. *Journal of Macroeconomics* 3 (2): 177–203.

Mankiw, G. N., and D. N. Weil. 1989. The Baby Boom, the Baby Bust, and the Housing Market. *Regional Science and Urban Economics* 19 (2): 235–58.

National Association of Home Builders, 1990. Will Home Prices Collapse? Washington, D.C.

Poterba, J. 1984. Tax Subsidies to Owner-Occupied Housing: An Asset-Market Approach. *Quarterly Journal of Economics* 99:729–52.

3   Housing Finance in Japan

Miki Seko

3.1 Introduction

The main issue of housing in Japan is affordability. Due to social and economic factors, the price of housing in Japan is extraordinarily high. Moreover, Japanese financial institutions do not lend on as generous terms as in other countries, placing significant liquidity constraints on aspiring homeowners.

In this paper I examine several problems of financing the purchase of housing in Japan in order to identify directions for future reform in Japanese housing finance in the context of ongoing financial liberalization initiatives. Housing finance in Japan is predominantly generated from the deposit-taking system, whether by commercial banks or public-sector lending institutions. Reforms, therefore, should focus on means to broaden the source of funds as one strategy to remove credit constraints and to mobilize capital more efficiently for housing finance.

Public-sector lending plays an important role in the Japanese housing finance system. The government-run Japan Housing Loan Corporation (JHLC) is the largest single mortgage lender in the world and accounts for some 25 to 35 percent of housing loans in Japan. Unlike other advanced industrial nations, Japan has no major private-sector institutions that specialize in housing finance, like the savings and loan associations in the United States and building societies in the United Kingdom.

Section 3.2 is an overview of the Japanese housing finance market and hous-

Miki Seko is professor of economics at Nihon University, Japan. The final version of the paper was written while she was a visiting scholar at the Department of Economics at MIT and the Center for Real Estate and Urban Economics at the University of California at Berkeley.

The author is thankful to Martin Feldstein, Takatoshi Ito, Yukio Noguchi, Seiritsu Ogura, James Poterba, Jonathan Skinner, Toshiaki Tachibanaki, and William Wheaton for their useful comments and suggestions.

ing finance systems. Section 3.3 examines JHLC home financing policy in terms of efficiency and equity. Section 3.4 briefly describes other aspects of the Japanese housing finance system related to recent steps toward financial liberalization.

3.2   Overview of the Housing Finance Market and Systems in Japan

3.2.1   The Housing Finance Market

The structure of the mortgage market in Japan is shown in figure 3.1. The state-run JHLC is the lender of last resort. Recently, there have been considerable efforts to develop specialized private-sector mortgage-lending entities. Mortgage companies and banks are becoming increasingly active in the housing finance market, although their presence is still small relative to their counterparts in the United States and the United Kingdom.

The Japan Housing Loan Corporation

The JHLC was established in 1950 as a special public corporation that provides long-term capital at a low rate of interest for the construction and purchase of housing. The JHLC obtains its funds from the postal savings system, not directly from public revenues.

The flow of loans by JHLC is indicated in figure 3.2. The JHLC draws funds from the Fiscal Investments and Loans budget. The amount of money to be loaned and the number of houses to be built with these loans each year are determined by the budget for the Fiscal Investments and Loans program. This program draws funds from the postal savings system through the Trust Fund Bureau, from postal life insurance and postal annuities, and from bonds offered for public subscription by government agencies. Its budget is submitted to the

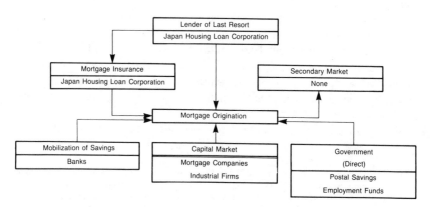

Fig. 3.1   Structure of the mortgage market in Japan
Source: McGuire 1981, fig. 13-1.

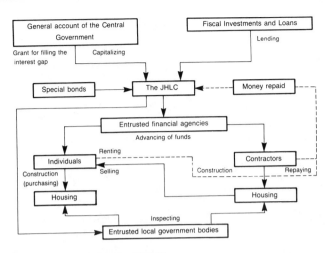

Fig. 3.2   The flow of loans by the JHLC
Source: Ministry of Construction, 1987, fig. 60.

Diet each year during deliberations on the overall budget bill. The JHLC makes loans at a lower rate of interest (currently about 5.4 percent) than the rate of interest on the funds drawn from the Fiscal Investments and Loans program (currently about 6.7 percent) and receives a government grant covering the interest-rate differential. In 1989, about 14.5 percent of the total budget for the Fiscal Investments and Loans program was allocated for housing construction through the JHLC. It is important to emphasize that capital for housing-purchase loans in Japan is primarily mobilized from the deposit-taking system (i.e., through short-term savings) by both the JHLC and commercial banks.

Table 3.1 shows the distribution of JHLC loans in 1989. Loans are made to private individuals who intend to acquire their own houses, private individuals and local housing-supply corporations that intend to build rental housing, local housing-supply corporations and enterprises such as commercial developers that intend to build houses for sale, and enterprises that intend to undertake urban renewal projects. On the demand side in 1989, about 78.3 percent of the JHLC loans were allocated to construction and purchase of new owner-occupied housing, and only 6.2 percent were allocated to the purchase of sec-ondhand owner-occupied housing. Generally, JHLC lending favors new hous-ing, with much stricter limits and lending criteria for used housing, thus acting to depress resale value of homes and discouraging the development of a mort-gage market in used homes. As for supply-side policy, only 4.7 percent of the JHLC loans were allocated to construct rental housing.

Other Institutions

The other large lenders are the commercial banks and housing loan compa-nies that are subsidiaries of commercial banks. These banks began providing

Table 3.1   Japan Housing Loan Corporation Loans, 1989

Type of Loan	Amount Lent (billions of yen)	Percentage
Construction of owner-occupied housing	2,555	44.2
Purchase of owner-occupied housing	1,969	34.1
Purchase of secondhand owner-occupied housing	359	6.2
Rented housing	274	4.7
Development of housing sites	129	2.2
Rehabilitation of owner-occupied housing	277	4.8
Urban renewal projects	69	1.2
Multistoried dwellings	16	0.3
Other	132	2.3
Total	5,780	100.0

Source: Housing Loan Corporation 1990.

housing loans in 1961. Figure 3.3 shows the proportion of outstanding loans of commercial banks to construction and real estate industries and the share of funds allocated to housing. Both proportions have shown a marked increase in the 1980s as a result of the real estate boom. It is important to bear in mind that there are no major private-sector institutions specializing in housing finance in Japan, as exist in the United States and the United Kingdom.

In addition, there are several other public housing finance institutions in Japan, but their role in housing finance is small compared to the JHLC.

Mortgage Market

The striking characteristic of Japanese housing finance in general is the virtual absence of a mortgage market for used houses. Unlike in the United States, mortgages are not bought and sold as commodities. This absence of trade in mortgages acts as an impediment to the flow of capital into housing finance markets. Among the factors that explain why an active mortgage market has not yet emerged in Japan, it appears that the government's longstanding informal policy of maintaining low interest rates on housing loans has rendered mortgages unattractive investment instruments. The absence of private-sector institutions specializing in mortgages has also hindered the development of a mortgage market. In addition, there is a limited legal foundation for a mortgage market, since gaining clear title to real estate pledged as collateral on a loan is difficult.

Private versus Public Loans

The housing finance systems in Japan comprise an unusual combination of private- and public-sector loans. Figure 3.4 indicates the origin of housing loans since 1965. Before 1965, almost all of the housing loans were public, because private financial institutions had to allocate their funds to the huge demand for business investment (for industrial capital formation). During the

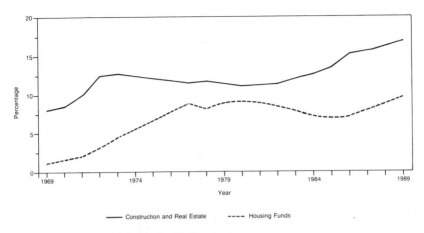

Fig. 3.3   Commercial loans oustanding by industry
Source: Economic Statistics Monthly (Bank of Japan), various issues.

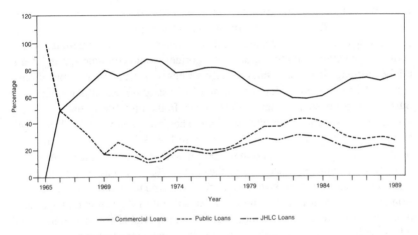

Fig. 3.4   Source of housing loans
Source: Housing Loan Corporation 1990.

1980s, commercial lending markedly increased, while JHLC loans fluctuated between 20 and 30 percent of total housing loans. The percentage of housing loans outstanding since 1965 is indicated in figure 3.5. The housing finance market in Japan has expanded greatly since 1965, marked by a decreasing reliance on public loans and a rapid increase in private loans. After 1975, the share of private loans decreased because their rate of growth declined. In the 1980s, however, there was a marked increase in property-related lending by commercial banks. In 1990, the share of bank loans outstanding for households rose to 16 percent of the total, for the first time exceeding the share for manufacturing

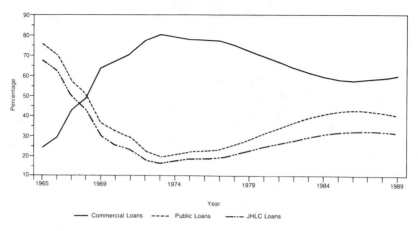

Fig. 3.5   Housing loans outstanding
Source: Housing Loan Corporation 1990.

firms, while the share for property companies rose from 4 percent in 1970 to 12 percent in 1990.[1] The surge of household and private-sector money into property sparked a self-perpetuating land price spiral, fed by continued hectic commercial lending and the certainty that prices would continue soaring. Generally, mortgage loans are available only for new construction, but speculators, construction companies, developers, and real estate offices all have access to other funds for property-related investments. In the mid-1980s, banks actively sought to boost property-related lending. They mistakenly credited the myth that land prices always go up and thus ran little risk if loans were secured by property. The banks had traditionally lent heavily to manufacturing firms, but this source of business dried up in the mid-1980s as manufacturers increasingly turned to equity markets to raise money. Given the unprecedented expansion of Japan's money supply in the 1980s, a result of the yen's rapid appreciation and low interest rates, ample funds were available for speculators and others with minimal monitoring. This explains the current severe problems of housing loan corporations and banks; with the bursting of the bubble, the rate of nonperforming loans has risen dramatically.

Interest Rates for Housing Loans

Figure 3.6 shows interest rates for housing loans in Japan. Government policy has deliberately kept mortgage rates low, although they have risen since 1989 in line with government policies aimed at curbing real estate speculation in the overheated property market. In the Japanese financial system, key interest rates are established by the government through the Bank of Japan. Exact levels of key interest rates and deposit-rate ceilings are determined by both

1. "Survey: The Japanese Economy," *Economist,* March 6, 1993, 6.

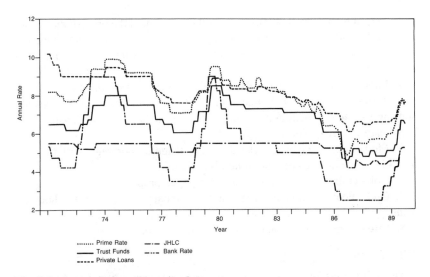

Fig. 3.6 Interest rates of housing loans
Source: Housing Industry Newspaper Company, various issues.

negotiation and discussion among other monetary authorities. Once the key interest rates are determined, all other rates find their levels in the market. The rate of interest charged by the JHLC is modest and below market interest rates.

Until recently, private loans for housing have been provided largely on a fixed-interest basis.[2] The proportion of private housing loans provided on a variable-interest basis has risen sharply since they were introduced in 1983, by 1989 constituting about two-thirds of private housing loans (46.5 percent in 1987, 57.2 in 1988, and 66.5 in 1989). The introduction of floating rates is part of the process of financial liberalization, as banks scramble to adjust to interest-rate deregulation; as long as the government kept interest rates low, banks could extend fixed-interest loans at little risk; now they must move to reduce their vulnerability to interest-rate increases.[3]

3.2.2 Homeowner Financing

Commercial Housing Loans

The standard conditions for private housing loans are
1. Borrowers: Twenty to sixty years old (less than seventy when repayment is completed).

2. Using time-series data, Seko (1991) has shown that, under inflation, credit constraints in Japan exist where standard fixed-payment mortgage is dominant.
3. See Arima (1986), Association for Promoting Housing Finance (1986), Boleat (1985), Horioka (1988), Ichimura (1981), Izu (1988), Mills and Ohta (1976), and Muramoto (1986) for more details about Japanese housing markets and housing finance systems.

2. Size of loan: Usually between 70 and 80 percent of the price of the house, and less than 30 million yen; a maximum of three to four times annual income. There is no legal down-payment requirement, but the usual self-financing ratio is more than 30 percent.

3. Interest rate: 6.78 percent fixed-rate, 6.00 percent variable-rate.

4. Terms of repayment: A maximum of twenty-five years for a fixed-rate housing loan and a maximum of thirty years for a variable-rate housing loan in the case of city banks.

5. Method of repayment: Usually the standard mortgage system (i.e., monthly payments are constant in nominal terms).

6. Collateral: The first rights to the mortgaged property.

7. Guarantee: By contracted guarantee company or security for housing loans.

8. Life insurance: Contracted group life insurance.

JHLC Loans

The JHLC puts limits on the amount and cost of its loans. Conditions on loans by the JHLC for new individual home purchasers as of 1992 are as follows (Ministry of Construction, Housing Bureau 1985, 1989).

1. Size of loan: The size of a loan is specified according to the floor space of a house, the region in which the house is built, the structure of the house, and so forth. For instance, an individual can normally borrow a total of 14.0 million yen, consisting of 7.3 million yen for the house and 6.7 million yen for the land, if the borrower acquires a wooden house in a large metropolitan region. This amount of money corresponds to 30–40 percent of the cost of the house and the lot, and the borrower must add funds on hand, loans from a private financial agency, and so forth, to this amount to purchase the house. If a borrower wants to borrow money just to build a house, the land area owned by the borrower must exceed one hundred square meters. It should be pointed out that lending criteria favor borrowers who already own land. The JHLC has special provisions for providing additional loans to households with aged or handicapped people, in cases where two households live together, and for energy-efficient houses.

2. Interest rates: The interest rate is classified for ten years after a loan is made by the size of a house, except for a person with an income over 10 million yen. The initial rate for the first ten years is 4.9 percent for 70–125 square meters, 5.25 percent for 125–55 square meters, and 5.6 percent for 155–220 square meters. From the eleventh year on, the rate of interest is fixed at 5.6 percent. The rate of interest applied to a person who earns an income of more than 10 million yen in the preceding year is fixed at 5.6 percent from the outset.

3. Terms of repayment: A loan must be repaid within twenty-five years for wooden housing of noncombustible construction, within thirty years for housing of quasi-fire-resistant construction, and within thirty-five years for housing of fire-resistant construction.

Table 3.2   **Source of Funding for Purchase of Custom-made Housing**
                     (percentage of contribution)

Source of funds	1984	1985	1986	1987	1988	1989
Proportion of self-financing						
Personal savings	29.2	29.1	29.2	29.9	26.7	26.0
Selling real estate	6.3	7.1	9.8	10.9	11.0	14.7
Inheritance and gifts	0.5	2.0	2.1	2.0	1.9	1.6
Other	2.5	1.6	4.0	2.7	2.5	1.9
Total	38.6	39.8	45.1	45.6	42.2	44.2
Loans						
Relatives	1.7	1.6	1.7	1.2	1.0	0.9
Government-related	39.6	38.0	34.5	35.3	42.6	39.3
Employer	9.2	7.7	8.8	5.9	4.4	3.6
Private-Sector financial institutions	10.6	12.3	9.8	11.5	9.5	11.8
Other	0.2	0.6	0.0	0.5	0.3	0.3
Total	61.4	60.2	54.9	54.4	57.8	55.8
Total	100.0	100.0	100.0	100.0	100.0	100.0

Source: Ministry of Construction 1989.

4. Method of repayment: A loan must be repaid on a principal-and-interest-equality basis: the step repayment system, which reduces monthly payments for the first five years, is also available.

5. Housing construction standards: Housing built with loans from the JHLC must not only conform to the Building Standard Law and other laws and ordinances, but also meet the housing construction standards established by the JHLC. The JHLC enforces these requirements through design inspections and field inspections made by local government bodies, thereby ensuring good-quality housing.[4]

Source of Funds

Table 3.2 outlines the wide variety of financing strategies that Japanese owners use when purchasing a dwelling.[5] The proportion of self-financing is about 40 percent, of which about 25–30 percent is from personal savings. This ratio may be biased downward: if a new owner borrows money from parents without collateral and applies it toward the down payment to the developer, the amount of money would still be counted as loans instead of down payment (Hayashi, Ito, and Slemrod 1988). About 40 percent of the purchase price is financed by public loans. One of the anomalies of the Japanese housing finance system is the relatively small role of commercial lending, about 12 percent of the total. Another anomaly is the relatively large role of personal savings; home buyers raise about one-quarter of the purchase price from their own savings.

4. See Okazaki and Urabe (1986) for more details.
5. Figure 3.4 indicates the origin of housing loans for all kinds of housing; table 3.2 indicates detached houses only.

3.3   JHLC Home Financing Policy

3.3.1   JHLC Housing Construction Policy

In Japan, the Housing Construction Program Law was enacted in 1966 to promote further housing construction through the united efforts of the central government, local government bodies, and the public. The law prescribes that the minister of construction submit a draft of a five-year plan for housing construction by considering the Housing and Housing Land Council's opinion. The final draft is decided upon by the Cabinet.

In each five-year plan, the government must decide the specific goals for housing conditions and set the target of the number of units to be built by both the private and public sectors. Local government bodies, the JHLC, and the Housing and Urban Development Corporation (HUDC) are given targets for the number of units to be built within the planned period.[6] The minister of construction divides the nation into ten regions and decides on a five-year program for local housing construction in each region. Each prefecture decides on a five-year program for housing construction based on the regional program.

Five five-year programs have been enacted in conformity with the Housing Construction Program Law.

In the first program (1966–70), the planned share of JHLC-funded housing was 44.4 percent, and its rate of achievement was 100.7 percent. In the second program (1971–75), the planned share was 39.7 percent, and its achievement ratio was 121.5 percent. In the third program (1976–80), the planned share was 57.4 percent, and its actual achievement ratio was 134.1 percent. In the fourth program (1981–85), the planned share was 65.5 percent, and its actual achievement ratio was 111.7 percent. In the fifth program (1986–90), the planned share was 71.4 percent, and its actual achievement ratio was 110.3 percent.

Each successive plan raised the JHLC target level, and in each period the JHLC exceeded this target, indicating that its lending program has been successful and popular. Clearly the JHLC has filled a need for subsidized housing loans, but past successes notwithstanding, the present JHLC home financing policy has problems both in terms of efficiency and equity.[7]

3.3.2   Efficiency

At present, the JHLC determines the amount of subsidized loans based on floor space. Thus, lending levels are solely based on the quantity of housing.

---

6. The HUDC was founded in 1981 by the government for the purpose of furthering the supply of housing and housing land of good quality to middle-class workers in large metropolitan regions, encouraging urban redevelopment, and furthering the development of urban parks in order to enhance the living environment. HUDC public housing is available on a lottery basis, regardless of income, at relatively reasonable prices.

7. See Ministry of Construction (1990) and Statistics Bureau (1983, 1988) for Japanese housing data.

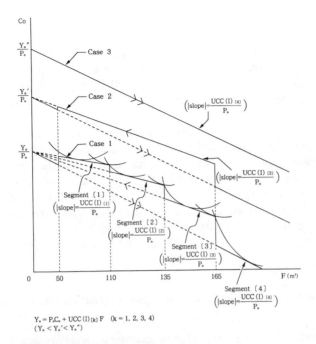

Fig. 3.7   **Nonlinear budget constraints**
Source: Seko 1993, fig. 1.
Notes: F = floor space; C_o = composite goods; P_o = price of C_o; y_o = nominal income; Y_o = y_o/P_o = real income; $UCC(I)_{[k]}$ = the user cost of capital of owner-occupied housing for kth segment (k = 1, 2, 3, 4); I = quality of housing.

Housing decisions of home purchasers, however, depend not only on quantity (in this case, floor space) but also on quality. This suggests that the current Japanese home financing system distorts borrowers' housing decisions.

Kato (1988) and Akiho (1984) examined the effects of the JHLC home financing policy on housing choice and the efficiency of home purchasers based on hedonic regression (Quigley 1982). They found that the JHLC lending criteria had a negligible impact on housing decisions in terms of floor space. Seko (1993) also examined the effect of the JHLC's home financing policy on housing decisions and the efficiency of home purchasers based on cross-sectional micro data, using econometric analysis. I found that the budget constraint becomes nonlinear and has jumps (as in figure 3.7), because the interest rate on JHLC loans is determined by the floor space (see section 3.2.2).[8] In response to the established criteria for access to subsidized credit, each household distorts its housing decision by overconsuming housing quantity and underconsuming housing quality under the present JHLC home financing system.

8. See Seko (1990) for nonlinear estimation of this aspect.

3.3.3   Equity

Current JHLC lending policies favor borrowers who already have land, thus conferring an advantage on those who have substantial assets. In addition, when we look at the income distribution of the JHLC borrower, the proportion of upper-income borrowers is relatively high (13.4 percent on average from 1986 to 1989).[9]

Moreover, because the JHLC makes loans at a lower interest rate than on the funds drawn from the Fiscal Investments and Loans program and receives a government grant financed by tax revenues from all Japanese taxpayers to cover the interest-rate differential, critics argue that this constitutes a redistribution of income from taxpayers to JHLC borrowers.[10] The fact that JHLC lending policies favor those who can most easily borrow from commercial banks (i.e., borrowers who own land or have a high income) suggests that the subsidies are not addressing the problems of those who most need assistance.

3.4   Some Recent Proposals for the Japanese Housing Finance System

Generally speaking, the housing finance system is characterized by borrowing short and lending long. That is, short-term savings of individuals are channeled into long term housing loans by housing finance institutions. This is the usual recipe for banking disaster because of a mismatch between assets and liabilities. Usually a housing finance institution overcomes this problem, either by raising its funds on a long-term basis, or by ensuring that the rate of interest on its long-term loans can be changed in line with the rate of interest on the short-term savings that it has attracted.

In Japan, as noted in section 3.2.1, variable-rate mortgages were introduced by commercial banks in 1983 as part of the overall process of Japanese financial liberalization, partially reducing the banks' vulnerability. However, a housing finance institution bears the risk that borrowers will prematurely redeem their loans. That is, loans are constantly being paid off as houses with mortgages are resold. Premature redemptions are also a danger if interest rates go down and borrowers seek better terms. Moreover, as variable-interest rates for mortgages in Japan are based on the long-term prime rate and not fully adjusted to market interest rates, changes in the rates are not sufficient to overcome those risks.

Under these circumstances, securitization of mortgages has been recommended recently in Japan as a complementary housing finance policy.[11] That is, mortgage loans should be converted into a security that can be actively

---

9. Upper-income borrowers denote households of annual income exceeding 10 million yen.
10. For example, Iwata (1977).
11. Securitization here is different from that in Noguchi's paper (ch. 1 in this volume).

traded in secondary mortgage markets, as in the United States Secondary mortgage markets are important to finance real estate transactions because they move real estate funds from investors to house buyers, and from areas of capital surplus to areas of deficit. The JHLC is well positioned to play a key role in securitizing mortgages in Japan.

In section 3.2, I noted that the JHLC obtains almost all of its funds from the Trust Fund Bureau, which mainly obtains funds from postal savings deposits. It is difficult to expand these funds under current Japanese fiscal conditions, especially given the elimination of tax incentives for postal savings and the consequent shift of savings into alternative accounts. (The rate of growth of postal savings deposits outstanding is declining. The ratio of the Fiscal Investments and Loans budget to GNP is around 8 percent.) This credit squeeze is likely to worsen in the near future due to financial liberalization and the prospects that heightened competition for deposits will raise interest rates. Given these prospects, subsidized housing loans will be difficult to sustain at current levels. These changed circumstances suggest a need to modify the role of the JHLC consistent with fiscal constraints and the evident need to develop a mortgage market that can more effectively channel funds to borrowers while covering associated risks.

In section 3.3, I noted how the present JHLC home-financing policy introduces inefficiency and inequity. It is possible to reform the state-run JHLC, transforming its role as a direct mortgage lender. It would be possible to expand commercial loans and rely on the JHLC to enhance the flow of funds from capital markets to the housing market via the purchase of mortgages and the sale of guaranteed mortgage-backed securities like the Government National Mortgage Association (GNMA), the Federal Home Loan Mortgage Corporation (FHLMC), and the Federal National Mortgage Association (FNMA) in the United States. Alternatively, the JHLC could serve as a buyer of mortgages held by private financial institutions and their mortgage-backed securities. This would have the same impact as if the JHLC were financing housing loans at private loan rates through private financial institutions.

It is also possible to securitize mortgages held by the JHLC. However, under present circumstances wherein interest rates of JHLC loans are artificially low due to subsidies, these securities may not be attractive to investors because of the increase in the danger of premature redemptions.

Although the JHLC can play a positive role in the process of securitization, this may entail some negative consequences. There are potential risks and social costs of having a large central institution insuring securitized mortgages as practiced in the United States. The JHLC's lack of experience and expertise is a serious drawback and could swell the costs to taxpayers. The imbalance in the rewards and costs of risk taking in financial markets also suggests that the JHLC should weigh carefully its potential impact on private institutions and in terms of public trust. Alternatively, private institutions could play a leading role in mortgage securitization. However, there are concerns that those most in need may be bypassed by market forces. In addition, funding constraints may limit the viability of such an approach. Initial forays into commercial property mortgage securitization in Japan have not been very successful, because the returns have been low. Raising returns to spark private-sector interest would have an adverse impact on those seeking mortgages (or paying rents), exacerbating credit constraints and inequities.[12]

3.5 Conclusion

Financial liberalization in Japan is encouraging the introduction and proliferation of more sophisticated financial instruments and a process of market deepening. The recent "problem loan" crisis that has devastated housing loan companies and generated concerns about commercial banks is a good reminder about the need for building a stable, efficient, and diversified mortgage market in line with financial liberalization. The relatively undeveloped nature of the Japanese housing finance system is evident in the absence of both a mortgage market for used houses and private-sector institutions specializing in housing finance. The current woes in the property sector suggest the need for some dramatic changes encompassing institutional arrangements and policy prescriptions.

Currently, the commercial housing loan market is stagnant even though interest rates are very low. The recession and administrative guidelines issued by the Ministry of Finance have served to dampen property-related lending. This is seen as a necessary corrective to the excesses of the so-called bubble economy and a means to bring about an orderly decline in property prices. Declining land prices would certainly lessen liquidity constraints on house-purchasing behavior. However, uncertainties about the market clearing level of property prices have dampened buying and selling activity. In this regard, the development of a securitized mortgage market could have desirable consequences in terms of providing accurate market information, hedging risks, and attracting capital to a moribund market and in that way providing some support for sliding real estate prices. However, the need for accurate price assessments would require individuals and companies to admit substantial losses on property acquired during the peak of the bubble between 1987 and 1989. This would also carry implications for loans secured by inflated property assets.

The recognized need to revitalize the troubled property sector has created a receptiveness to innovation and reform. The JHLC and commercial lenders have a vested interest in a revitalized property sector and could collaborate to draw up measures facilitating the emergence of a securitized mortgage market. This may entail a modified role for the JHLC in line with changing market needs. The government may also want to consider mortgage tax credits to

---

12. Kamoike (1988) and Miyao (1989) also mentioned recent proposals in Japan. See Altman and McKinney (1986) and Light and White (1979) for the American housing finance system.

lessen liquidity constraints. The introduction of a reverse annuity mortgage to convert housing stock into flow is another alternative, as Japanese society enters a period of rapid aging.[13]

The source of funding for housing in Japan remains skewed toward personal savings, while commercial lending remains a relatively untapped source at about 12 percent of the purchase price. Given the high cost of housing in Japan, marked by a rapid price increase in the 1980s, it is increasingly difficult for households to mobilize sufficient savings to make down payments that average close to 40 percent. Such levels are unheard of in other industrialized nations, where there is a much greater reliance on commercial housing loans. Introducing a mortgage tax credit as in the United States would significantly lower the real cost of commercial lending.

References

Akiho, Y. (1984). One Consideration of the Evaluation of Housing Policy (in Japanese). *Monthly Housing Finance Review* 390:34–43.

———. 1988. On Securitizing Mortgages (in Japanese). *Research on Housing Problems* 4 (2): 36–50.

Altman, E. I., and M. J. McKinney. 1986. *Handbook of Financial Markets and Institutions.* Sixth edition. New York: John Wiley and Sons.

Arima, T. 1986. Current Situations and Problems of Japanese and U.S. Housing Finance (in Japanese). *Research on Housing Problems* 2 (4): 2–20.

Association for Promoting Housing Finance. 1986. *Housing Policy and Housing Finance in Europe and the U.S.* (in Japanese). Tokyo: Association for Promoting Housing Finance.

Boleat, M. 1985. *National Housing Finance Systems: A Comparative Study.* London: Croom Helm.

Hayashi, F., T. Ito, and J. Slemrod. 1988. Housing Finance Imperfections, Taxations, and Private Saving: A Comparative Simulation Analysis of the U.S. and Japan. *Journal of the Japanese and International Economies* 2 (3): 215–38.

Horioka, Charles Y. 1988. Tenure Choice and Housing Demand in Japan. *Journal of Urban Economics* 24 (3): 289–309.

Housing Industry Newspaper Company. 1990, 1991. *Housing Economy Databook* (in Japanese). Tokyo: Housing Industry Newspaper Company.

Housing Loan Corporation. 1990. *Housing Loan Corporation Yearbook* (in Japanese). Tokyo: Housing Loan Corporation.

Ichimura, S. 1981. Economic Growth, Savings, and Housing Finance in Japan. *Journal of Economic Studies* 8: 41–64.

Iwata, K. 1977. *The Economics of Land and Housing* (in Japanese). Tokyo: Nihon Keizai Shinbun-sha.

Izu, H. 1988. *New Housing Economy* (in Japanese). Tokyo: Gyosei.

Kamoike, O. 1988. Financial Intermediaries and Housing Finance (in Japanese). *Research on Housing Problems* 4 (1): 55–64, (2): 51–59, (3): 44–54, (4): 63–70.

---

13. By 2025, an estimated 25 percent of Japan's population will be over age sixty-five.

Kato, H. 1988. The Effects of Housing Finance Policy on Consumer Housing Choice (in Japanese). *Research on Housing Problems* 4 (2): 2–35.

Light, J. O., and W. L. White. 1979. *The Financial System.* Homewood, Ill.: Richard D. Irwin.

McGuire, C. C. 1981. *International Housing Policies.* Lexington, Mass.: Lexington Books.

Mills, E., and K. Ohta. 1976. Urbanization and Urban Problems. In H. Patrick and H. Rosovsky, eds., *Asia's New Giant.* Washington, D.C.: Brookings Institution.

Ministry of Construction. Housing Bureau. 1985, 1989. *A Quick Look at Housing in Japan.* Tokyo: Building Center of Japan.

———. 1987. *The Results of the Survey on Financing Private Housing* (in Japanese). Tokyo: Housing Bureau, Ministry of Construction.

———. 1990. *Construction Statistics Yearbook* (in Japanese). Tokyo: Construction Price Research Foundation.

Miyao, T. 1989. *The Age of the Stock Economy* (in Japanese). Tokyo: Nihon Hyour-onsha.

Muramoto, T. 1986. *The Housing Finance System in Modern Japan* (in Japanese). Tokyo: Chikura.

Okazaki, T., and K. Urabe. 1986. *Knowledge of Housing Finance* (in Japanese). Tokyo: Nihon Keizai Shinbun-sha.

Quigley, J. M. 1982. Nonlinear Budget Constraints and Consumer Demand: An Application to Public Programs for Residential Housing. *Journal of Urban Economics* 12 (2): 177–201.

Seko, Miki. 1990. Nonlinear Budget Constraints and Estimation: Effects of Subsidized Home Loans on Floor Space Decisions in Japan. Paper presented at the Thirty-seventh North American Regional Science Meetings, Boston, November 10.

———. 1991. The Effect of Inflation on Japanese Homeownership Rates: Evidence from Time-Series. *Economic Studies Quarterly* 42 (2): 155–63.

———. 1993. Effects of Subsidized Home Loans on Housing Decisions and Efficiency in Japan: Tradeoff between Quality and Quantity. *Journal of Real Estate Finance and Economics* 6 (1): 5–23.

Statistics Bureau. Management and Coordination Agency. 1983, 1988. *Housing Survey of Japan* (in Japanese). Tokyo: Japan Statistics Association.

4   Housing Finance in the United States

Patric H. Hendershott

4.1 Introduction

During the 1960s and the 1970s, the U.S. government closely regulated the single-family housing finance system. The regulation manifested itself in a highly specialized system with four notable characteristics. First, because federally chartered depository institutions were prohibited from originating adjustable-rate mortgages (ARMs), virtually all home buyers used the long-term (twenty- to thirty-year) fixed-rate mortgage (FRM). Second, portfolio restrictions and tax inducements led nonbank depository institutions (savings and loans [S&Ls] and mutual savings banks [MSBs]) to supply two-thirds of all funds to the home mortgage market. Moreover, the tax inducement caused home mortgage rates to be roughly a half percentage point lower than they would otherwise have been. Third, because depository institutions were funding their FRMs with short-term deposits, deposit rate ceilings were imposed when interest rates rose significantly. Fourth, because the capital market could not compete with "cheap" deposit money, few conventional mortgages (those not government insured) were pooled into mortgage pass-through securities. As a result of these four characteristics, the U.S. housing sector was extremely vulnerable to increases in interest rates that caused deposits to flow out of the depository institutions, thereby restricting credit availability.

Portfolio restrictions, tax inducements, prohibitions against ARMs, and deposit rate ceilings were all removed in the 1980s, and, not surprisingly, the housing finance system changed markedly. Between early 1982 and 1989, two-fifths of all new loans had adjustable, not fixed, rates, and S&Ls *reduced* their holdings of FRMs (both whole loans and mortgage pass-throughs) by 15 to 20

Patric H. Hendershott is professor of finance and public policy and holder of the Galbreath Chair in Real Estate at Ohio State University and is a research associate of the National Bureau of Economic Research.

percent. Moreover, the fraction of conventional FRM originations that have been pooled into pass-throughs rose from less than one-twentieth before 1981 to over one-half after 1985. With the opportunity of borrowers to shift to lower coupon ARMs when rates rise and with the integration of the home mortgage market with capital markets generally, one would expect that the U.S. housing sector is now less sensitive to rising interest rates than it was in the 1960s and 1970s.

In this paper, I begin by documenting these changes in the U.S. housing finance system and then describe the impact of these changes on the FRM market in the 1980s. In sections 4.4 and 4.5, I attempt to relate changes in real house prices and home ownership to these changes and survey recent studies of housing demand and supply in the United States to determine whether the interest sensitivity of housing production has been reduced. A final section offers some concluding thoughts.

4.2   U.S. Housing Finance, 1961–89

I begin with a general overview of U.S. housing finance, with emphasis on the pre-1982 period. I then examine the major finance evolutions of the 1980s: the widespread securitization of conventional FRMs, the development of a national primary market for ARMs, and the decline of the S&L industry.[1]

4.2.1   An Overview Emphasizing the 1960s and 1970s

Table 4.1 lists, for four-year periods from 1962–65 to 1986–89, the fraction of the increase in outstanding home mortgages absorbed by each of three investor groups: nonbank depository institutions (S&Ls, MSBs, and credit unions), commercial banks, and others. S&L and MSB net purchases of agency securities are assumed to be purchases of mortgage pass-throughs and are thus included in their mortgage absorptions.

The far right column gives the ratios for the total 1962–77 period. As can be seen, the nonbank depository institutions absorbed two-thirds of the increase in outstandings (S&Ls alone accounted for 60 percent between 1969 and 1977) and the other third was split about equally between commercial banks and other investors (federally sponsored credit agencies, predominantly Federal National Mortgage Association [Fannie Mae], contributed over half of the other). There is some variation within the four four-year subperiods. In particular, thrifts absorbed only 54 percent of the increase in outstandings during the 1966–69 period, when deposit rate ceilings limited their ability to attract funds, and a full 72 percent in the 1970–73 period, when deposits surged (see figure 4.1). The other sector picked up the slack in 1966–69 (over half by the sponsored agencies) and added few home mortgages in 1970–73, when insurance companies liquidated a quarter of their holdings.

---

1. This overview draws, quite heavily at times, on Hendershott (1991).

Table 4.1   Ratio of Increases in Home Mortgage Holdings to Increases in Total Home Mortgages Outstanding

	1962–65	1966–69	1970–73	1974–77	1978–81	1982–85	1986–89	1962–77
Nonbank depository institutions[a]	.67	.54	.72	.66	.41	.38	.23	.66
Commercial banks	.16	.18	.22	.17	.16	.10	.17	.18
Other	.17	.28	.06	.17	.43	.52	.60	.16

[a]S&Ls, MSBs, and credit unions (the latter did not purchase as much as 1 percent of the increase in outstandings until the 1980s). Data for the S&Ls and MSBs include increases in agency securities, which are assumed to be mortgage pass-throughs.

Source: "Financial Assets and Liabilities Year-End, 1966–1989," Flow of Funds Accounts, Board of Governors of the Federal Reserve System, Washington, D.C., September 1990 (and Year-End, 1961–84, October 1985 for pre-1966 data).

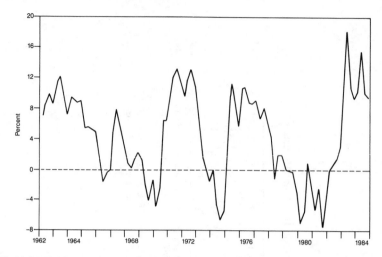

Fig. 4.1   Real deposits at thrift institutions (quarterly percentage of change at annual rates)
Source: Throop 1986, chart 1.

The 1978–81 period was a replay of the 1966–69 period in that deposit growth slowed, but the period of reduced growth was far longer, owing to the more prolonged and sharper rise in market interest rates (see figure 4.1). Many thrifts were reluctant to bid for deposits, in spite of a loosening of deposit rate ceilings with the June 1978 introduction of money market certificates and the Deregulation and Monetary Control Act of 1980, because the spreads between their asset portfolio yields and the cost of deposits became so large. The surge in other net purchases reflected greater participation by a broad spectrum of investors, with households (largely through owner financing of house sales) being the largest purchasers. Relative to the 1974–77 period, households increased their share of the market by 8 percentage points, and the federally sponsored credit agencies, state and local governments, and insurance companies each increased their share by 4 percentage points.

The post-1981 period showed a continued decline in thrift absorptions, in spite of substantial real deposit growth, and a continued rise in the other share to 60 percent in the 1986–89 period. The post-1981 period is marked by unprecedented regulatory changes and will be discussed in detail shortly. Before turning to it, I first explain the motivation for the heavy S&L and MSB investment in home mortgages in the 1960s and 1970s.

Portfolio restrictions on S&Ls (no corporate loans, bonds, or equity issues) encouraged investment in residential mortgages prior to the 1980s. Moreover, residential mortgages were especially profitable to thrifts (S&Ls and MSBs), owing to a special tax preference. The preference was the ability of thrifts to compute loan loss reserves that far exceeded a reasonable provision for normal losses, as long as thrifts invested a large fraction of their assets in housing-related loans or liquid assets (Hendershott and Villani 1980, appendix). That is, thrifts were allowed to transfer large portions of their pretax income to reserves, thereby reducing their tax liability. Between 1962 and 1969, the transfer was limited to 60 percent of taxable income; between 1969 and 1979, the fraction was gradually reduced to 40 percent; the 1986 Tax Reform Act lowered the fraction to 8 percent.

The incentive provided by the extraordinary loan loss provisions depends on the expected level of thrift taxable profits over the expected life of the investment (with no profits now or in the future, the incentive is zero), the income tax rate, and the statutory fraction of income that can be transferred to reserves. Assuming a 1 percent net pretax return on assets, the incentive was substantial in the 1960s and 1970s (Hendershott and Villani 1980). In the 1960s, S&Ls would have accepted a pretax return on tax-preferred housing-related assets 0.75 percentage point lower than on comparable nonpreferred assets. The maximum transfer fraction decline throughout the 1970s, and by 1979, when the transfer fraction was down to 40 percent, thrifts would have accepted 0.5 percentage point less. Of course, with a transfer fraction of only 8 percent, or minimal profit expectations, mortgages have virtually no advantage over other investments.

4.2.2 Securitization of Conventional Fixed-Rate Mortgages

In 1970, the Federal Home Loan Mortgage Corporation (Freddie Mac) was chartered to spur the development of a secondary market for conventional mortgages. Freddie Mac introduced the first conventional mortgage pass-through security in 1971. Fannie Mae initiated a conventional pass-through program similar to Freddie Mac's in 1981. Investors in pass-throughs receive a pro rata share of the underlying mortgage payments, both scheduled and early in the event of prepayment or default. A major attraction of these pass-throughs is that Fannie Mae and Freddie Mac guarantee the investors' payments even if the underlying mortgages default.[2]

The conventional loan volume that can be securitized by the sponsored agencies (Fannie Mae and Freddie Mac) is restricted by limits on the dollar value of loans that can be pooled into their pass-through securities. The dollar limit, known as the "conforming" limit, changes annually with a house price index and was $187,600 in 1989, up 63 percent since 1985 (the limit was virtually unchanged in 1990). In 1987, over 90 percent of home mortgage loans (80 percent of dollar volume) was eligible for pooling by the agencies, and this percentage has been fairly constant in the 1980s.

The best measure of the agencies' presence in the conforming FRM market is the share of new (generally defined as less than one year since origination) conventional FRMs eligible for agency securitization (under the conforming

---

2. The guarantee is especially attractive to investors because of the general view that the federal government implicitly stands behind the debt of these agencies.

limit) that is, in fact, securitized by Fannie Mae and Freddie Mac. This share rose from 4 percent in the 1977–81 period, to almost 25 percent in the 1982–85 period, and to over 50 percent since 1986, including 69 percent in 1989 (Hendershott 1990).[3] That is, in less than a decade, the agencies and their pass-throughs have gone from being a negligible factor to being the driving force in the market.

Two major factors drove the increase in conventional loan securitization in the 1980s.[4] First, thrifts maintained their share of mortgage originations but reduced their relative investment in home mortgages (sold some of the originated mortgages). Most strikingly, the share of S&L total assets in home mortgages and agency securities (largely Fannie Mae and Freddie Mac pass-throughs) fell from 72 to 59 percent during the 1982–84 period. This portfolio shift reflected the reduced profitability of S&Ls and the expansion of S&L asset powers. The reduced profitability eroded the tax incentives for residential mortgage investment, while the expansion of powers encouraged thrifts to invest more widely.[5] Second, Fannie Mae and Freddie Mac pass-throughs are excellent collateral for borrowing via Federal Home Loan Bank (FHLB) advances and security repurchase agreements, and in the 1980s these became cheaper marginal sources of funds than deposits for many S&Ls. During the 1984–88 period, S&Ls increased such debt by over $150 billion. That is, some loans were simply swapped for pass-throughs, and the pass-throughs were retained in portfolio and "repoed" or used as collateral for increased advances.

4.2.3   Adjustable-Rate Mortgages

Periodically in the 1960s and 1970s, increases in interest rates reminded thrifts of the problems of borrowing short and lending long, and thrifts lobbied for permission to offer borrowers an alternative to the FRM, the ARM, that would reprice more in line with thrift deposits. Congress made clear to the regulatory body (then the Federal Home Loan Bank Board) that it did not want borrowers to have that choice (Cassidy 1984). In December 1978, an exception was made for federally chartered S&Ls in California, allowing them to compete with state-chartered S&Ls, and in July 1979, nationwide authority to invest in ARMs with tight interest-rate caps was granted. However, tightly

3. The securitization of conventional conforming ARMs by Fannie Mae and Freddie Mac is less prevalent. It appears that only 2 to 3 percent were securitized in 1984–85 and that the percentage is still only 10 to 12 percent. The greater securitization of FRMs than ARMs likely reflects both the greater standardization of FRMs and the greater desire of originators to hold ARMs in their portfolio. (Some investment banks and large thrifts also securitize home mortgages, but these institutions largely—possibly exclusively—limit themselves to nonconforming or jumbo loans and they likely securitize only 10 to 20 percent of the market.)

4. Over 50 percent of new government-insured originations (Federal Housing Administration [FHA] and Veterans Administration [VA] mortgages) was securitized—put into GNMA pass-throughs—by 1976, 80 percent by 1981, and 100 percent by 1985. FHA/VA originations declined from 30 percent of the total FRM market in the early 1980s to 20 percent in the late 1980s.

5. The vengeance with which some S&Ls used the new asset powers was undoubtedly driven by a desire to "double their bets," given that the market value of their net worth was negative.

capped ARMs were not much of an alternative to the FRM, and these loans were not popular.

In April 1981, fairly liberal regulations were implemented for federally chartered thrifts, and in August 1982, these were loosened further and extended via the Deposit Institutions Act to all state-chartered institutions. Thrifts took advantage of this opportunity. In the middle of 1982, ARMs were only 10 percent of the single-family mortgage portfolio of FSLIC-insured S&Ls. By March 1989, 48 percent of the thrift single-family loan portfolio (including mortgage pass-throughs) was in ARMs (Hendershott and Shilling 1992). Moreover, over the 1984–89 period, ARMs accounted for 43 percent of the conventional single-family loan volume originated by all lenders.

The expansion of ARMs could significantly reduce the volatility of housing demand. At any point in time, the initial coupon on an ARM is less than that on a FRM, but the coupon on the ARM can easily rise above the original FRM contract rate during the life of the contract. Thus a borrower is faced with trading off a lower initial coupon against greater uncertainty about the coupon in later years. Borrowers prefer a lower initial coupon because it allows them to qualify for a larger loan and thus reduces the "affordability" problem, but they dislike interest-rate risk.

Which mortgage a specific borrower will choose at any point in time depends largely on the level and structure of interest rates. With high interest rates generally or with lower rates but a steeply upward-sloping yield curve, borrowers will be more likely to choose ARMs. High interest rates force the borrower to the ARM (there is great utility to lowering the initial rate); relatively low short-term rates induce the borrower to the ARM. However, with lower rates and a flat term structure, borrowers will tend to select the FRM: no affordability problem "forces" the ARM and no relatively low short rates induce the ARM.

Figure 4.2 illustrates both how the ARM share of conventional mortgages has varied over the 1984–89 period and the relationship between this variation and changes in the spread between the coupons on FRMs and ARMs. Large rate spreads (2.5 percentage points) in 1984–85 and mid-1987 to the end of 1988 were associated with 40 to 60 percent ARM shares, while small spreads (1.5 points) in 1986 to mid-1987 and in late 1989 were associated with 20 to 25 percent shares.

Research by Brueckner and Follain (1989) provides econometric evidence on ARM demand. Table 4.2 computes probabilities of the ARM being selected under different interest-rate assumptions, using the Brueckner-Follain estimates. In the first computation, the FRM rate and the FRM-ARM rate spread are put at their mean values over the 1984–89 period (commitment rate data collected by Freddie Mac in its weekly survey of 125 major lenders), and all other variables in their equation are placed at their mean values over the estimation period. The computed ARM probability, 31 percent, is slightly less than Freddie Mac's estimate that ARMs made up 39 percent of conventional

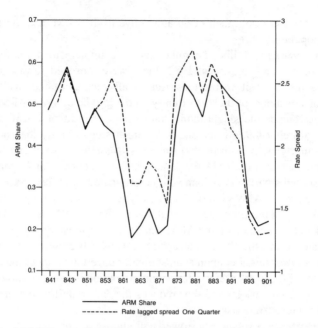

Fig. 4.2   ARM share and FRM minus ARM rate spread quarterly, 1984–89
Source: Federal Home Loan Mortgage Corporation.

Table 4.2   Probability of choosing an ARM in Different Interest-Rate Environments

Experiment	FRM Rate	FRM-ARM Spread	Probability of Choosing ARM
Mean values	11.23	2.15	.31
Changing FRM rate	10.00	2.15	.28
	15.00	2.15	.99
Raising spread, low FRM rate	11.23	1.30	.12
	11.23	2.75	.50
Raising spread, high FRM rate	14.00	1.30	.82
	14.00	2.75	.95

Source: Hendershott 1990, table 1.

mortgage originations during this period. The next two calculations show the sensitivity of the mortgage choice to the level of the FRM rate: an increase in the FRM rate to 15 percent would raise the ARM share from 31 to 99 percent (assuming an FRM-ARM initial coupon spread of 2.15), while a decrease to 10 percent would only lower the share to 28 percent. The last four rows show the impact of variations in the FRM-ARM rate spread at two different levels of the FRM rate. Raising the spread from its historic low (1.3 percent) to its high (2.75 percent) increases the ARM share by 13 (high FRM rate) to 38 (low FRM rate) percentage points.

4.2.4   A Closer Look at the Thrifts

Figure 4.3 provides data on both S&L behavior and the relative role of S&Ls as home mortgage investors over the past quarter century. The behavior of S&Ls is reflected in the proportion of S&L assets invested in home mortgages either directly or indirectly through holdings of agency securities. The S&Ls' presence in the home mortgage is measured as the ratio of S&L total (direct and indirect) home mortgage holdings to total home mortgage debt outstanding. This presence is the product of the other two series in the figure, the fraction of S&L assets invested in home mortgages and the ratio of S&L total assets to the book value of all outstanding home mortgages.

The share of S&L assets in home mortgages varied within a narrow 72 to 74 percent range until 1981, before plummeting to 59 percent at the end of 1984. The ratio slipped further to 57 percent at the end of 1987, but has since risen to 61 percent. The sharp decline in 1983 and 1984 reflected accelerated

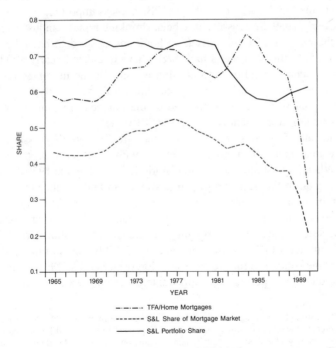

Fig. 4.3   Share of S&L total financial assets (TFA) in home mortgages, S&L share of total home mortgage market, and ratio of S&L TFA to total home mortgages outstanding

Source: Flow of Funds Accounts. First three quarters of 1990 annualized.

growth in the S&L industry (18 percent annual growth rate), not an actual shift out of mortgages.

Beginning in 1961 with 42 percent of the home mortgage market, the S&L presence rose gradually throughout most of the 1970s, reaching a peak of 51 percent in 1977. Since then the S&L presence has been halved. The increase between 1969 and 1977 and subsequent decline through 1981 reflected swings in the size of the S&L industry relative to the size of the home mortgage market. The ratio of the S&L total financial assets to total home mortgage debt outstanding rose from 0.56 in 1969 to 0.70 in 1977, before declining to 0.63 in 1981. While S&L total financial assets grew between 1984 and 1988, they grew at a slower rate than the home mortgage market; with a constant S&L mortgage portfolio share, the S&L share of the home mortgage market fell from 73 to 63 percent.

The role of MSBs is more straightforward. The MSB share of the home mortgage market was roughly constant between 1961 and 1972, as was the ratio of MSB total financial assets to home mortgages outstanding. Since then, this ratio has declined almost monotonically, and the MSB share has dropped from 15 percent to 6 percent. To a large extent, this decline is due to the shift of the U.S. population from the Northeast, where MSBs are relatively important, to the South and West, where MSBs are less important.

Since early 1989, S&L assets have been shrinking rapidly; in just a year and a half, the ratio of S&L total assets to home mortgage debt has fallen from 0.36 to 0.25. In this year and a half, S&Ls have liquidated nearly $90 billion in agency securities and over $50 billion in direct home mortgage holdings. The recent decline in S&L mortgage holdings follows directly from the increased capital requirements mandated by the Financial Institutions Reform, Recovery, and Enforcement Act of 1989 (FIRREA).[6]

The decline of the S&L industry stemmed directly from their asset-liability maturity mismatch, the funding of FRMs with short-term deposits (Kane 1989). When interest rates surged to historic levels in the late 1970s and early 1980s, capital in the S&L industry was wiped out and the incentive for risk taking took over. It is perhaps noteworthy that the vulnerability of S&Ls to periods of sustained increases in interest rates continued to exist at least as late as 1989. S&Ls were still using roughly 40 percent of their short-term deposits to fund long-term FRM investments, and the $400 billion so funded slightly exceeded the volume so funded in 1978. Moreover, S&L ARMs have rate caps that would bind in a period of sustained interest-rate increases. If interest rates

---

6. FIRREA strongly encourages relative home mortgage investment by S&Ls. S&Ls must now keep 70 percent of assets in qualified loans, versus 60 percent formerly, and fewer non-housing-related loans are now classified as qualified than was previously the case. In addition, restrictions on non-housing-related loans are substantially increased. While some of these restrictions are not yet fully in force, the decline in the home mortgage portfolio share of S&Ls has already been arrested.

Table 4.3   **Correlation between Mortage Rates and Capital Market Rates**

Year	Correlation[a]	Year	Correlation[a]
1972	−0.22	1982	0.80*
1973	0.19	1983	0.81*
1974	0.46	1984	0.65*
1975	−0.18	1985	0.76*
1976	0.16	1986	0.58*
1977	−0.49	1987	0.90*
1978	0.42	1988	0.88*
1979	0.34	1989	0.91*
1980	0.33	1990	0.86*
1981	0.42		

Sources: Roth 1988, table 1, for 1972–87; after 1987, my computations.

[a]Correlations are between month-to-month changes in the Freddie Mac survey FRM rate and the ten-year Treasury rate.

*Significantly different from zero at a 5 percent confidence level.

should repeat their 1977–86 pattern, taxpayers could well lose another $50 billion or more in present-value dollars (Hendershott and Shilling 1992).

4.3   The Impact of Securitization on FRM Coupon Rates

Mortgage securitization should cause mortgage rates to be more closely connected to capital market rates. The impact of securitization on the general level of mortgage rates is less clear. Empirical evidence relating to each of these impacts is discussed below.[7]

4.3.1   Timing of Conventional FRM Rate Adjustment to Capital Market Rates

Roth (1988) analyzed the integration of mortgage and capital markets by looking at trends in the month-to-month correlation of changes in coupon rates on conventional mortgages and ten-year Treasuries annually from 1972 to 1987. His results are reproduced and extended to include 1988–90 in table 4.3. Prior to 1982, the correlation of the changes ranged from −.5 to +.5 and was never statistically different from zero. After 1981, the correlation was never less than .58 and was always statistically positive. Moreover, after 1986, the correlation has been nearly .9.

A potential problem with Roth's analysis is that the mortgage rate incorporates a call premium while the Treasury rate does not, and in some periods the value of the call premium may have changed markedly, possibly disguising a close relationship between the noncall components of the mortgage coupon

---

7. This section, too, draws heavily on Hendershott (1991).

and the Treasury coupon. Hendershott and Van Order (1989) attempted to eliminate this problem by constructing a perfect mortgagelike capital market rate and estimating the adjustment of conventional mortgage rates to this perfect rate (rather than to a Treasury rate). The analysis consisted of two parts. First, they estimated a price equation for government-insured mortgage pass-through. Second, they regressed conventional mortgage coupon rates on current and past values of the estimated perfect-market coupon rate taken from the Government National Mortgage Association (GNMA) equation.

The price equation was estimated on weekly GNMA price and coupon data from the January 1981–July 1988 period. In this equation, the GNMA price was regressed on the coupon (adjusted to a bond-equivalent basis), the seven-year Treasury rate, and two determinants of the value of the borrower's call option—the term structure slope (seven-year rate less six-month rate) and an estimate of the volatility of the seven-year rate. Various interactions of these variables were included to allow for nonlinear price responses.

To obtain the perfect-market rate, the estimated price equation was solved for the coupon rate after the mortgage price was set equal to one hundred less the actual points charged in the conventional market (less one point presumed to equal origination costs). This coupon was then converted to a mortgage (rather than bond-equivalent) basis, and fifty basis points were added for servicing and other costs. As the degree of integration increased, changes in the perfect-market coupon rate should have been reflected more quickly in the conventional rate (the data are again from Freddie Mac's survey of 125 major lenders).

Conventional rates were regressed on the current and lagged one-to-eight-week values of the perfect-market rates for various parts of the 1971–88 period. Table 4.4 reports the cumulative adjustment of the conventional rate currently and over lags of two, four, six, and eight weeks. The shift toward integrated markets is striking. The percentage of the change in the perfect-market rate that is reflected instantaneously in the conventional rate rose monotonically from effectively 0 in the 1970s to 8 in the 1980–82 period, 16 in the

Table 4.4   Time Response of Conventional Rates to Fictional Perfect-Market Rates

Period	Adjustment to One-Point Rise in Perfect Rate				
	Current	3 Weeks	5 Weeks	7 Weeks	9 Weeks
1986–88	0.59	0.95	0.96	0.87	0.84
1983–85	0.16	0.55	0.68	0.83	0.88
1980–82	0.08	0.45	0.75	0.93	1.05
1976–79	0.01	0.36	0.62	0.66	0.86
1971–75	0.06	0.17	0.37	0.56	0.74

Source: Hendershott and Van Order 1989, table 5.

Table 4.5   **Actual and Perfect-Market Effective Conventional FRM Rates (%)**

	Actual	Perfect Market	Difference
1971	7.54	8.33	−.79
1972	7.38	7.92	−.53
1973	8.04	8.97	−.93
1974	9.19	9.78	−.60
1975	9.05	9.92	−.87
1976	8.86	9.22	−.35
1977	8.84	9.09	−.24
1978	9.64	10.08	−.44
1979	11.20	11.34	−.14
1980	13.76	14.24	−.48
1981	16.69	16.55	.13
1982	15.97	15.24	.73
1983	13.23	12.86	.37
1984	13.89	13.52	.37
1985	12.43	11.95	.48
1986	10.19	9.69	.49
1987	10.21	10.01	.20
1988	10.23	10.21	.02

Source: Hendershott and Van Order 1989, table 6.

1983–85 period, and 59 in the 1986–88 period. The fraction of the change in the perfect-market rate reflected in the conventional rate within two weeks rose monotonically from a sixth in the first half of the 1970s, to almost half in the early 1980s, to over half in the 1983–85 period, and to nearly one in recent years.

4.3.2 Securitization and the Level of Mortgage Rates

Table 4.5 lists annual values of the actual conventional rate, the Hendershott–Van Order fictional perfect-market rate, and the difference between them for the 1971–88 period. The precise differences are, of course, subject to some error: the actual rate is a survey rate and the perfect rate is computed from an empirical equation estimated with error. Nonetheless, the overall pattern of the differences seems both systematic and plausible. The actual rate was three-quarters of a percentage point below the perfect-market rate in the 1971–75 period; a third of a point below in the 1976–80 period; and roughly half a point above the perfect rate in the 1982–86 period.

As explained earlier, the low mortgage rate in the 1970s can be attributed to tax advantages for thrift mortgage investments and portfolio restrictions against nonmortgage investments, and the switch in the 1980s reflects a sharp relative shift of thrifts out of home mortgage investments owing to the reduced (non-) profitability of S&Ls and the expansion of S&L asset powers. The half-percentage-point premium in the early 1980s provided the incentive for the securitization of conforming conventional FRMs. The premium covered the start-up cost of the securitizers and the liquidity premium demanded by investors.

Beginning in the middle of 1986, the actual rate is very close to the perfect-market rate, the conventional conforming mortgage market seemingly being fully integrated into capital markets. That is, as the volume of mortgage pools grew, bid/ask spreads were bid down (and thus the liquidity premium fell), and the per dollar costs of the securitizers declined. This suggests that the rates on conforming loans, which are eligible for purchase by the agencies, should have declined relative to rates on nonconforming or jumbo loans.

Hendershott and Shilling (1989) explained the relationship between rates on individual loans and a number of factors, using California data during the May–June period of 1978 and 1986. The factors were loan-to-value ratio, loan size, precise month the loan was closed, dummy variables for geographic regions in the state, and whether the loan was on a new property, was under the conforming limit, or was just above the limit. The loan-to-value ratio had the expected positive impact; the loan size and the new property dummies had the expected negative impacts; and the responses in the two years were remarkably similar. For those two years, however, the effects of the conforming limit differed markedly. In 1986, conforming loans had a rate thirty basis points lower than well-above-the-limit loans, and soon-to-be-conforming loans had a rate fifteen basis points lower (standard errors were only five basis points). In 1978, however, the point estimate for the conforming loan coefficient was only three basis points.

It should be emphasized that the perfect-market rate listed in table 4.5 is computed from a GNMA price equation, not from an equation explaining prices on seven- or ten-year Treasury bonds. The working assumption of Hendershott and Van Order was that the GNMA market has been integrated with capital markets since 1981. This assumption seems plausible because GNMAs have full faith and credit guarantees and have traded like Treasuries, with comparably low transactions costs and high volume, at least since 1981.

4.4   Real House Prices and Home Ownership, 1960–89

Systematic deviations of the conventional FRM commitment rate from the perfect-market estimates—0.33 to 0.75 percentage points prior to 1981 and +0.5 point in the 1982–86 period—provided a general stimulus for owner-occupied housing in the 1970s and a deterrent in the first half of the 1980s. This would translate into higher real house prices and home ownership rates in the 1970s and lower real prices and ownership in the first half of the 1980s. Of course, many other things, such as changes in real capital market interest rates, tax law, and so forth, can affect real prices and ownership (Hendershott 1988). Thus, we certainly would not want to attribute all observed behavior to relative changes in mortgage rates. Nonetheless, a look at changes in real prices and home ownership is interesting.

4.4.1   Real House Prices

Figure 4.4 contains two alternative measures of U.S. real house prices, as well as a measure of real after-tax interest rates for the 1963–89 period: the residential investment deflator divided by the GNP deflator and the constant-quality new house price series computed by the Bureau of Census (old series through 1977, new one thereafter) divided by the GNP deflator. The latter relates to single-family housing only and includes a land component. The two series tell basically the same story. Real house prices rose sharply between 1965 and 1980 (by 21 to 26 percent) and fell in the first half of the 1980s by 6 percent.

The real after-tax interest rate in figure 4.4 equals an after-tax adjusted ten-year Treasury rate less the average appreciation rate in the residential investment deflator during the previous three years. The adjustment reflects the earlier evidence of deviations between the actual and perfect-market home mortgage rates; the ten-year Treasury rate is lowered by three-quarters of a percentage point for the years before 1976 and by one-third point for the 1976–80 period, and is raised by one-half point for the years 1982–86. The tax rate is the average marginal tax rate on interest income and varies between 0.24 and 0.3.

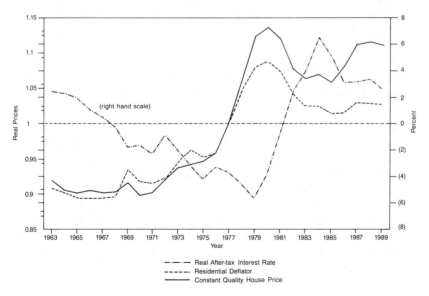

Fig. 4.4   Real house prices and after-tax interest rate

Hendershott (1991) relates the rate of change in real house prices (the change in the logarithm) to both the level and change in the unadjusted real after-tax interest rate, as well as the rate of change in real GNP and a demographic demand variable. Reestimation using the adjusted interest-rate variable (*RAT*) yields

$$d\ln p = z - .00419\ \Delta RAT - .00281\ RAT, \qquad R^2 = 0.58,\ DW = 2.00,$$
$$(.00222) \qquad\quad (.00135)$$

where z represents the contribution of the other variables and 1960–89 is the estimation period. Coefficients on both interest-rate variables are statistically negative at the 0.05 confidence level.

I have used these coefficients to compute what real house price inflation would have been over the 1956–89 period if the real after-tax interest rate had stayed at its 0.24 percent average value over the entire period. The observed real residential investment deflator rose by 21 percent between 1965 and 1980 and then fell by 6 percent between then and 1985. The recomputations say that two-thirds of the real increase is attributable to the low real after-tax rate during the 1966–79 period and that all of the real decrease is attributable to the high real after-tax rates in the first half of the 1980s.

4.4.2   Home Ownership

Home ownership varies enormously with age and household type. The average ownership rate of married couples age 35–44 years has exceeded that of couples under age 25 by roughly 50 percentage points over the past quarter century. The rates for singles and other household heads increase similarly with age, but the rates are 20 to 40 percentage points lower for comparable-age singles than for marrieds. Rates for young other household heads are comparable to those of singles, but those of older other heads are closer to those of older married couples.

Research on home ownership indicates a strong correlation with economic factors such as income (Haurin, Hendershott, and Ling 1988), wealth (Jones 1989) and the relative costs of owning versus renting (Hendershott and Shilling 1982; Rosen and Rosen 1980). These factors are correlated with age and family structure to varying degrees and thus explain at least part of the overall correlation of ownership with age and family type.

Table 4.6 shows a sharp increase in the ownership rate of married couples between 1960 and 1980. For every age class, the increase is 11 to 14 percentage points, with two-thirds of the increase coming in the 1970s. Table 4.7 contains data for married couples and single households for five age classes for three years: 1974, 1980, and 1987. These data indicate an even greater surge to ownership between 1974 and 1980 by single households than by married couples. For the four cohorts between ages 25 and 44, the increase was 7 to 11 percentage points in these six years alone.

These movements are consistent with those of real after-tax interest rates.

Table 4.6   **Home Ownership Rates of Married Couples (%)**

Age of Head	1960	1970	1980
Under 25	23	26	37
25–29	44	49	58
30–34	62	66	75
35–44	73	77	84
45–64	75	81	88
Over 64	78	79	84

Source: Census of Housing, 1960, 1970, 1980.

Table 4.7   **Home Ownership Rates by Household Types and Age of Head, Selected Years (%)**

Age of Head	Married Couples			Singles		
	1974	1980	1987	1974	1980	1987
Under 25	32.7	34.9	29.9	7.0	11.5	9.7
25–29	54.2	58.2	52.5	13.0	20.2	19.4
30–34	71.9	74.7	69.2	22.5	30.5	28.8
35–39	78.1	82.2	78.0	26.2	37.1	35.7
40–44	82.4	84.7	83.1	29.2	36.6	44.0
45–49	85.1	86.2	86.0	35.3	35.5	44.0
Over 49	83.7	87.1	88.9	54.4	57.4	59.5

Sources: Annual Housing Survey and *Housing Vacancy Survey.* Data kindly supplied by David Crowe of the National Association of Home Builders.

As figure 4.4 indicates, the 1970s were a period of negative and declining real after-tax rates. In contrast, these rates jumped sharply in the early 1980s, and the home mortgage rate rose especially, moving from a third of a point "below market" in 1980 to a half point above in 1982. Ownership by married couples under age 40 fell by roughly 5 percentage points.

4.5   The Interest Sensitivity of Housing Production

Increases in market interest rates have traditionally been viewed as restricting housing demand through two channels. First, higher interest rates raise the ratio of mortgage payments to income. Because lenders set qualification standards in terms of this ratio, borrowers will be constrained to purchase smaller houses when interest rates rise, if they are unable to provide a larger down payment. (Households will want to purchase smaller houses if the real after-tax interest rate has risen.) Second, with deposit rate ceilings in place, substantial increases in market interest rates cause deposit outflows and lead depository lenders to ration credit—to require sufficiently larger down payments so that the demand for their credit is reduced to the available supply. In the absence of a ready supply of other credit, such as is supplied by a secondary mortgage market, the total volume of credit is reduced. With both of these channels operating, some households will be unable to move up to larger houses, and some households will not be formed. Housing starts will drop, the average real value of starts will decline, and real house prices will soften. Arguably, the prominent changes in housing finance in the 1980s—the removal of deposit rate ceilings, the widespread introduction of ARMs, and the securitization of conforming FRMs—should have reduced the sensitivity of housing demand to increases in interest rates.

4.5.1 Multiple Regression Analysis

Three relatively recent studies have used multiple regression analysis to examine possible changes in the sensitivity of housing activity to increases in interest rates. Akhtar and Harris (1986–87) and Throop (1986) both explain quarterly real residential investment over roughly the 1960–85 period. Ryding (1990) explains quarterly real single-family residential investment over the 1965–88 period. The models are similar in that real disposable income, real after-tax interest rates, and a variety of disintermediation or credit-rationing dummy variables are the primary determinants of investment demand.[8]

One advantage of regression analysis is that it allows a direct test of the impact of thrift deposit contraction in the early 1980s, the last period of contraction prior to 1989–90. If the 1979–82 contraction did not lead to credit rationing, subsequent contractions are not likely to do so. The empirical results are mixed. Ryding estimates only one-third as large a response to his rationing proxy—the spread between the three-month bill rate and the passbook savings rate—in 1979–82 as in the 1969–70 and 1973–75 periods. Akhtar and Harris estimate two-thirds as large a response in 1979–82 as in the earlier period, using zero-one dummies for periods of credit rationing. Finally, Throop finds no rationing in 1979–82.

Figure 4.5 reproduces a simulation of Ryding's model (the residential investment equation plus some interest-rate relationships) for different regimes. A permanent one percentage point increase in the federal funds rate reduced investment by about 15 percent between the late 1960s and middle 1970s, but by only 7 percent in the early 1980s. Moreover, if one assumes that credit rationing will no longer occur, the reduction is only 3 percent. That is, housing may only be a fifth as sensitive to interest rates now as it was in the 1970s.

4.5.2 Vector Autoregressions

An alternative to multiple regression analysis is estimation of vector autoregression models. Kahn (1989) and Pozdena (1990) both compare models

---

8. The existence of credit rationing in some periods does not mean that the housing stock will be lower in the long run. Increased production after the rationing may make up for reduced production during the rationing period (Hendershott and Van Order 1989).

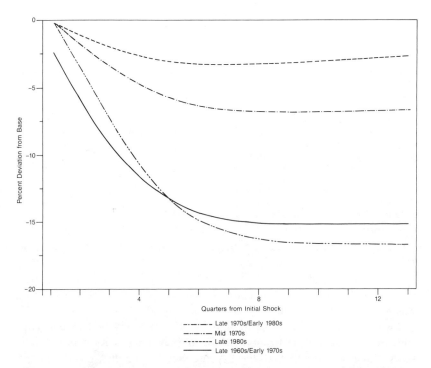

Fig. 4.5   Housing investment: response to a permanent monetary tightening
Source: Ryding 1990, chart 10.

estimated over the 1983–89 period with models estimated in earlier periods (1956–79 for Kahn and 1960–82 for Pozdena). Pozdena explains total housing starts (monthly), and Kahn explains total real fixed residential investment (quarterly). Both relate the activity variable to its lagged values and lagged short-term interest rates (three-month bills and the federal funds rate, respectively) over the prior year. Pozdena also includes lagged values of the term structure slope (his bill rate less the AAA corporate bond rate) in his second model.

Table 4.8 shows the percentage of variance in starts explained by Pozdena's models that is accounted for by lagged starts, lagged bill rates, and the lagged term structure spread (in his second model). As can be seen, lagged bill rates account for only a third to a half as much of the explanation in the 1980s as in the earlier period. Pozdena also traces out the effect on housing starts of a one-standard-deviation increase in bill rates for both the pre-1983 and post-1982 periods. For the pre-1983 period, the response peaks at a 60,000 decrease in starts over the fourth to sixth quarters. The post-1982 response is less stable, and the average decrease over these quarters is only about 20,000.

Kahn does not report empirical estimates, but he does trace out his results in a figure analogous to that of Pozdena. A permanent one percentage point

Table 4.8   Interest-Rate Variation and Housing-Starts Variation (%)

Explanation	VAR 1		VAR 2	
	Pre-1983	Post-1982	Pre-1983	Post-1982
Starts	39.6	78.5	32.9	43.9
T-bills	60.4	21.5	56.9	28.2
Lagged term structure spread	—	—	10.2	27.8

Source: Pozdena 1990, table 1.

Note: Variance decomposition of starts, from twelfth-lag vector autoregressions (VARs); in percentage of variation explained, measured at twenty-four months.

increase in the federal funds rate reduces real residential investment by about 4 percent in the pre-1980 period versus 1.5 percent in the post-1982 period. The maximum decline is reached roughly seven quarters after the increase in rates.

The Pozdena and Kahn results are remarkably similar (and are also consistent with Ryding's results). Kahn has a slightly longer lag, but he is explaining expenditures, which slightly lag starts. Both find the 1980s' response to be only about a third of the earlier response. Not surprisingly, both authors conclude that mortgage securitization and the introduction of ARMs have significantly reduce the volatility of the housing industry. Further, greater contracyclical shifts in interest rates will be needed to obtain the same degree of monetary tightness and ease as was achieved with smaller movements in earlier decades. Finally, a less volatile housing industry could well lead to a more capital intensive and productive industry.

4.6   Concluding Thoughts

In the 1980s, the U.S. housing finance system was transformed from a one-instrument (FRM), deposit-based (and subsidized) system to a two-instrument (FRM and ARM), largely capital market system. In the 1960s and 1970s, mortgage rates were "too low" and real house prices and home ownership rose rapidly, but bouts of credit rationing led to severe housing production cycles. In the 1980s, mortgage rates have been relatively higher but more closely tied to capital market rates, and an ARM was introduced for households to shift to when housing became less affordable—when interest rates rose generally or when long rates rose relative to short rates. As a result, housing production is now less volative and (hopefully) will be more efficient.

Two uncertainties seem to exist today regarding U.S. housing finance. The first relates to the collapsing thrift industry. While no large impact seems likely for conforming FRM rates owing to the securitization of that market, a decline in the correlation between mortgage and Treasury rates in 1990 has been observed. More important, major disruptions could occur in the ARM and jumbo

FRM markets, with these rates getting out of line relative to capital market rates just as conforming FRM rates did in the first half of the 1980s. (Unfortunately, we have no evidence on whether or not this is occurring.) This could lead to reduced housing demand, real prices, and home ownership. At some point, though, securitization of these markets should occur, by Fannie Mae and Freddie Mac below the conforming limit and by fully private sector entities in the jumbo market.

The second uncertainty concerns the government-insured FHA/VA market. I have not discussed these FRMs because this market was effectively securitized prior to the 1980s and did not undergo major changes in the 1980s. However, in response to a marked deterioration in the soundness of the basic single-family insurance fund, legislation was enacted in 1990 to substantially increase the cost of this insurance (Hendershott and Waddell 1990). Insurance premiums are rising by 45 to 85 percent (greater percentage increases for higher loan-to-value loans), and borrowers are being required to supply more money up front. FHA loans are used more heavily by younger, less wealthy households; survey data indicate that the FHA/VA share of the total home mortgage market during the 1984–89 period was twice as great for married couples under age 25 as for those above age 34 (Hendershott 1990, table 2). I conclude that the changes in the FHA program are likely to lead to further shrinkage in the FHA share of the FRM market and declines in home ownership rates of younger households.

References

Akhtar, M. A., and E. S. Harris. 1986–87. Monetary Policy Influence on the Economy: An Empirical Analysis. *Federal Reserve Bank of New York Quarterly Review* (Winter): 19–34.

Brueckner, Jan, and James R. Follain. 1989. ARMs and the Demand for Housing. *Regional Science and Urban Economics* (May): 163–87.

Cassidy, Henry J. 1984. A Review of the Federal Home Loan Bank Board's Adjustable-Rate Mortgage Regulations and the Current ARM Proposal. Research Working Paper no. 113, Federal Home Loan Bank Board. August.

Haurin, Donald R., Patric H. Hendershott, and David C. Ling. 1988. Homeownership Rates of Married Couples: An Econometric Investigation. *Housing Finance Review* (Summer): 85–108.

Hendershott, Patric H. 1988. Home Ownership and Real House Prices: Sources of Change, 1965–1985. *Housing Finance Review* (Spring): 1–18.

———. 1990. The Composition of Mortgage Originations in the Year 2000. *Journal of Housing Research* 1 (1): 43–62.

———. 1991. The Market for Home Mortgage Credit: Recent Changes and Future Prospects. In *Recent Changes in the Market for Financial Services,* 15th Annual Economic Policy Conference, Federal Reserve Bank of St. Louis.

Hendershott, Patric H., and James D. Shilling. 1982. The Economics of Tenure Choice,

1955–1979. In *Research in Real Estate,* ed. C. F. Sirmans, 1:105–33. Greenwich, Conn.: JAI Press.

———. 1989. The Impact of the Agencies on Conventional Fixed-Rate Mortgage Yields. *Journal of Real Estate Finance and Economics* 2:101–15.

———. 1992. The Continued Interest Rate Vulnerability of Thrifts. In *Financial Markets and Financing Crises,* ed. Glenn Hubbard, 259–82. Chicago: University of Chicago Press.

Hendershott, Patric H., and R. Van Order. 1989. Integration of Mortgage and Capital Markets and the Accumulation of Residential Capital. *Regional Science and Urban Economics* 19 (2): 188–210.

Hendershott, Patric H., and K. E. Villani. 1980. Secondary Residential Mortgage Markets and the Relative Cost of Mortgage Funds. *Journal of the American Real Estate and Urban Economics Association* 8:50–76.

Hendershott, Patric H., and James Waddell. 1990. The Changing Fortunes of FHA's Mutual Mortgage Insurance Fund and the Legislative Response. *Journal of Real Estate Finance and Economics* 5:119–32.

Jones, Lawrence D. 1989. Current Wealth and Tenure Choice. *Journal of the American Real Estate and Urban Economics Association* 17 (1): 17–40.

Kahn, G. A. 1989. The Changing Interest Sensitivity of the U.S. Economy. *Federal Reserve Bank of Kansas City Economic Review* (November): 13–34.

Kane, Edward J. 1989. *The S&L Insurance Mess: How Did It Happen?* Washington, D.C.: Urban Institute Press.

Pozdena, Randell J. 1990. Do Interest Rates Still Affect Housing? *Federal Reserve Bank of San Francisco Economic Review* (Summer): 3–14.

Rosen, Harvey S., and Kenneth T. Rosen. 1980. Federal Taxes and Homeownership: Evidence from Time Series. *Journal of Political Economy* 88:59–75.

Roth, H. L. 1988. Volatile Mortgage Rates: A New Fact of Life. *Federal Reserve Bank of Kansas City Economic Review,* 16–28.

Ryding, John. 1990. Housing Finance and the Transmission Mechanism of Monetary Policy. In *Studies on Financial Changes and the Transmission of Monetary Policy.* New York: Federal Reserve Bank of New York, May.

Throop, Adrian. 1986. Financial Deregulation, Interest Rates, and the Housing Cycle. *Federal Reserve Bank of San Francisco Economic Review* (Summer): 63–78.

5 Housing and the Journey to Work in the Tokyo Metropolitan Area

Tatsuo Hatta and Toru Ohkawara

5.1 Introduction

Why are land prices in Tokyo so high compared to those in other major cities of the world? Many explanations have been given, such as Land Lease and Building Lease Laws, low assessments of land under the inheritance tax, and the "bubble."[1] These are not mutually exclusive explanations, and no doubt the accumulated effect of these factors accounts for a good portion of the high land prices in Tokyo.

Yet the most basic factor is often neglected: Tokyo is by far the largest metropolitan area in the industrialized world. Figure 5.1, which is based on table 5.1, shows that it is twice as large as the second largest—New York—in both population and employment.[2]

As Mills (1967, 1972) and Muth (1969) pointed out, a city with lower com-

Tatsuo Hatta is professor of economics at Osaka University. Toru Ohkawara is senior economist at the Central Research Institute of the Electric Power Industry in Japan.

The authors would like to thank Bob Dickle, Bruce Hamilton, Kenichi Inada, Takatoshi Ito, Kikuo Iwata, David Merriman, Ryohei Kakumoto, Yukio Noguchi, John Quigley, Michelle White, and Fukuju Yamasaki for useful comments and suggestions. They would also like to thank Orie Ando, Yasunori Goto, Hiroshi Nozue, Rehana Siddiqui, and Margaret Pasquale for their competent research assistance. Hatta gratefully acknowledges the financial support by the Science Promotion Grant of the Japanese Ministry of Education.

The authors would like to dedicate this paper to Takao Fukuchi, their common teacher, who many years ago ignited their interest in the issues discussed here.

1. See Noguchi (ch. 1 in this volume) and Ito (ch. 9 in this volume), for example.

2. Kobayashi, Komori, and Sugihara (1990) make a detailed comparison of Tokyo, London, and Paris, including the comparisons in table 5.1. However, they do not compare these cities against New York. Kakumoto (1986, 139–42, 154–56) conjectures that the population and employment sizes of the comparable metropolitan area of Tokyo must be twice as large as that of New York based on the comparison of employment in an area of six hundred square kilometers. Table 5.1 verifies Kakumoto's conjecture and fills the gap in the Kobayashi, Komori, and Sugihara study by supplying the New York data for an area of fourteen thousand square kilometers.

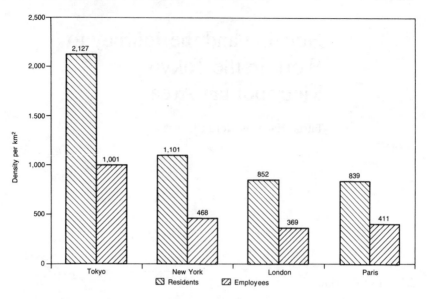

Fig. 5.1   Metropolitan areas of the world

Table 5.1   Metropolitan Areas of the World

	Toyko	New York	London	Paris
Area (km²)	13,495	14,812	15,437	12,012
Year	1980	1980	1987	1982
Residents (in thousands)	28,699	16,303	13,152	10,073
Density (1000/km²)	2.13	1.10	0.85	0.84
Employees (in thousands)	13,515	6,925	5,702	4,933
Density (1,000/km²)	1.00	0.47	0.37	0.41

Sources: Tokyo: Shutoken Seibi Kyokai 1988, 2:10, 62, 190; New York: U.S. Bureau of the Census 1986, 202, 214–15; London: British Central Statistical Office (1989); Paris: INSEE (1988).

Notes: The metropolitan areas here cover Tokyo, Kanagawa, Chiba, and Saitama prefectures for Tokyo; seven PMSAs listed in table 5.2 for New York; Greater London and the surrounding six counties; and the Île de France. A more detailed comparison among Tokyo, London, and Paris is found in Kobayashi, Komori, and Sugihara (1990, 21), though New York is not included in the comparison. Kakumoto (1986) compares Tokyo and New York for the areas of six hundred square kilometers and less.

muting cost per kilometer will have a larger population and higher residential land prices than another city with the identical labor productivity at its central business district (CBD) but with a relatively higher commuting cost per kilometer. If the population of New York were doubled, keeping the current commuting facilities intact, traffic congestion would become prohibitive. In this sense, the availability of a network of well-developed commuter railroads keeps the commuting cost in Tokyo lower than in New York. This may be the main reason why population size and land price are higher in Tokyo than in New York.

Government intervention also contributes to make the commuting cost in Japan artificially low. In fact, Japanese commuters generally pay no commuting expenses at all; their employers reimburse them. Employers do this because the additional wage payment earmarked to cover the commuting expenses is, up to a generous limit, not taxable under personal and corporate income taxes. Employers can reduce the combined tax payments made by themselves and their employees by reimbursing the commuting fares while reducing the average of the regular wage rate. Note that under this scheme the larger the city size is, the larger the government subsidy given to the average resident.

Free commuter riding gives strong incentives to the employees to live farther from the city center. This makes the city grow in terms of both geographical size and population. Moreover, the free ride makes the population density and land price distribution from the CBD flatter than otherwise, as the Mills-Muth theory implies.

The present study has three major aims. First, we study differences in the population and employment distributions of Tokyo and New York, and examine how the different commuting environments of the two areas explain these distributions. As the Mills-Muth theory shows, the population density function in the residential district of a city has an intimate relationship with the land price function there. The employment density function in the CBD also has a close relationship with the land price function there. Although data on land prices are not available for New York, population and employment density data are available for both Tokyo and New York. A comparison of the latter will shed light on the distribution of land prices in Tokyo.

Kakumoto (1970, 1986) and Mills and Ohta (1976) compare population densities between Tokyo and New York for 1960, 1970, and 1980, respectively. In this article, we examine the two metropolitan areas for 1980, but larger and more detailed areas than Kakumoto (1986) does. This reveals that even in 1980 the CBD of Tokyo had much lower employment density than that of New York, unlike the implication of Kakumoto's data. Our data also show that the difference in population densities between the two CBDs is more dramatic than Kakumoto's data show. While Mills and Ohta show that the density of manufacturing employment in the CBD of Tokyo is greater than that of New York, we reveal the opposite for the total employment.

Second, we will empirically examine the impact of abolishing the preferential tax treatment of free commuter riding upon the land price structure and the size of the Tokyo metropolitan area. Our result shows, for example, that the land price at Toyoda, which is fifty-four minutes away from the Tokyo station, would be realized in Nishikokubunji, which is forty-seven minutes away from the Tokyo station, if commuters themselves are made to pay commuter-pass fares. To this end, we will first estimate the land price function for Tokyo using microdata on residential land price and distance from the Tokyo station.

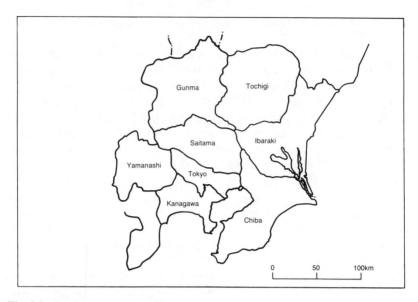

Fig. 5.2   Prefectures around Tokyo
Note: A more detailed map of Tokyo prefecture is found in figure 5.10.

Third, we will evaluate the current urban economic policies in Tokyo regarding the CBD development and commuter transportation from the viewpoint of whether they help attain an efficient resource allocation. It will be shown that the various existing policies have consistently made both population and employment density distributions flatter than efficiency requires.

The existing literature on the estimation of the land price function, such as Muth (1969), Mills (1972), Kau and Sirmans (1979), Mills and Hamilton (1984), Ohkawara (1985), and Alperovich (1990), assumes that commuters pay the monetary expense of commuting. In estimating our land price function for Tokyo, we take into account the fact that commuters actually pay commuting costs only in terms of time and fatigue.

Haurin (1983) studies the effects of the reimbursement of commuting expenses upon profits of the CBD firms, the population density distribution, and efficiency, assuming that the city is closed. When an open city is considered, however, entry of new firms bids up the land price until profits are wiped out. In the present paper, we examine the effect of the reimbursement on the land price as well as on population density, assuming that such competition exists at least in the long run.

Section 5.2 compares the population and employment densities of Tokyo and New York and makes three observations. Section 5.3 presents a simplified version of the Mills-Muth model. Section 5.4 explains the observations in the theoretical framework of section 5.3. Sections 5.5 through 5.7 empirically esti-

mate the land price function of Tokyo. Section 5.8 discusses the policy implications of our theoretical and empirical observations. A summary of the paper is
given in section 5.9.

5.2   Tokyo's Population and Employment: Facts

5.2.1   Residential Population

Table 5.1 compares the residential population in the metropolitan areas of
Tokyo, New York, London, and Paris. It shows that the residential population
of the Tokyo metropolitan area, 29 million, is approximately twice as large as
that of New York, 16 million, and more than twice as large as London or Paris.

The metropolitan area of Tokyo in this table consists of Tokyo, Kanagawa,
Chiba, and Saitama prefectures, shown in figure 5.2. For the three other metropolises, areas of similar geographical size were chosen. In the case of New
York, for example, the seven most densely populated primary metropolitan
statistical areas (PMSAs) in the New York–New Jersey–Connecticut consoli-
dated metropolitan statistical area (NY-NJ-CT CMSA) are chosen, as listed in
table 5.2. This area is the NY-NJ-CT CMSA minus Monmouth-Ocean, the NJ
PMSA and Orange County, and the NY PMSA; the area includes Fairfield, CT,
Middlesex, NJ, and Hunterdon, NJ, for example.

The above statistics are apparently in conflict with the obvious observation
that downtown Tokyo has far fewer skyscrapers than Manhattan. Indeed, figure
5.3 and table 5.3 show that the population density of the central sixty square
kilometers in Tokyo is one-half of that in New York. (In this paper, the population density measures the gross density, which is population/urban area, rather
than the net density, which is population/residential area.) The area of Tokyo
we chose for this comparison consists of the Chiyoda, Chuo, Minato, and Shinjuku wards, the map of which is shown in figure 5.4. The counterpart in New
York is Manhattan. Table 5.3 shows that the population density of the Chiyoda
ward is less than one-sixth of a CBD area in Manhattan that has a population
twice as large the Chiyoda ward. This is also illustrated in figure 5.3.

Tables 5.4 through 5.6 further break down the population density figures of
the various areas of the Tokyo metropolitan area in table 5.7. Table 5.8 breaks
down the figures for the New York metropolitan area. Figure 5.3 is ultimately
based on these tables.

Figure 5.3 indicates that the population density of New York is the highest
near the CBD and declines as the area expands. In Tokyo, on the contrary,
population density is very low at the central districts and increases as the area
is expanded up to 240 square kilometers. As a result, Tokyo has a higher population density than New York in an area with the size of Manhattan plus Brooklyn. As the area becomes larger, the gap in the population density grows. Thus
the population density of New York starts out at a high level near the center

Table 5.2   PMSAs in the New York Area, 1980

Primary Metropolitan Statistical Area (PMSA)[a]	Area		Population		Employment[b]				
	mi²	km²	Size (1,000s)	Density (1,000s/km²)	Private Sector (1,000s)	Federal Govt. (1,000s)	Local Govt. (1,000s)	Total (1,000s)	Density (1,000s/km²)
Jersey City	46	119	557	4.68	180	11	22	213	1.79
New York	1,146	2,968	8,275	2.79	3,282	85	392	3,759	1.27
Bergen-Passaic	424	1,098	1,293	1.18	527	5	42	574	0.52
Nassau-Suffolk	1,198	3,103	2,606	0.84	778	18	96	892	0.29
Newark	1,226	3,175	1,879	0.59	731	20	74	825	0.26
Fairfield[c]	632	1,637	807	0.49	364	4	24	392	0.24
Middlesex, etc.[d]	1,047	2,712	886	0.33	248	2	21	271	0.10
Total	5,719	14,812	16,303	1.10	6,110	145	671	6,926	0.47

Source: U.S. Bureau of the Census 1986, 202, 214–15.

[a]The seven most densely populated PMSAs in the NY-NJ-CT CMSA.

[b]Private sector, federal govt., and local govt. stand for private nonfarm, federal government, and state and local government employ-ments. Private nonfarm and state and local government employment data are for 1982, while federal government employment data are for 1983.

[c]Fairfield is the CT–New England County metropolitan area called Bridgeport-Stamford-Norwalk-Danbury.

[d]Middlesex, etc., is the NJ PMSA called Middlesex-Somerset-Hunterdon.

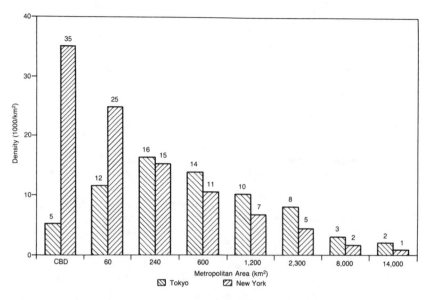

Fig. 5.3   Population density: Tokyo versus New York

and drops sharply as the area is expanded, while the density of Tokyo starts out at a lower level, increases first, and then declines more slowly than that of New York.

5.2.2   Employment

Table 5.1 shows 13.5 million people employed in the Tokyo metropolitan area while the New York metropolitan area has only 6.9 million (roughly one-half of the employment in the Tokyo metropolitan area), and London and Paris metropolitan areas have even less. Table 5.7 compares the employment densities of Tokyo and New York for various area sizes, and figure 5.5 illustrates this. Tokyo has twice as many people employed as New York in six hundred square kilometers, which is the twenty-three ward district in Tokyo and the combined area of Manhattan, Queens, the Bronx, and Brooklyn in New York. Moreover, this table shows that Tokyo has more people employed than New York even in a central sixty square kilometers, which is the combined area of Chiyoda, Chuo, Minato, and Shinjuku wards in Tokyo and Manhattan in New York.[3]

Near the center of the city, however, the opposite is observed. Figure 5.5, which is based on table 5.7, illustrates that the combined twenty square kilometers of Chiyoda and Chuo wards has a smaller population than a comparable area of south Manhattan. Moreover, the Chiyoda ward itself has less than three-

---

3. Kakumoto (1986, 154–56) was the first to make comparisons of the two cities with respect to areas of sixty and six hundred square kilometers.

Table 5.3 **Tokyo versus New York: Population Density, 1980**

Tokyo			New York		
Area (km²)	Residents (1,000s)	Density (1,000s/km²)	Area (km²)	Residents (1,000s)	Density (1,000s/km²)
		CBD area			
	Chiyoda ward[a]			Midtown[b]	
10.4	55	5.29	3.6	128	35.16
		60 km² area			
	Four central wards[c]			Manhattan	
58	683	11.68	57	1,423	24.96
		240 km² area			
	Fifteen central wards[d]		Manhattan and Brooklyn		
236	3,889	16.48	237	3,659	15.44
		600 km² area			
			Manhattan, Queens, Bronx, and		
	All twenty-three wards		Brooklyn		
598	8,352	13.97	629	6,719	10.68
		1,200 km² area			
	"Urban area"[e]			Top six counties	
1,232	12,746	10.35	1,230	8,479	6.89
		2,300 km² area			
	"Urban area" plus "suburban area"[f]			Top nine counties	
2,292	18,736	8.17	2,240	10,305	4.60
		8,000 km² area			
	Tokyo metropolitan area[g]			Top fifteen counties[h]	
8,415	27,348	3.25	8,107	14,642	1.81
		14,000 km² area			
	Four prefectures[i]			Top seven PMSAs[j]	
13,495	28,699	2.13	14,812	16,303	1.10

Sources: Tokyo: Shutoken Seibi Kyokai 1988, 2:10, 62, 190, 204, 205–12; New York: New York City 1988; U.S. Bureau of the Census 1986, 202, 214–15; CACI 1990, 425.

[a]The part of the Imperial Palace that is closed to the public is excluded from the area figure of Chiyoda ward in the first three rows. It is included in the area figures of larger areas of Tokyo, since its inclusion hardly affects density figures.

[b]"Midtown" is defined as the area bounded by 59th Street, 14th Street, and Lexington Avenue. It is District 5 of New York City (1988).

[c]The four central wards are Chiyoda, Chuo, Shinjuku, and Minato.

[d]The fifteen central wards are the first fifteen wards listed in table 5.4.

[e]"Urban area" (Kisei Shigaichi) is defined by the Tokyo Metropolitan Area Refurbishment Act. (Shotoken Seibi Ho) and consists of the twenty-three wards of Tokyo Musashino, and Mitaka, Kawasaki, Kawaguchi, and Yokohama except for Seya ward.

[f]Table 5.6 lists the thirty-eight suburban cities of Tokyo in the "suburban area" (Kinko Seibi Chitai) as defined by the law.

[g]"Tokyo metropolitan area" (Tokyo Daitoshi Chiiki) combines the "urban area" and "suburban area" defined above.

[h]The fifteen counties in the New York area with the highest population densities are listed in table 5.8 in order of density.

[i]Tokyo, Kanagawa, Chiba, and Saitama prefectures.

[j]The seven SMSAs in the New York area with the highest population density are listed in table 5.2.

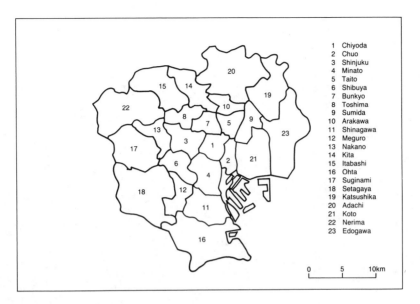

Fig. 5.4   The ward district of Tokyo

Notes: Wards are listed in the order of the density of population during the day, as in tables 5.4 and 5.9. Figure 5.10 locates the ward district of Tokyo within Tokyo prefecture.

fourths of the number of employees that New York has, with roughly the same area.[4] A detailed breakdown of population densities is given in table 5.9 for the ward district of Tokyo, and in table 5.10 for south Manhattan.

5.2.3   Summary Observations

Our observations may be summarized as follows:

1. Population and employment sizes of the entire metropolitan area of Tokyo are twice as large as those of New York.

2. The CBD of Tokyo is underutilized relative to the CBD of New York. The employment density of the CBD of Tokyo is less than three-fourths of the corresponding area in New York, while population density of the CBD of Tokyo is less than one-sixth of that of New York.

3. The population density curve is flatter in the Tokyo suburbs than in the New York suburbs. (As the area size increases, the population density increases first and then declines in Tokyo, while it monotonically declines in New York.) The employment density curve is flatter in Tokyo than in New York in all area sizes.

4. The Tokyo figure includes government as well as private-sector employees, but the New York figure does not include employees of federal or local governments. Thus the actual employment density of New York is even higher than the figure given in table 5.7.

Table 5.4   The Twenty-three Wards of Tokyo: Population, 1980

Day Population Density[a] (1,000s/km²)	Ward	Area (km²)	Residential Population (1,000s)	Density (1,000s/km²)	Cumulative Area (km²)	Cumulative Population (1,000s)	Cumulative Density (1,000s/km²)
94.2	Chiyoda	10.39[b]	55	5.3	10.39	55	5.3
65.5	Chuo	10.05	83	8.3	20.44	138	6.8
38.1	Shinjuku	18.04	344	19.1	38.48	482	12.5
35.3	Minato	19.99	201	10.1	58.47	683	11.7
33.7	Taito	10.00	186	18.6	68.47	869	12.7
30.8	Shibuya	15.11	247	16.3	83.58	1,116	13.4
29.4	Bunkyo	11.44	202	17.7	95.02	1,318	13.9
28.5	Toshima	13.01	289	22.2	108.03	1,607	14.9
19.5	Sumida	13.82	233	16.9	121.85	1,840	15.1
19.4	Arakawa	10.34	198	19.1	132.19	2,038	15.4
19.1	Shinagawa	20.91	346	16.5	153.10	2,384	15.6
19.0	Meguro	14.41	274	19.0	167.51	2,658	15.9
16.9	Nakano	15.73	346	22.0	183.24	3,004	16.4
16.6	Kita	20.55	387	18.8	203.79	3,391	16.6
14.5	Itabashi	31.90	498	15.6	235.69	3,889	16.5
13.4	Ohta	49.42	661	13.4	285.11	4,550	16.0
12.3	Suginami	33.54	542	16.2	318.65	5,092	16.0
11.6	Setagaya	58.81	797	13.6	377.46	5,889	15.6
10.7	Katsushika	33.90	420	12.4	411.36	6,309	15.3
10.2	Adachi	53.25	620	11.6	464.61	6,929	14.9
10.1	Kota	36.89	362	9.8	501.50	7,291	14.5
9.6	Nerima	47.00	564	12.0	548.50	7,855	14.3
9.1	Edogawa	48.26	495	10.3	596.76	8,350	14.0
Total[c]		597.89	8,352	14.0			

Souce: Shutoken Seibi Kyokai 1988, 2:204, 205.

[a]The density of population during the day, which includes employees, students, and residents who are in the ward during the daytime.

[b]The area of Chiyoda ward is 11.52 km². The part of the Imperial Palace that is closed to the public is 1.13 km². The area listed here is what is open to the public.

[c]The last row gives the total area of the ward district including the Imperial Palace. The total population figure is corrected for rounding error. The impact of these corrections upon the total population density is negligible.

Table 5.5   **Cities in the Urban Area of Tokyo: Population, 1980**

City	Area (km²)	Population (1,000s)	Density (1,000s/km²)
23 wards of Tokyo	598	8,352	14.0
Musashino	11	137	12.5
Mitaka	17	165	9.7
Kawasaki	136	1,041	7.7
Kawaguchi	56	379	6.8
Yokohama	414	2,673	6.5
Urban area total	1,232	12,746	10.3

Source: Shutoken Seibi Kyokai 1988, 2:205–12.
Note: "Urban area" is defined in the notes to table 5.3.

5.3   A Theory of Commuting Costs, Land Prices, and Population Densities

As a preparation to explaining the reasons for the above differences between Tokyo and New York in section 5.4, we now discuss the relevant aspects of the Mills-Muth model of an urban economy.

5.3.1   Commuting Cost and Metropolitan Size

The fundamental reason why megalopolises like Tokyo and New York exist is the agglomeration economies in production, that is, the benefits that firms can obtain from each other when they are located in the same city. When a firm is located in the CBD of a large city, costs of communication with other firms in the city are reduced both in terms of face-to-face and telephone contacts. Besides, a firm in a large city can enjoy business support services, such as computer maintenance, elevator maintenance, office cleaning, and business consulting. Moreover, public facilities such as communication and transportation facilities are subject to considerable scale economies. Thus new firms are attracted to a large city. These newcomers to the city further emit external economies to other firms in the same city, and encourage even more firms to move into the city.

This virtuous cycle of agglomeration economies increases the productivity of the firms at the CBD, enabling them to pay much higher wage rates than the rural firms. This wage-rate difference attracts workers from the rural area to the city.

But the immigration will not continue indefinitely. The urban workers have to pay commuting costs, which consist of train fares, auto expenses, time, and fatigue. We will call the CBD wage rate minus the monetary equivalent of the commuting cost at a given location the *net urban wage rate* at the location. It declines as the distance between the CBD and the location increases. At a location too far from the CBD, the net urban wage rate would become lower than the rural wage rate.

Table 5.6   **Cities in the Suburban Area of Tokyo: Population, 1980**

City	Area (km²)	Population (1,000s)	Density (1,000s/km²)
Komae	6	71	11.8
Hoya	9	91	10.1
Tanashi	7	67	9.6
Hatagaya	6	56	9.3
Koganei	11	102	9.3
Kami Fukuoka	7	58	8.3
Kokubunji	11	91	8.3
Higashi Kurume	13	107	8.2
Chofu	22	181	8.2
Kunitachi	8	64	8.0
Kodaira	21	155	7.4
Higashi Murayama	17	119	7.0
Soka	28	187	6.7
Matsudo	61	401	6.6
Ichikawa	56	364	6.5
Fuchu	30	192	6.4
Kiyose	10	62	6.2
Narashino	21	125	6.0
Seya, Yokohama	17	101	5.9
Tachikawa	24	142	5.9
Shigi	9	51	5.7
Funabashi	85	480	5.6
Hino	27	145	5.4
Akishima	17	89	5.2
Zama	18	94	5.2
Niiza	23	119	5.2
Urawa	71	358	5.0
Asaka	18	90	5.0
Fussa	10	49	4.9
Sagamihara	91	439	4.8
Chigasaki	36	171	4.8
Higashi Yamato	14	66	4.7
Tama	21	95	4.5
Ooi	8	36	4.5
Toda	18	78	4.3
Kamakura	40	173	4.3
Fujisawa	70	300	4.3
Yokosuka	99	421	4.3
Total	1,060	5,990	5.7
Urban area[a]	1,232	12,746	10.3
Grand total	2,292	18,736	8.2

Source: Shutoken Seigi Kyokai 1988, 2:205–12.

Note: These are the thirty-eight most densely populated cities within the "suburban area" (Kinko Seibi Chitai) as defined by the Act on Suburban Development in the Tokyo Metropolitan Area (Shutoken no Kinkou Seibi Chitai oyobi Toshi Kaihatsu Kuiki no Seibi ni Kansuru Horitsu).

[a]"Urban area" is defined in table 5.3.

Table 5.7   **Tokyo versus New York: Employment Density**

Tokyo			New York		
Area (km²)	Employment (1,000s)	Density (1,000s/km²)	Area (km²)	Employment (1,000s)	Density (1,000s/km²)
			11 km² and less		
	Chiyoda ward[a]		Midtown amd Downtown[b]		
			(a) 5.34	760	142.4
10.39	768	73.9	(b) 10.99	11,961	108.4
			20 km² area		
	Two central wards		South Manhattan[c]		
20	1,386	69.3	21.48	1,609	74.9
			60 km² area		
	Four central wards		Manhattan		
59	2,406	40.8	57	1,949	34.2
			600 km² area		
			Manhattan, Queens,		
	All twenty-three wards		Bronx, and Brooklyn		
598	6,234	10.4	629	3,223	5.1
			14,000 km² area		
	Four prefectures		Top seven PMSAs		
13,495	13,515	1.0	14,812	6,925	.05

Sources: Tokyo: Shutoken Seibi Kyokai 1988, 2:62, 204, 205; New York: U.S. Bureau of the Census 1986, 202, 214–15; CACI 1990, 425.

Notes: Data for Midtown, Downtown, and South Manhattan are for 1987 and include only private-sector employment. All other data are for 1980 and include both private-sector and government employment.

[a]The part of the Imperial Palace that is closed to the public is excluded from the area figure of Chiyoda ward.

[b]Midtown and Downtown of Manhattan (a) is the first eight zip code areas in table 5.10, while (b) is the first ten zip code ares of the same table.

[c]South Manhattan is defined to be the area consisting of the first eighteen zip code areas in table 5.10. See notes to table 5.3 for the definitions of other areas.

Assume that people are homogeneous and free migration takes place between the city and the rural area. Then a resident at a border between the metropolitan area and the rural area should be indifferent between commuting to the CBD and working in the rural area. If we assume that the rural workers pay zero commuting costs, the net urban wage rate at the border must be equal to the rural wage rate.

Figure 5.6(a) illustrates the determination of the boundary of the metropolitan area. The rural wage rate, $\bar{w}$, and the CBD wage rate, w^0, are marked on the vertical axis. The net urban wage rate at each location is depicted by the thick line, under the assumption that the commuting cost is proportional to the distance from the CBD. The metropolitan area ends at a distance where

Table 5.8   **Counties in the New York Area: Population, 1980**

County	Area (mi²)	(km²)	Population Size (1,000s)	Population Density (1,000s/km²)	Cumulative Area (km²)	Cumulative Population (1,000s)	Cumulative Density (1,000s/km²)
Manhattan	22	57	1,428	25.0	57	1,428	25.0
Brooklyn	70	181	2,231	12.3	238	3,659	15.4
Bronx	42	109	1,169	10.7	347	4,828	13.9
Queens	109	282	1,891	6.7	629	6,719	10.7
Jersey City, NJ	46	119	557	4.7	749	7,276	9.7
Essex, NJ	127	329	851	2.6	1,077	8,127	7.5
Richmond	59	153	352	2.3	1,230	8,479	6.9
Union, NJ	103	267	504	1.9	1,497	8,983	6.0
Nassau	287	743	1,322	1.8	2,240	10,305	4.6
Bergen, NJ	238	616	845	1.4	2,857	11,150	3.9
Passaic, NJ	187	484	448	0.9	3,341	11,598	3.5
Westchester	438	1,134	867	0.8	4,476	12,465	2.8
Middlesex, NJ	316	818	596	0.7	5,294	13,061	2.5
Rockland	175	453	260	0.6	5,747	13,321	2.3
Suffolk	911	2,359	1,321	0.6	8,107	14,642	1.8

Source: U.S. Bureau of the Census 1986, 202.

Note: Listed are the fifteen most densely populated counties in the NY-NJ-CT CMSA. The sixteenth is Fairfield County, CT.

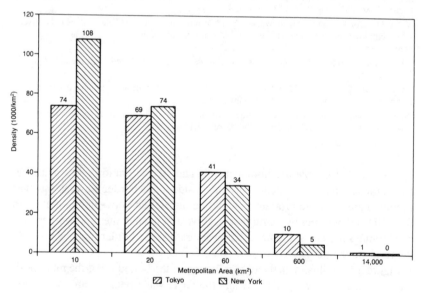

Fig. 5.5 Employment density: Tokyo versus New York

Table 5.9   **The Twenty-three Wards of Tokyo: Employment, 1980**

Day Population Density[a] (1,000s/km²)	Ward	Area (km²)	Emp.[b] (1,000s)	Density (1,000s/km²)	Cumulative Area (km²)	Cumulative Employees (1,000s)	Cumulative Density (1,000s/km²)
94.2	Chiyoda[c]	10.39	767	73.8	10.39	767	73.8
65.5	Chuo	10.05	619	61.6	20.44	1,386	67.8
38.1	Shinjuku	18.04	446	24.7	38.48	1,832	47.6
35.3	Minato	19.99	574	28.7	58.47	2,406	41.1
33.7	Taito	10.00	257	25.7	68.47	2,663	38.9
30.8	Shibuya	15.11	285	18.9	83.58	2,948	35.3
29.4	Bunkyo	11.44	167	14.6	95.02	3,115	32.8
28.5	Toshima	13.01	205	15.8	108.03	3,320	30.7
19.5	Sumida	13.82	173	12.5	121.85	3,493	28.7
19.4	Arakawa	10.34	112	10.8	132.19	3,605	27.3
19.1	Shinagawa	20.91	242	11.6	153.10	3,847	25.1
19.0	Meguro	14.41	130	9.0	167.51	3,977	23.7
16.9	Nakano	15.73	115	7.3	183.24	4,092	22.3
16.6	Kita	20.55	159	7.7	203.79	4,251	20.9
14.5	Itabashi	31.90	223	7.0	235.69	4,474	19.0
13.4	Ohta	49.42	360	7.3	285.11	4,834	17.0
12.3	Suginami	33.54	161	4.8	318.65	4,995	15.7
11.6	Setagaya	58.81	241	4.1	377.46	5,236	13.9
10.7	Katsushika	33.90	177	5.2	411.36	5,413	13.2
10.2	Adachi	53.25	246	4.6	464.61	5,659	12.2
10.1	Koto	36.89	211	5.7	501.50	5,870	11.7
9.6	Nerima	47.00	172	3.7	548.50	6,042	11.0
9.1	Edogawa	48.26	193	4.0	596.76	6,235	10.4
	Total	597.89	6,234	10.4			

Source: Shutoken Seibi Kyokai 1988, 2:204, 205.

[a]The density of population during the daytime, which includes employees, students, and residents who are in the ward.

[b]Emp. stands for the number of employees.

[c]See note *b*, table 5.4.

the thick line reaches the level of the rural wage rate. The distance between the CBD and a border is represented by $\bar{x}$ on the horizontal axis.

The figure makes it clear that the commuting cost at the border reflects the labor productivity difference between the CBD and the rural area. If the CBD productivity is increased, the thick line in figure 5.6(a) will shift right, and the city size will increase both geographically and demographically. If the transportation cost is reduced, the thick line in figure 5.6(a) will become flatter and $\bar{x}$ will increase. This of course implies that, if the transportation cost of a city is cheaper in one city than in another city with an identical CBD productivity, the geographic and demographic sizes of the former city will be greater than the latter.

Table 5.10   **South Manhattan: Employment, 1987**

Zip Code[a]	Area (km²)	Employee (1,000s)	Density (1,000s/km²)	Cumulative Area (km²)	Cumulative Employee (1,000s)	Cumulative Density (1,000s/km²)
10020	0.09	41.5	441.9	0.09	42	441.9
10005	0.26	71.9	278.5	0.35	113	322.1
10047–48	0.12	33.7	276.1	0.47	147	310.3
10017	1.18	195.1	165.9	1.65	342	207.4
10006	0.28	39.4	142.8	1.93	382	198.1
10022	1.62	183.6	113.6	3.54	565	159.6
10004	0.67	73.0	108.7	4.21	638	151.5
10018	1.13	122.4	108.7	5.34	760	142.4
10016	1.20	110.4	92.2	6.54	871	133.2
10036	1.63	123.1	75.7	8.16	994	121.8
10038	0.92	65.1	70.6	9.09	1,059	116.6
10001	1.91	132.2	69.4	10.99	1,191	108.4
10019	2.35	145.2	61.9	13.34	1,337	100.2
10010	1.08	63.3	58.8	14.41	1,400	97.1
10007	0.92	33.4	36.2	15.34	1,433	93.4
10003	1.84	63.4	34.6	17.17	1,497	87.2
10013	2.09	57.8	27.6	19.26	1,554	80.7
10011	2.21	54.6	24.7	21.48	1,609	74.9
10012	1.24	21.9	17.7	22.72	1,631	71.8
10014	1.96	22.6	11.5	24.68	1,653	67.0
10002	2.51	20.1	8.0	27.19	1,674	61.6
10009	1.69	10.2	6.0	28.88	1,684	58.3
Total	28.88	1,683.7	58.3			

Sources: CACI 1990, 425, for the employment figures. Rehana Siddiqui of Columbia University computed the area of each zip code district from a Manhattan map.

Note: The employment figures are for the private sector only.

[a]Zip code 10020 is Rockefeller Center, 10005 is Wall St., and 10047–48 are the twin towers of the World Trade Center.

5.3.2   Land Prices and Population Density

Due to the assumption of free migration, a person must be indifferent between living at any location in the city and living in the rural area at an equilibrium. Suppose that a worker living close to the CBD enjoyed a higher living standard than a border worker. Then all of the rural residents would want to migrate near the CBD. Hence the housing rent near the CBD would go up until the living standard of the residents there became exactly equal to the living standard at the rural area.

The thick line in figure 5.6(b) represents the housing rent curve, which is derived from the net urban wage rate curve depicted in figure 5.6(a). When nonhousing consumption is substitutable for housing floor space in consump-

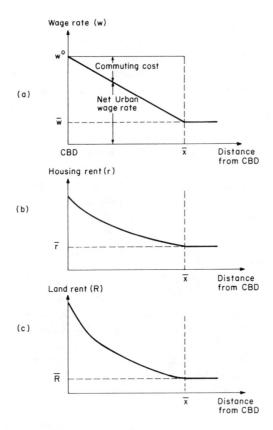

Fig. 5.6   The rent curves

tion, the population density increases as the location becomes closer to the city center, and hence the housing rent curve is convex to the origin.[5]

5. If the demand for housing floor space were fixed regardless of the level of rent, the housing rent curve would be linear. In fact, if we choose the unit of housing services so that each consumer consumes one unit of housing floor space, $r - \bar{r} = w - \bar{w}$ will hold at each location within the city. If housing floor space and nonhousing consumption are substitutable, however, the rent curve becomes convex to the origin. Suppose that the rent curve is linear in such a way that it just enables a resident at an interior location to purchase the same combination of floor space and nonhousing consumption as a border resident, guaranteeing at least the utility level of a border resident. If an interior resident chose this option, he would not be maximizing his utility under the given expenditure; he would be able to improve his utility by reducing the consumption of the floor space and increasing that of the nonhousing consumption goods. This is because he faces a higher relative price of the floor space than a border resident does. Thus the utility-compensating rent has to be higher than the rent that just enables this resident to buy the same bundle as the border resident. We can similarly compare this resident and the third resident living even closer to the center, showing that the rent for the third resident again has to be higher than a linear rent curve based on the second resident's consumption bundle. When nonhousing consumption is substitutable for housing floor space, therefore, the housing rent curve must be convex to the origin.

If land and capital are substitutable in housing production, moreover, the increase in the housing rent will encourage construction of high-rise buildings, and the floor space per square kilometer of land will expand near the CBD. The land rent curve then becomes more curved toward the origin in comparison to the housing rent curve.[6] Thus the shape of the housing rent curve and the factor substitutability in the housing industry determines the curvature of the land rent curve, as depicted in figure 5.6(c).

If either the utility function or the production function or both are substitutable, the land space per resident becomes smaller, that is, the population density increases for locations closer to the CBD. The reasoning above suggests that this causes the land rent function to be curved to the origin. We might conclude, therefore, that the steeper the population density curve, the steeper the land rent curve.[7] Indeed, we will show in equation (8) that the land rent curve and the population density curve are proportional in the economy with Cobb-Douglas utility and production functions when the commuting cost consists of only time and fatigue.

The land price curve is vertically proportional to the land rent curve if the land price is equal to the present value of the future land rent and if a proportional future increase in the land rent is expected regardless of the location. The equality between the land price and the present value of the rent income stream does not hold if "bubbles" prevent the fundamentals from being reflected in the land prices. But so long as the bubble effect is proportional to the present value of the future land rent stream regardless of the location in the city, we may still view the land price curve to be vertically proportional to the land rent curve.

These observations yield the following proposition regarding the effect of a change in the commuting cost upon the land price curve and the population density curve.

Proposition 1. Suppose that the commuting cost per kilometer is reduced, keeping the CBD productivity constant. Then the following hold: (1) the y-axis intercept of the land price curve remains the same. However, the slope of the land price curve becomes flatter, and the level of $\bar{x}$ increases. (2) The y-axis intercept of the population density curve remains the same, but the slope of the population density curve becomes flatter.

---

6. If a fixed amount of land is necessary to produce a given floor space, the housing rent difference between two locations will be proportional to the land rent difference. If land and capital are substitutable, the land rent difference will grow more than proportionally as the housing rent difference grows. The reason is similar to the one given for the convexity of the housing rent curve.

7. If housing and other consumptions are not substitutable in the utility function and if capital and land are not substitutable in the production function, population density at any location of the city should be equal to that in the rural area. The above argument suggests, moreover, that the land rent function should be linear in that case.

5.3.3   Agglomeration Economies

It was pointed out in section 5.3.1 that agglomeration economies are the source of the high labor productivity at the CBD in large metropolitan areas. In the present section, however, we have so far implicitly assumed that the labor productivity at the CBD is kept constant while the per-kilometer commuting cost is changed. Since a change in commuting cost implies a change in the urban population size, this amounts to implicitly assuming that the agglomeration economies are already exhausted at the CBD, and the production function obeys constant returns to scale at a high level of efficiency.

This artificial separation between the urban population size and the CBD productivity is conceptually convenient. But proposition 1 can be easily modified to the situation where an increase in the employment size at the CBD still causes agglomeration economies. We will assume external economies of scale. Thus each firm perceives its production function to be constant returns to scale, but the production in the CBD as a whole obeys increasing returns to scale.

Then we have the following proposition.

Proposition 2. Suppose that the commuting cost per kilometer is reduced in an economy where the CBD technology is subject to external economies of scale. Then the following hold: (1) The y-axis intercept of the land price curve increases, the slope of the land price curve becomes flatter for each land price, and the level of $\bar{x}$ increases. (2) The y-axis intercept of the population density curve increases, and the slope of the population density curve becomes flatter for each density level.

Roughly speaking, the effect of changing the per-kilometer transportation cost is magnified when the CBD technology is subject to external economies of scale.

5.3.4   Idiosyncratic Consumers

In deriving the above propositions, we assumed that all consumers are alike. But the existence of a relatively small number of idiosyncratic consumers does not affect the shapes of the land price and population density curves.

Suppose, for example, that there is a group of talented persons who get higher wages at the CBD than other workers, even though they earn the same wages as others if they work in the rural area. Their reservation land price at an urban location, that is, the one that would make them feel indifferent about the choice between that location and the border, will be higher than the reservation land price for the homogeneous consumers. If there is a sufficiently small number of these talented people, however, the amount of land demanded of a given location at their reservation land price will be below the amount supplied. In this case, the talented people will not be the marginal buyers of land;

the market clearing price will be the one obtained from the homogeneous consumers.[8]

5.3.5   Business Land Use

So far we have implicitly assumed that the CBD firms use a minuscule amount of land. Obviously this is not the case in reality. Suppose that the CBD production uses land, capital, and labor. Also assume that the productivity decreases as a firm is located farther from the city center. Then the line AC in figure 5.7(a) depicts the business land price curve that shows the land prices for various locations under which business firms would be indifferent in their locational choice. If the business firms demand large enough amounts of land in the CBD district to become the marginal buyers, they will outbid the demand for residential use; consequently, the business land prices become the market prices, and the line ABD will become the market price line.

The commuters working in the AB region may first go to the city center by train and then reach their workplace from the city center through other transportation modes. In that case, the firms must compensate the additional trip cost from the city center to the workplaces, and it will be a cause of the reduced productivity of the firms represented by the declining AB curve.

Some workplaces near B may be less expensive for commuters to reach directly without detouring through the city center. If these commuters received the same wage rate as the workers at the center, they would be better off than the workers at the center, which would entice more people to work near B. This would drive down the wage rate near B until it became equal to the location's net urban wage rate for the workers at the center.

Some grocery shops may find it more profitable to be located at S in the middle of the suburbs rather than near the CBD. Their demand curve for the land at S is downward sloping. For the CBD commuters, on the other hand, the land at S and any other suburban location is a perfect substitute. Their demand curve for the land at S is horizontal at the level of the land price given by figure 5.7(a). The combined demand curve of the grocery shops and the commuters for the land at this location is downward sloping at first and becomes flat at the demand price level of the CBD commuters. If the vertical supply curve of this land intersects with the combined demand curve at the flat portion, we say the CBD commuters are the "marginal land buyers" and the grocery shop owners "inframarginal land buyers." If the grocery shops are not marginal land buyers, they will not affect the market land prices.

---

8. As another example, suppose that there is one deviant person in this economy who hardly minds commuting up to twenty minutes but dislikes the additional commuting more intensely than others. Then the price curve that would make him indifferent about the choice of residential location is relatively flat at a high level near the CBD up to a location with the twenty-minute commuting distance and then precipitously declines. At the location within twenty minutes of the CBD, he is thus willing to pay more for the land than others. But to the extent he is a minority, he will not be the marginal buyer, and his taste will not affect the land prices.

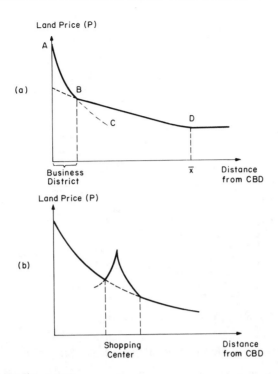

Fig. 5.7   Land price curves

If a shopping center in a suburb is large enough to be a local marginal land buyer, however, it will outbid the residents, and the land price curve will become like figure 5.7(b). Workers commuting to these suburban workplaces will bid down their wage rates at the center.

These observations suggest that, when small workplaces are spread all over the metropolitan area, workers commute from suburbs farther away from the CBD to non-CBD workplaces, but they do not affect the shape of the market land price curve for the residential districts. Figure 5.7(b) suggests that, even if a major shopping center exists, it will not necessarily affect the residential land prices in the area away from the CBD and the shopping center.

5.3.6   Summary

In the present section, we have shown that, in a Mills-Muth model of a concentric city, a reduction in transportation costs makes a city larger both geographically and demographically, while it makes the land price and population density curves flatter. We have also demonstrated that the land price and population density curves will stay the same even if the assumptions of homogeneous consumers and concentration of employment at the city center are violated to some extent.

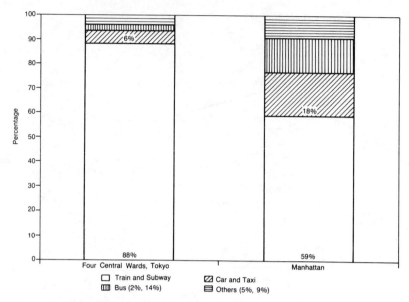

Fig. 5.8   Modes of transportation for commuting

5.4   Tokyo's Population and Employment: An Explanation

We are now in a position to explain the three major differences between Tokyo and New York in structural characteristics, using the theoretical framework outlined above.

5.4.1   The Size of the Metropolitan Area

Dependence on the Railroad System

We have seen in the previous section that the higher the productivity at the CBD is and the lower the cost of commuting is, the larger is the city size. Since the major source of the high productivity at their CBD of Tokyo or New York is the agglomeration economies, the size of the CBD employment itself affects the productivity of the city. Thus commuting cost must be the major independent factor that determines the difference in the sizes of New York and Tokyo.

Figure 5.8, which is based on table 5.11, indicates that 59 percent of the commuters to Manhattan and 88 percent of the commuters to the four central wards of Tokyo use the railroad. Table 5.11 shows that 93 percent of the commuters to the Chiyoda ward use the railroad for commuting.

Passenger cars play a negligible role in commuting to the CBD of Tokyo. In 1980, only 5 percent of the commuters to the four central wards of Tokyo used passenger cars and taxis. On the other hand, 18 percent used passenger cars and taxis to commute to Manhattan. Moreover, many railroad commuters to Manhattan use passenger cars from home to railroad stations, while Tokyo

Table 5.11   Mode of Transportation for Commuting, 1980 (%)

| | Tokyo[a] | | |
Mode of Transportation	Chiyoda	4 Wards[b]	Manhattan[c]
(a) Train and subway[d]	93.0	88.2	59.1
(b) Car	3.2	4.2	16.5
(c) Taxi	1.0	1.1	1.3
(d) Bus	0.9	1.6	13.9
(e) Bicycle and motorcycle	0.3	0.9	0.3
(f) Walk	1.0	3.1	8.2
(g) Other means[e]	0.6	0.8	0.7
Total commuters (1,000s)	753	2,313	1,921

Sources: New York: Barry 1985; Tokyo: Japanese Agency of General Affairs 1985.

[a]Tokyo figures include those who commute to attend schools as well as those who commute to work. The figures for *b* through *f* represent those who use the respective mode only.

[b]The four wards are Chiyoda, Chuo, Minato, and Shinjuku.

[c]The New York figures represent only those who commute to work in Manhattan. The figures represent the percentage of those who use the respective mode for the most distance. The only exception is mode *e*.

[d]Includes Tokyo commuters who use train or subway in conjunction iwth another mode. A commuter who uses three or more modes is also classified in this category, since the original data do not decompose this category. Those who use three or more modes are 8.8 percent of the total in both four wards and Chiyoda.

[e]"Other means" for Tokyo represents a combination of two means among *b–e*. "Other means" for New York represents a mode other than *a–f* for the most distance.

railroad commuters walk, bicycle, or take the bus to railroad stations. Compared with New York commuters, therefore, Tokyo commuters rely less on passenger cars and more on railroads.

Table 5.12 shows that subways carry twice as many passengers in Tokyo as in New York. Moreover, suburban commuter trains play a even more important role than subways in Tokyo, while the opposite is the case in New York. The subway system carries only 21 percent of the railroad passengers in Tokyo, while it carries 83 percent of them in New York.

Indeed, the Tokyo railroad system carries at least five times as many commuters as the New York system. In 1980, the total number of passengers with commuting passes was 7.1 billion for the railroad system in the Tokyo commuting area as defined by Unyu Keizei Kenkyu Center. In the same year, the total number of commuters (to work) was 1.4 billion for the railroad system in the Tri-State region as defined by the Tri-State Regional Planning Commission.[9] The Tri-State region has an area of more than twice the size of the Tokyo commuting area.

9. The size of Tokyo commuting area is 6,400 square kilometers and is smaller than the Tokyo metropolitan area defined in table 5.3. Its population was 25.804 million. In 1980, the total number of passengers with commuting passes in this area per year was 7,117 million for the entire railroad system, while it was 1,486 million for subways. See Unyu Keizai Kenkyu Center (1989, 108–9).

Table 5.12   International Comparison of Subway Networks

City	Annual Volume of Passengers (millions) (A)	Kilometers of Services Provided (km) (B)	Annual Number of Kilometers Served (millions, km) (C)	Average Passengers per Operating Kilometer (A)/(C)
Moscow	2,417	184	408	5.9
Tokyo	2,181	199	230	9.5
Paris	1,376	295	248	5.5
Mexico City	1,038	78	134	7.7
New York	991	370	434	2.3
Osaka	857	91	74	11.6
Leningrad	763	73	141	5.4
London	498	388	325	1.5
Nagoya	414	58	47	8.9
Budapest	362	26	27	13.5

Source: Union Internationale de Transport Publique 1983.

If the population of New York were doubled, keeping the current commuting facilities intact, traffic congestion would become prohibitive. In this sense, the availability of a network of well-developed commuter railroads keeps the commuting cost in Tokyo lower than in New York. This may be the main reason why population size is higher in Tokyo than in New York.

Demand and Supply for the Railroad Systems

In Tokyo, a higher railroad-to-automobile ratio than in New York is demanded for commuting for two reasons.

First, the commuter train service runs more frequently in Tokyo than in New York, making a train ride more attractive to commuters in Tokyo than those in New York. For example, a Chuo Line train for Tokyo station stops at Mitaka every two minutes during the rush hour, but a New Haven Line train for Grand Central Station stops at Larchmont every twenty minutes; both Mitaka and Larchmont are thirty minutes away from the respective terminal stations.

Second, commuting cost from home to the nearby suburban train station is cheaper in Tokyo than in New York. Frequent and inexpensive bus service is available to most suburban train stations in Tokyo, while driving passenger cars is often necessary to reach suburban train stations in the New York area. Suburban communities in Tokyo were developed in such a way that the residents can walk, ride a bicycle, or take a bus to railroad stations, because suburbs were developed before motorization. The resulting high population den-

---

The Tri-State region is an area greater than the top seven PMSAs defined in table 5.3. In 1980, the total number of people commuting to work in this region was 1.443 million, while it was 1.150 million for subways. See Barry (1985, 17, 19).

sity in suburbs makes frequent bus service to the train station possible. In the New York area, where many suburbs were developed after motorization, it was taken for granted that most commuters drive cars to the suburban railroad stations. Hence suburban communities with low population densities emerged. As a result, relatively few people live within walking distance of a suburban train station, and bus service to many suburban train stations is not even available.

On the supply side, the railroad services in Tokyo are widespread and frequent for two reasons.

First, a higher level of fixed investment was made in the train system than in the highway system during the period when Tokyo was suburbanized. This is because the suburbanization of Tokyo took place before passenger cars became affordable to most residents.

Second, the high population density in the Tokyo area makes frequent commuter services profitable. Except for interest subsidies for certain types of investments, commuter train firms in Tokyo operate in the black without government subsidies.[10] This makes them remarkably different from their American and European counterparts.

An examination of demand and supply factors above implies that agglomeration economies exist in the production of mass transit services. Scale economies can always give rise to multiple equilibria. Once the density exceeds a critical level, an equilibrium in a metropolitan area is reached with high population density and with a profitable mass transit system. But if the critical level is not attained, a different equilibrium is reached, with a low density requiring passenger cars as a mode of commuting. It appears that the historical accident helped Tokyo reach the level of suburban density above the "critical level."

5.4.2   Underutilization of the CBD

Employment

The Tokyo metropolitan area has a population size twice as large as that of the New York metropolitan area, owing partly to a better-developed transit system. Thus it would be only natural if the CBD of Tokyo should have a higher employment density than that of New York.

In reality, the employment density of Tokyo is lower than that of New York; the space of the CBD area of Tokyo is considerably underutilized relative to that of New York. Three historical and institutional factors explain this phenomenon.

The first factor is the building code used to restrict the height of buildings in Japan until 1970, when advancement in aseismic construction technology made the restriction unnecessary. In the area with convenient traffic access,

---

10. See Nippon Min'ei Tetsudo Kyokai (1989, 12–13, 44–47).

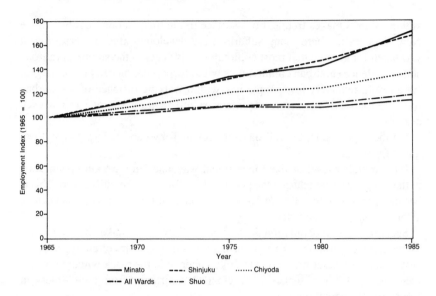

Fig. 5.9   Employment trend, central wards in Tokyo

low-level buildings had been constructed by the time the restriction was re-moved.

Second, Land Lease and Building Lease Laws have prevented conversions of one- and two-story residential housing into skyscrapers.[11]

Third, other restrictions on building size such as the Sunshine Law make construction of skyscrapers more expensive.

Owing to these historical and institutional frictions, therefore, Tokyo is out of equilibrium with respect to its CBD employment density. It appears, how-ever, that the CBD in Tokyo is in the adjustment process and is moving toward an equilibrium with a high employment density. Evidence for this is that the employment in the Tokyo CBD has been rapidly expanding relative to the larger business districts, as figure 5.9 and table 5.13 indicate.

Besides, the market seems to realize that the CBD in Tokyo is in an adjust-ment phase. Noguchi (ch. 1 in this volume) points out that the land price in Tokyo is much higher than the present value of the future office rent stream if the rent is assumed to increase in proportion to GNP. When the potentially high employment density is realized in the future by overcoming the above frictions, a square kilometer of land in the CBD will be able to command a much higher land rent than now. In a competitive economy, such future produc-tivity increases in land must be already capitalized in the present land price. Noguchi's observation seems to imply that the market expects such a rapid increase in the land productivity at the CBD.

11. See Noguchi (ch. 1 in this volume) and Ito (ch. 9 in this volume) for details.

Table 5.13   Dynamics of Employment in the CBD of Tokyo (in thousands)

	1965	1970	1975	1980	1985	Growth Rate 1965–85 (%)
Chiyoda	610	673	745	767	850	39.3
		10.3%	10.7%	3.0%	10.8%	
Chuo	565	587	621	619	658	16.5
		3.9%	5.8%	−0.3%	6.3%	
Minato	398	461	537	574	694	74.4
		15.8%	16.5%	6.9%	20.9%	
Shinjuku	300	351	400	446	512	70.7
		17.0%	14.0%	11.5%	14.8%	
Total, ward district	5,537	5,891	6,118	6,234	6,681	20.7
		6.4%	3.9%	1.9%	7.2%	

Note: The percentage under each employment figure gives the growth rate of employment in the preceding five years.
Sources: Japanese Agency of General Affairs 1986; Shutoken Seibi Kyokai 1988.

Moreover, the market seems to expect Tokyo to have an even higher CBD land rent than New York. Currently, we observe a higher CBD land price in Tokyo than in New York despite a lower employment density. It is certainly possible to explain a part of this gap in terms of the "bubble," as Noguchi does. But the gap is also consistent with the hypothesis that the market expects Tokyo to have a higher employment density in the CBD than New York will, to match Tokyo's larger population and employment in the entire metropolitan area. Suppose that the equilibrium is restored and the CBD of Tokyo attains a higher employment density than that of New York. Then agglomeration economies would enable Tokyo to have a higher labor productivity, and hence higher rents and land prices, than New York. The gap in the CBD land prices of the two cities is consistent with such a business expectation.

Residential Population

The population density of the CBD is also lower in Tokyo than in New York. But Tokyo's low CBD density does not require special explanations; the business sector can outbid the household sector for the CBD land use in any city in any country. Moreover, the three explanations for the low employment density in the CBD of Tokyo account for the low population density.

It is the high density in the CBD of New York that requires a special explanation, although we will not venture into this topic here except to note that strict zoning in New York protects residential areas in the middle of its CBD.

5.4.3   Flat Population Density Curve

Figure 5.3 shows that the population density curve for the suburbs of Tokyo is flatter than the curve for New York. One possible explanation may lie in the fact that the commuter trains in Tokyo maintain fast, accurate, and frequent services, which keep the per-kilometer cost of travel in Tokyo low.

In addition, employers' reimbursements of commuting expenses help keep the per-kilometer cost of travel low. Indeed, among those who bought commuter passes for the railroad in major metropolitan areas of Japan in 1985, only 5 percent paid the full amount of the commuting passes by themselves.[12] Employers reimburse commuting expenses because the additional wage payment earmarked to cover the commuting expenses, up to 50,000 yen per month, is not taxable under the personal income tax. This preferential tax treatment encourages employers to shift a portion of the initial total wage payment to the reimbursement of commuting expenses.[13]

Free commuter riding gives strong incentives to employees to live farther from the city center than otherwise. This flattens the population density and land price distribution from the CBD. Moreover, the free ride makes the city grow in terms of both geographical size and population. In 1985, the average commuter working in Chiyoda, Chuo, and Minato wards spent sixty-seven minutes in commuting one way, according to the Ministry of Transportation (1985).

5.5   The Land Price Function: The Model

In sections 5.5–5.7 we will expound on the impact of the reimbursement of commuting expenses by estimating the residential land price functions with and without reimbursement.

The basic idea for the estimation is simple. Tokyo commuters pay no monetary expenses for commuting. Hence the nonmonetary costs of commuting, time and fatigue, are the only reason why the land prices in Tokyo fall as the distance of a location from the CBD increases. Thus the observed land price distribution will reveal the nonmonetary costs of commuting, and we should be able to estimate the parameters of the utility function and the housing production function from the land price distribution. Once these parameters are estimated, we can derive the land price equation that would prevail when commuters have to pay their monetary commuting expenses as well.

The model we use is a formal version of the model developed in section 5.3. The readers not interested in technicalities may want to skip to section 5.7.3.

---

12. According to the Japanese Ministry of Transportation (1987, 164), 94.9 percent of those who bought commuter passes for the railroad in Tokyo, Osaka, and Nagoya metropolitan areas in 1985 received some reimbursement from their employers, 93.4 percent were reimbursed more than one-half of the purchase amount, and 86.5 percent received full reimbursement.

13. Suppose a firm decides to reimburse its employees' commuting expenses by appropriating a portion of the initial total wage payment. This action will reduce its employees' aggregate income tax payments without increasing the firm's total labor costs.

5.5.1 The Demand Price Equation

Consider a household that consumes h square meters of housing services, z units of composite consumption good, and ℓ minutes of leisure. Let

$$u(h, z, \ell) = h^\beta z^{1-\beta} \ell^\alpha$$

represent its utility function. Suppose that the hours of work is fixed. Let δ represent leisure endowment minus the sum of the time for work and the time required for minimum subsistence such as sleeping and eating. Then the leisure time ℓ is obtained by subtracting the commuting time from δ. Assume that the household is at a point with the commuting distance of x minutes from the CBD (hereafter we will refer to it simply as a point with distance x). Then we have $\ell = \delta - x$. We define the reduced utility function U by substituting this for ℓ in the function u to get

(1) $$U(h, z, x) = h^\beta z^{1-\beta}(\delta - x)^\alpha.$$

We assume that the household located at a point with distance x maximizes its utility level under the following budget constraint:

(2) $$r(x)h + z = Y - tx,$$

where $r(x)$ is the housing rent at distance x, Y is income, and t is the per-kilometer fare for commuting that the commuter has to pay. The unit of the compound good is so chosen as to make its unit price equal to one.

A consumer living at distance x will maximize the value of (1) subject to (2) by choosing h and z for the given Y, t, x, and $r(x)$. The maximum utility level that the household attains under the budget constraint is given by the indirect utility function $v^0(r(x), Y - tx, x)$.

It is assumed that the rural residents do not have to commute to work, and their utility level is $\bar{v}$. Since we assume that the household can freely migrate between the metropolitan area and the rural area seeking a higher utility level, the utility level of a household living in the metropolitan area has to be equal to that in the rural area, regardless of the distance of the residence from the CBD. At the equilibrium of the model, therefore, $r(x)$, $Y - tx$, and x have to satisfy[14]

(3) $$v^0(r(x), Y - tx, x) = \bar{v}.$$

---

14. If the housing rent $r(t)$ at an x were so low that $v^0(r(x), Y - tx, x) > \bar{v}$ holds, every household would want to move to this location and the housing rent will be bid up until equation (6) is restored. Were $r(t)$ so high so as to make this inequality reversed, households would leave this location until equation (6) holds.

Merriman and Hellerstein (1993) use discrete choice techniques to estimate the parameters of utility function similar to equation (1) with the data on commuting flows in Tokyo. They find strong empirical evidence that commuters are sensitive to both land prices and commuting times when choosing residential locations.

Let

$$r(x) = r^*(Y - tx, x, \bar{v})$$

be the solution function for $r(x)$ in equation (3). Since Y, t, and $\bar{v}$ are constant in our model, this shows that the housing rent is a function solely of the commuting distance x. The function r^* is the *demand price equation* for the housing service at distance x. This is drawn in figure 5.6(b).

5.5.2   The Supply Price Equation for Housing Services

We assume that the production function of the housing service industry is given by

$$H(x) = \lambda L(x)^v K(x)^{(1-v)},$$

where $L(x)$ is the size of the land area that the housing service industry employs at distance x, $K(x)$ is the amount of capital that the housing service industry employs at distance x, and, $H(x)$ is the floor space of housing that the housing service industry produces at distance x. We assume that each firm maximizes profit under the given technological constraint, taking prices as given, and that free entry takes place in this industry, deriving the profit to zero. Then $r(x)$, the price of unit output of housing, must be equal to the unit cost. Thus we must have

$$r(x) = c(R(x), i),$$

where $c(R(x), i)$ is the unit cost function, $R(x)$ is the land rent at distance x, and i is the interest rate. This is the *supply price equation* for the housing service that governs the relationship among the housing rent $r(x)$, the land rent $R(x)$, and the interest rate i at the distance x from the CBD.

5.5.3   The Market Equilibrium

The market equilibrium requires that the demand and supply prices must be equal, and we have

(4) $$c(R(x), i) = r^*(Y - tx; x, \bar{v}).$$

This equilibrium condition implicitly determines the land rent function. Let

(5) $$R(x) = R^*(Y - tx, x, \bar{v}, i)$$

be the solution function for $R(x)$ in (4). This is depicted in figure 5.6(c).

Let us assume that the land price of a given location is the present value of the future stream of the land rent at that location. Then the land price function $P(x)$ is obtained by dividing (5) by i. Under our specifications of the utility and the production functions, $P(x)$ is explicitly written as[15]

15. First consider the following cost minimization problem for unit output:

$$\text{Min } r \equiv R\frac{L}{H} + i\frac{K}{H}$$

(6) $$P(x) = B(Y - tx)^{1/\beta\nu}(\delta - x)^{\alpha/\beta\nu},$$

where B is a constant containing i. Clearly, the first and the second parentheses on the right-hand side represent the contributions of the monetary and non-monetary commuting costs, respectively, in determining the land price. This is the basic equation in our model determining the land price at each distance from the CBD.

5.5.4 Estimation Procedure

Equation (6) is the land price equation to be estimated.

We cannot, however, directly estimate equation (6). The Japanese commuter does not have to pay the monetary expense of commuting, and hence $t = 0$ holds in (6), yielding

(7) $$P(x) \equiv C(\delta - x)^{\alpha/\beta\nu},$$

where $C \equiv BY^{1/\beta\nu}$. We will estimate the parameters C, $\alpha/\beta\nu$, and δ by running a regression of equation (7).

Although this does not give us an estimate of the parameter mix $1/\beta\nu$ that appears in equation (6), we can estimate it by taking advantage of the relation-

---

$$\text{S.T. } 1 = \lambda \left\{ \frac{L}{H} \right\}^{\nu} \left\{ \frac{K}{H} \right\}^{1-\nu}$$

The solution functions for L/H and K/H are

$$\frac{L}{H} = \frac{1}{\lambda} \left\{ \frac{\nu i}{(1-\nu)R} \right\}^{1-\nu} \quad \text{and} \quad \frac{K}{H} = \frac{1}{\lambda} \left\{ \frac{\nu i}{(1-\nu)R} \right\}^{-\nu},$$

respectively. At the free-entry, perfectly competitive equilibrium, the minimized unit cost is equal to the housing price. Hence we have

$$r = \frac{R}{\lambda} \left\{ \frac{i \nu}{(1-\nu)R} \right\}^{1-\nu} + \frac{i}{\lambda} \left\{ \frac{i \nu}{(1-\nu)R} \right\}^{-\nu}.$$

Thus we get the supply price function

$$r(x) = ER(x)^{\nu},$$

where

$$E \equiv \frac{1}{\lambda} \left[\frac{1}{\nu} \right]^{\nu} \left\{ \frac{i}{(1-\nu)} \right\}^{1-\nu}.$$

The expenditure minimization under the given utility level $\bar{\nu}$ similarly specifies the demand price equation as

$$r(x) = A(Y - tx)^{1/\beta}(\delta - x)^{\alpha/\beta},$$

where

$$A \equiv \beta(1 - \beta)^{(1-\beta)}\bar{\nu}^{1/\beta}.$$

Equating the demand and supply price equations and applying the fact that $P(x) = R(x)/i$, we get equation (6), where

$$B \equiv \frac{1}{i} \left[\frac{c}{D} \right]^{1/\nu}.$$

ship between the land price function and the population density function. Define the population density function $M(x)$ by

$$M(x) = \frac{H(x)}{L(x)h(x)}$$

Then we obtain[16]

(8) $$M(x) = \frac{1}{\beta v} \cdot \frac{i}{Y} \cdot P(x).$$

Since i and Y are constant, we can estimate the parameter mix $1/\beta v$ by running a regression of this equation.

5.6 The Land Price Function: Data

We estimate the land price function (7) and the population density function (8) by using the land price and population density data along the Chuo Line, which is a major commuter line in the Tokyo metropolitan area. (Figure 5.10 is a map of this line and a few stations along it.) The income variance of the suburban residents along different commuter lines is considered to be wider than that along a given line. In particular, the Chuo Line is among those that are recognized for the homogeneity of income and social class along them. Besides, this line takes commuters directly to the Tokyo station without transferring. These are our reasons for choosing the Chuo Line as our object of study.

To estimate the two equations we need the following data: residential land price per square meter (P), the number of households per square meter (M), and the commuting time cost (t) at various locations along the Chuo Line; the average income (Y); and the interest rate (i).

For the land price and the time distance, the government benchmark land prices (Koji Chika) of 1985 are employed. The data contain the land price, the name of the nearest train station, and the distance from the nearest train station for each sample. We employ only the residential household samples along the Chuo Line, but exclude those samples whose nearby stations are closer than Nakano station to the CBD. We deem that the land prices of the residential area to the east of Nakano station strongly reflect the commercial value of the land.

---

16. Since the production function of the housing service industry is Cobb-Douglas, the share of the land rent $R(x)L(x)$ in the total revenue $r(x)H(x)$ of this industry is v. Thus we have $R(x)L(x) = vr(x)H(x)$. This and the definition of $M(x)$ yield

$$M(x) = \frac{R(x)}{vr(x)h(x)}.$$

When $t = 0$, on the other hand, the Cobb-Douglas utility function yields $r(x)h(x) = \beta Y$. Thus we get equation (8).

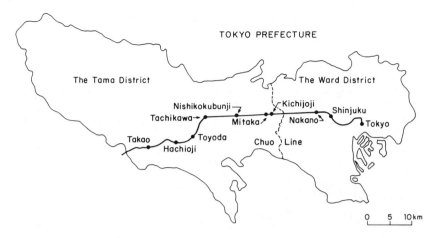

Fig. 5.10   Tokyo prefecture and the Chuo Line
Notes: The ward district consists of twenty-three wards, as shown in figure 5.4. The Tama district consists of counties and cities, some of which are listed in tables 5.5 and 5.6. Figure 5.2 locates Tokyo prefecture within the Tokyo metropolitan area.

Among these data we choose all that are located within 1.5 kilometers, that is, walking distance, of the nearest station. It would be difficult to estimate the commuting time between the train station and the residential location for those who live farther away from the train station for a number of reasons. First, they may use a variety of traffic modes. Second, even if we assume that most of them use buses, the bus route may be roundabout and the actual time cost of riding the bus may not be proportional to the geographical distance found in the data. Third, the different frequency of the bus service would greatly affect the actual time cost. Fourth, many passengers may take trains at stations that are not geographically closest to their residences. On the other hand, the households living relatively near the station mostly walk or ride a bicycle, and in case they use the bus, the time cost is likely to be monotonically related to the geographical distance from the nearby station.

Seventy-seven samples in the data satisfy the above qualifications. The unit of measurement of the land price in the present study is 10,000 yen per square meter.

The commuting consists of the trip from the residential location to the nearby station and the train ride from the nearby station to the CBD. We estimate the former from the data of the geographical distance between the residential location and the station. The latter is estimated from the data on the trip time by the rapid train (*kaisoku*) and by the special rapid train (*tokubetsu kaisoku*). The unit of measurement of the time distance from the CBD is minutes required for one-way commuting per day. Table 5.14 lists the one-way commuting time to Tokyo station from each station of the Chuo Line west of

Table 5.14   **Time Distance from Tokyo Station**

Station[a]	S	One-Way Commuting Time		X[b]
		Rapid Train	Special Rapid Train	
*Shinjuku	0	14	14	14.00
Okubo	0	16	16	16.00
Higashi Nakano	0	18	18	18.00
*Nakano	0	18	18	18.00
Koenji	0	20	20	20.00
Asagaya	0	22	22	22.00
Ogikubo	0	24	24	24.00
Nishi Ogikubo	0	27	27	27.00
Kichijoji	0	29	29	29.00
*Mitaka	1	32	28	27.53
Musashi Sakai	0	34	30	31.63
Higashi Koganei	0	36	33	34.22
Musashi Koganei	1	39	36	35.12
Kokubunji	0	42	38	39.63
Nishikokubunji	0	44	40	41.63
Kunitachi	0	46	42	43.63
*Tachikawa	0	54	40	45.69
*Hino	0	57	43	48.69
*Toyoda	0	61	46	52.10
*Hachioji	0	65	50	56.10
*Nishi Hachioji	0	68	54	59.69
*Takao	0	72	57	63.10

Source: Japan Travel Bureau 1985.
[a]Asterisks indicate the stations where special rapid trains stop.
[b]The constructed time distance.

Shinjuku. Figure 5.11 shows the relationship between the time distance, which is estimated by the procedure discussed later, and the land price.[17]

The benchmark land price data do not include population density in the location of each sample. We use the census data of 1985 instead. First, for each of our samples, we compute the population density (N) in the basic cell district of the survey in which the sample is located. (Each cell is five hundred meters square.) Second, assuming that each household has one commuter to the CBD, we estimate the density of the commuters denoted M by $M = N/2.52$, where 2.52 represents the average number of household members in Tokyo metropolitan prefecture, based on the *Basic Survey of the Residents* of 1985.

For the sake of consistency, we use the same time period in measuring com-

17. Each selected station in figure 5.11 shows the one-way commuting time distance to the Tokyo station. On the other hand, each sample in the figure is located at the time distance that includes the commuting time from home to the nearby station as well as the time from the nearby station to the Tokyo station. Thus samples for which the nearby station is Mitaka are shown in the figure midway between Mitaka and Tachikawa, for example.

muting time, interest rate, income, and commuting expense. Since we have used one-half day for the strategic variable of commuting time, we also use one-half day for measuring the other two variables. It is assumed that commuters work twenty-two days a month. To convert monthly figures of income and interest into a half-day basis, we therefore divide them by forty-four.

We assume that the personal income of all of the residents in the metropolitan area is constant regardless of the distance from the CBD. Our estimate of income of the representative resident is based on the figure of 4,932 thousand yen, which is the average annual earnings of an employee in the Tokyo metropolitan prefecture in 1985, as reported in Japanese Economic Planning Agency (1988). Assuming that there is only one employee (i.e., commuter) in each household, monthly income per household is $493.2/12 = 41.1$ (10,000 yen per one-half day). Half-day income per household is $y = 41.1/44 = 0.93409$.

As for the data of interest rates, we employed the national average loan interest rate of banks converted to one-half day as reported by the Japanese Economic Planning Agency (1989), which is 0.012 percent.

5.7   Land Price Function: Estimation

5.7.1   Estimation of Equation (7)

Before explaining the estimation procedure, let us first state the final form of our estimation of equation (7):

(9) $$P = e^{-9.7091+D}(174.89 - X)^{2.6750.}$$

where D is the dummy variable for the samples near Nakano and Kichijoji stations (see fig. 5.10). The variable D takes the value of 0.23309 for the sam-

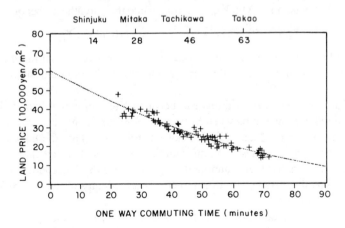

Fig. 5.11   Land price distribution

ples near Nakano station, 0.1458 for those near Kichijoji station, and zero for all other samples. It reflects the fact that the residential land prices of Nakano and Kichijoji are shifted upward because of their proximity to the commercial districts. Figure 5.11 gives a scatter diagram of $(X, P/e^D)$ combinations, which means that the samples of Nakano and Kichijoji are adjusted by the dummy variables. This figure also depicts the graph of equation (9) with $D = 0$.

The time distance variable X is the sum of the trip time from home to the station and the trip time on the train, and it is defined by

(10) $X = 5.2911L + (X_R + 0.59332D_E - 2.0969S)$,

where L is the geographical distance between the residential location of the sample and the nearby station; X_R is the time period of a one-way ride by rapid train between Tokyo and the nearby station of the sample; X_E is the time period of a one-way ride by special rapid train between Tokyo and the nearby station of the sample; $D_E = X_E - X_R$ if the special rapid train stops at the nearby station of the sample, and zero otherwise (the special rapid train stops at Mitaka, Tachikawa, and all the stations to the west of Tachikawa); and S is the dummy that takes the value of one for the samples near Mitaka or Koganei and zero otherwise.

The coefficient of L indicates that it takes an average commuter 5.2911 minutes per kilometer (approximately 11 kilometers per hour) to make a trip between residence and station. This implies that many of the residents living within 1.5 kilometers of a station use either bicycles or buses.

The terms in the parenthesis of equation (10) represent time spent on the train. If the special rapid trains do not stop at the nearest station for the given sample, and if the station is not Nakano or Mitaka, both D_E and S take the value of zero, and hence the time cost of the train ride is equal to the time required by the rapid train.

If special rapid trains stop at the nearby station of a given sample, and if the station is not Nakano or Mitaka, the terms inside the parentheses become

$$X_R + 0.59332 D_E = 0.40668 X_R + 0.59332 X_E.$$

This implies that the resident living near a station where special rapid trains stop takes these trains about 60 percent of the time and rapid trains 40 percent of the time.

An additional number of trains run between Koganei and Tokyo stations, and even more trains run between Mitaka and Tokyo stations. This means that the passengers from Koganei or Mitaka for Tokyo can take the unoccupied trains that originate at these stations, and the passengers have a better chance of getting seats rather than standing during the train ride. The coefficient of S indicates that this privilege is worth the extra 2.1 minutes of the train ride, or 4.2 minutes per day.

Finally, note that equation (9) indicates that $\delta = 175$ (minutes per one-half day). the value of δ, therefore, is approximately six hours per day, a quite reasonable number in view of its definition.

Equation (9) is based on the following estimation based on the maximum likelihood method:

$$\log P = -9.7091 + 0.2331D_N + 0.1452D_K$$
$$(-0.8822) \quad (3.3644) \quad (2.7875)$$

$$+ 2.6750 \log[174.89 - \{5.2911L + (X_R + 0.59332D_E - 2.0969S)\}],$$
$$(1.4189) \quad (1.9689)(3.2247) \quad (4.1913) \quad (-2.6358)$$

$$R^2 = 0.923748,$$

where the numbers in the parentheses are t values.

5.7.2 Estimation of Equation (6)

Let us now derive equation (6). For this purpose, we need to estimate $1/\beta v$ by estimating the population density function, as we argued earlier. The OLS estimate of (8) is

$$M = 5.58861 \cdot \frac{i}{Y} \cdot P, \qquad \hat{R}^2 = 0.686902.$$
$$(36.3666)$$

Thus we obtain

(11)
$$\frac{1}{\beta v} = 5.5886.$$

Finally, we have to estimate t in equation (6). We assume that for our samples households have to pay monetary travel expense only for the train. Thus we run a regression of the half-day-equivalent of the cost of a one-month train pass (Z, unit 10,000 yen) against commuting time required for a one-way trip to Tokyo station.

$$F = 0.00065824 X \qquad \hat{R}^2 = 0.951762$$
$$(118.20)$$

Thus our estimate of t is 0.00065824.

From this, (6), (9), and (11), we obtain the following:

(12) $P = e^{-9.32806+D}(0.93409 - 0.00065824X)^{5.5886}(174.89 - X)^{2.6750.}$

The power of e is chosen so that the right-hand sides of equations (9) and (12) give the same land price when $X = 0$. Equation (12) gives the land price at the hypothetical residential location with a zero distance to the station that is X minutes away from the Tokyo station.

5.7.3 Implications of the Estimated Land Price Function

The thick line in figure 5.12 depicts the graph of equation (12) for the case where $D = 0$. This shows the land price function after commuters are made to pay the train fare equal to the commuter pass in 1985. The dotted line of figure 5.11 is duplicated in figure 5.12. The difference between the two curves shows

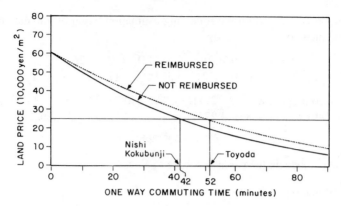

Fig. 5.12   The effect of fare reimbursement upon land prices

the effect of the reimbursement of the commuting fare on the structure of the land price in the Tokyo metropolitan area. For example, figure 5.12 indicates that the land price that was realized at Toyoda, which is fifty-four minutes away from Tokyo in 1985, would have been realized in Nishikokubunji, which is forty-seven minutes away from Tokyo.

It should be noted at this point that the effect of stopping reimbursements represented by figure 5.12 is a long-run effect that would be realized after the emigration process from the urban area had been completed. Immediately after the reform, the utility level of the suburban residents living near the border would be reduced. People living closer to the city center, who have lower commuting costs, would suffer a milder loss in utility. It is perhaps unrealistic to assume that many suburban residents can change jobs and emigrate to the rural area within several years after the reform. But it is likely that many of them would migrate to a location closer to the city center, keeping their jobs at the CBD. This would increase the land price curve near the CBD more than figure 5.12 indicates until the urban utility became equal regardless of location. This would discourage young people looking for jobs for the first time from working in the Tokyo metropolitan area. The population size of the metropolitan area would be reduced, and the urban land price curve would come down in the long run until the land price curve as indicated by the thick line of figure 5.12 is restored. In this sense, figure 5.12 represents the long-run impact of stopping of reimbursement.

As pointed out earlier, firms in Tokyo reimburse the commuting expenses of their employees because of the preferential treatment of the commuting expenses in personal income taxes. We can interpret the thick curve in figure 5.12 to represent the land price curve after the preferential tax treatment is eliminated.

Let us now decompose the effect of the elimination of the deductibility of commuting expenses in two stages. Suppose that in the first stage the firms continue to reimburse commuting expenses, and that only at the second stage do the firms stop reimbursement. At the first stage, a Tokyo resident has to pay income tax for the reimbursement, which becomes his only monetary commuting expense. In this first stage, the land price curve will become steeper than the dotted curve in figure 5.12, but its change will be smaller than the change indicated by the thick line.

This, however, is not the end of the story for the first stage. Since the government subsidy for commuting is now eliminated, the population size of the Tokyo area will shrink. Proposition 2 indicates that this will reduce the CBD productivity. Thus the land price curve in the first stage has to start at a point lower than the y-axis intercept of the dotted curve in figure 5.12.

At the second stage, firms stop reimbursements. A firm adds the average of what it formerly paid as the reimbursement to the regular wage rate. This incremental payment, which is lump sum regardless of the residential locations of the workers, will raise the y-axis intercept of the land price curve.

Thus the first- and the second-stage effects work in opposite directions on the y-axis intercept, and the net effect is uncertain. Our thick curve in figure 5.12, starting at the same point as the dotted curve, may be taken as an approximation to this net effect.

5.8   Policy Implications

There are varied opinions as to whether the expansion of the population size of the Tokyo metropolitan area should be encouraged or discouraged. Kakumoto (1986), for example, reasons that investment in infrastructure in the business districts of Tokyo should be discouraged, because the commuting capacity has reached its limit. Hatta (1983), on the other hand, argues that, once the commuter industry is deregulated, the fare structure and the capital equipment size in the commuter industry will become optimal. He claims that given such deregulation, the government should encourage the expansion of employment in Tokyo so that the economy can take full advantage of agglomeration economies.

In this section, we examine the policy implications of our theoretical and empirical observations in earlier sections. In the process, we discuss the issues of whether the population of Tokyo has exceeded its efficient size and whether capital stocks in transportation and in the CBD infrastructure are at their efficient levels.

5.8.1   Efficiency Measure

We first need to establish a measure of efficiency. For this purpose, let us examine the welfare impact of a productivity improvement in the CBD in the model of section 5.3. By assumption, producers are competitive, and hence earn zero (economic) profit both before and after the productivity change. Also by assumption, people are mobile, and hence if there is any improvement in the urban living standard, rural residents will migrate into the city until the land price curve is shifted up by such an amount that the living standard at any location of the city becomes equal to the rural level. In the end, the owners of land—the immobile factor—reap all the benefit of the technological change.

Proposition 3. If productivity improvement takes place at the CBD, all of its fruits fall on the landowners. No one else makes economic gains: producers continue to get zero profits, and the living standard of the urban resident remains exactly the same as that of the rural resident.

In the model of section 5.3, therefore, the efficiency impact of technological improvement is measured by the increase in the total land value.

5.8.2   Urban Land Tax

The fruit of technological progress that goes to the landowners can be recouped and be shared by others if the land tax is imposed on the difference between the value of such urban land and the value of rural land the same size.

The urban land tax is an efficient tax. It will reduce the urban land price curve, but the sum of the urban land price and the present value of the future land tax obligations remain the same as the pretax land price at any location. This tax therefore will not affect the population density curve or the city size.

Often an urban land tax has been proposed in Japan on efficiency grounds, since it is considered to discourage the idle use of land. But this tax is neutral on efficiency. Its virtue lies in its redistribution capacity.

5.8.3   Government Subsidies for Commuting

The government subsidies on commuting expenses reduce efficiency. To see this, take a worker who commutes to the CBD from the city border. For him the rural wage rate is equal to his net urban wage rate. His net social productivity in the city is equal to his net urban wage rate minus government subsidies for commuting, while his social productivity in the rural economy is equal to the rural wage rate. Thus his net productivity is higher in the rural area than in the city by the amount of government subsidies. Social efficiency would require him to work in the rural economy. This indicates that the preferential tax treatment on commuting expenses creates inefficiency.

5.8.4   Efficient Fare Structure

Tokyo's commuter trains are notorious for their rush hour congestion. Indeed, the congestion rate during the rush hours in the national railroad in the Tokyo metropolitan area was estimated to be 244 percent, where the National Land Agency (1987) defines the congestion rate of 100 percent as a situation where "passengers can either be seated or hold onto poles or hanging rings comfortably."[18]

---

18. When the rate is 200 percent, "passengers feel considerable pressure from each other but can manage to read weekly magazines." When the degree is 250 percent, "passengers cannot move

Whether or not this is an excessive level of congestion for Tokyo, however, requires scrutiny. For this purpose, examining the fare structure is useful. Hatta (1983) has shown that in a large metropolitan area where many commuter railroad companies compete for customers, free market fare setting and no limitations on investment would automatically internalize congestion, resulting in efficient marginal cost pricing and efficient investment.

Thus the current free-ride system in Tokyo inefficiently encourages the demand for transit rides, causing an excessive degree of congestion during the rush hour and for a long-distance ride. Requiring the commuters to pay the current commuter-pass fares would reduce congestion and improve efficiency. In deriving the thick line in figure 5.12, we assumed that after the tax reform the commuters have to pay the train pass fares of 1985.

These commuter-pass fares, however, are much lower than profit-maximizing ones, and hence are below the socially efficient levels. This is because the following regulations force Japanese railroad companies to set pass fares artificially low: (1) A discount of approximately 50 percent is given on the commuter pass, making the peak-load fare 50 percent less than the off-peak fare. (2) Fares are set on a per-kilometer basis regardless of the degree of congestion. (3) Full cost pricing is required.

If correct peak-load prices were imposed on passengers, therefore, the fares during the rush hour would have to rise substantially beyond the monthly pass rates assumed in our study. Note that the inefficiently low fares not only cause excessive congestion in the short run, but also stymie incentives for the commuter rail firms to invest in improving the service in the long run.

If these regulations as well as the tax deductibility of commuting expenses were eliminated, the land price curve in figure 5.12 would become substantially steeper than the thick line. Besides, through the effect indicated by proposition 2, the y-axis intercept would come down. It is possible that the Tokyo population would be reduced. Our equation (12) can be modified for studying the impact of a further fare increase.[19]

5.8.5   Subsidizing the CBD Production

So far in this section we have explicitly ignored the agglomeration economy of the CBD production. Once this is taken into account, a free market mecha-

---

hands." When the degree reaches 300 percent, the official description states that "passengers can be physically endangered."

19. If train fares were increased to the level of the social cost of commuting, the combined monetary and nonmonetary commuting cost would not increase as much because of the reduced congestion level. In the long run, the offsetting reduction in the combined commuting cost would become even stronger for the following reasons: The fare increase would cause a substantial excess profit, since by and large Japanese commuter lines already make a profit. When profit induced the competitive commuter lines to expand, congestion would further decline, and the nonmonetary trip cost would be further reduced to offset the increase in monetary trip cost even more. Despite this possibility of moderation, increasing the fare to the efficient level would increase the combined commuting cost. After all, current commuters are facing the average rather than the marginal cost of congestion.

nism alone does not attain efficiency; the government needs to deliberately encourage production in the CBD area, since the proximity of many offices in a concentrated area increases productivity. Such policy measures include (1) elimination of the status quo–preserving regulations on construction and lease laws, (2) subsidies on the construction of high-density buildings in the CBD, and (3) an increased investment in the infrastructure in the CBD, such as water, sewage, and local streets, so as to accommodate high-density employment.

5.8.6   Summary

Efficiency requires two sets of policies. The first is the CBD development policies, such as revamping construction and lease laws, heavily investing in the infrastructure of the CBD, and subsidizing high-rise building construction. The second is marginal cost pricing of transportation and public utility services, such as the elimination of preferential treatment of commuting expenses, deregulation of fare and investment determination in the commuter industry, increasing the price of water, and charging a congestion tax on parking places.

The CBD development policies would increase the employment and population sizes, while making the employment density curve steeper. The marginal cost pricing would make the employment and population sizes smaller and the density curves steeper.

Thus various policies and regulations governing Tokyo have affected both population and employment sizes in conflicting directions relative to the efficient sizes. It is not clear whether Tokyo has exceeded optimal size. What is clear is that population and employment are allocated inefficiently within the metropolitan area. The current policies and regulations have consistently made both density distributions flatter than efficiency requires.

5.9   Conclusion

In the present paper, we compared the population and employment structures of the metropolitan area of Tokyo against those of New York. We made three empirical observations and explained the difference in the framework of the Mills-Muth urban model.

First, Tokyo is twice as large as New York with respect to both population and employment. The well-developed mass transit system in Tokyo is an essential factor that supports this size. In order for a mass transit system to be economically viable for the suppliers and convenient for the commuters, a critical level of suburban population density is necessary. Only then can the train system and the suburban bus system supply frequent service. The fact that the suburbanization of Tokyo took place before motorization occurred helped Tokyo attain a level of suburban density above the "critical level."

Second, the CBD of Tokyo is underused in terms of both employment and residential population densities. This may be explained by the technological limitations that existed until 1970 regarding constructing aseismic skyscrapers and by the Land Lease and Building Lease Laws.

Third, the residential area of Tokyo is more spread out, and its suburban population density curve is flatter than that of New York. This can be explained by the lower cost of commuting time due to the well-developed suburban transit system. In addition, it may be explained by the fact that the commuting expenses of the employees in Tokyo are reimbursed by their employers, which in turn is caused by the exclusion of commuting expenses under the personal income tax in Japan. Our empirical results shown in figure 5.12 demonstrate a substantial impact of this preferential tax treatment of commuting expenses upon the land price structure of the Tokyo metropolitan area.

The low cost of commuting time in Tokyo resulting from the well-developed commuter train system, which has enabled Tokyo to attain a large population size and high population densities in the suburban areas, explains the high residential land prices in Tokyo. Besides, government subsidies through preferential tax treatment make the land prices in the suburbs even higher.

On the other hand, high land prices should be accompanied by high employment densities in the business district. In the Tokyo CBD, however, relatively high land prices are accompanied by relatively low employment densities. This appears to reflect the fact that the Tokyo CBD is in the adjustment process toward an equilibrium with a high employment density as a result of the removal of the technological constraint on aseismic construction. In other words, the market seems to have capitalized the future high CBD productivity that will be attained when the potentially high density is realized in the eventual equilibrium. Also, a more rapid increase in the employment density at the CBD relative to the surrounding business districts seems to confirm that the Tokyo CBD is in the adjustment process.

Finally, we examined the normative economics of Tokyo. It was shown that a combination of the following two policies will attain an efficient resource allocation in the Tokyo metropolitan area: (1) a major redevelopment in the infrastructure of the CBD and (2) a substantial increase in the commuter fares through deregulation and the elimination of the preferential tax treatment.

These two policies will have offsetting effects on the total population size: the first will encourage the population inflow into the metropolitan area, while the second will discourage it. Thus the efficient size of the population in Tokyo may be greater or less than its current size. The efficient population and employment densities achieved by the above policies will be steeper than the current ones.

The two policies will also make the land price curve steeper. The first policy seems already expected as inevitable, and its future effects are capitalized in the current land prices in the CBD, but the second policy will reduce the land prices in the suburbs. In other words, to improve efficiency in the Tokyo metropolitan area, a substantial increase in the train fares is necessary, which in turn will depress the suburban land prices sharply.

References

Alperovich, G. 1990. An Empirical Test of a Model of the Urban Housing Market. Mimeo.
Barry, J. J. 1985. 1980 Census Comparisons No. 13: Tri-state Region, Journey-to-Work Tables, County-to-County. New York Metropolitan Council.
British Central Statistical Office. 1989. *Regional Trend 1989.* London: Central Statistical Office.
CACI. 1990. *The Sourcebook of Zip Code Demographics.* 7th ed. Arlington, VA: CACI Marketing Systems.
Hatta, T. 1983. Competition and Nationally Optimum Resource Allocation under the Presence of Urban Traffic Congestion. *Journal of Urban Economics* 14:145–67.
Haurin, D. R. 1983. The Effect of Reimbursement on Worker's Transport Costs: The Case of Urban Areas in Japan. *Journal of Urban Economics* 13:205–15.
Institut Nationale de Statistique de la France (INSEE). 1988. *Annuarire Statistique de la France.* Paris: INSEE.
Japanese Agency of General Affairs. Statistical Bureau. 1985. *Population Census of Japan.* Vol. 5. *Commutation; Part 4: Means of Transport to Work or to Attend School.* Tokyo: Ministry of Finance Printing Office.
———. 1986. *1986 Establishment Census of Japan.* Vol. 2. *Results for Prefectures; Part 13: Tokyo-to.* Tokyo: Ministry of Finance Printing Office.
Japanese Economic Planning Agency. 1989. *Keizai Yoran* (Economy in brief). Tokyo: Ministry of Finance Printing Office.
———. 1988. *Kenmin Keizai Keisan* (the annual report on prefectural accounts. Tokyo: Ministry of Finance Printing Office.
Japanese Ministry of Home Affairs. 1985. *Jumin Kihon Daicho ni Motozuku Zenkoku Jinko-Setai-su Hyo* (The basic survey of the residents). Tokyo: Ministry of Finance Printing Office.
Japanese Ministry of Transportation. 1987. *Daitoshi Kotsu Sensasu 1985* (Transportation census of metropolises 1985). Tokyo: Ministry of Finance Printing Office.
Japanese National Land Agency. 1985. *Chika Koji* (Government benchmark land prices). Tokyo: Ministry of Finance Printing Office.
Japan Travel Bureau. 1985. *Timetables, July 1985.* Tokyo: Japan Travel Bureau.
Kakumoto, R. 1970. *Toshi Kotsu Ron* (Urban transportation). Yuhikaku Press.
———. 1986. *Tokyo mo Bocho o Tomeru.* (Tokyo will also stop expanding). Tokyo: Waseda University Press.
Kau, J. B., and C. F. Sirmans. 1979. Urban Land Value Functions and Price Elasticity of Demand for Housing. *Journal of Urban Economics* 6:112–21.
Kobayashi, M., M. Komori, and H. Sugihara. 1990. Tokyo Ikkyoku Shuchu o Kangaeru (On the recent phenomenon of centralization into Tokyo). *Chosa* no. 142. Tokyo: Japan Development Bank.
Merriman, D., and D. Hellerstein. 1993. Compensation for Commuters in the Land and Labor Markets: Some Evidence from the Tokyo Metropolitan Area. Mimeo.
Mills, E. 1967. An Aggregative Model of Resource Allocation in a Metropolitan Area. *American Economic Review* 57:353–59.

————. 1972. *Studies in the Structure of the Urban Economy.* Baltimore: Johns Hopkins University Press.

Mills, E., and B. W. Hamilton. 1984. *Urban Economics.* 3d edition. Glenview, Ill.: Scott Foresman.

Mills, B., and K. Ohta. 1976. Urbanization and Urban Problems. In H. Patrick and H. Rosovsky, eds., *Asia's New Giant.* Washington, DC: Brookings Institution.

Muth, R. F. 1969. *Cities and Housing.* Chicago: University of Chicago Press.

New York City. Department of City Planning. 1988. *Community Districts: Facts-at-a-Glance: Manhattan.* New York: Department of City Planning.

Nippon Min'ei Tetsudo Kyokai (Japan Association of Nongovernment Railways). 1989. *Oote Mintetsu no Sugawo.* (The true picture of large nongovernment railway companies). Tokyo: Nippon Min'ei Tetsudo Kyokai.

Ohkawara, T. 1985. Urban Residential Land Rent Function: An Alternative Muth-Mills Model. *Journal of Urban Economics* 18:338–49.

Shutoken Seibi Kyokai. 1988. *Daitoshi Ken no Seibi* (Refurbishment of great metropolitan areas). Tokyo: Shutoken Seibi Kyokai.

Union Internationale de Transport Publique. 1983. *UITP Handbook.*

U.S. Bureau of the Census. 1986. *State and Metropolitan Area Data Book 1986.* Washington, DC: U.S. Government Printing Office.

Unyu Keizai Kenkyu Center. 1989. *Toshi Kotsu Nempo* (Annals of urban transportation). Tokyo: Unyu Keizai Kenkyu Center.

6 Housing and the Journey to Work in U.S. Cities

Michelle J. White

6.1 Introduction

This paper explores how the urban environment in the United States shapes the pattern of housing development. I focus on three major trends. First, during the postwar period, both housing and jobs in U.S. cities have suburbanized rapidly. As a result, U.S. cities have become very spread out and cover a great deal of land. New development on the fringes occurs at very low density levels. Second, urban commuters in the United States have shifted from commuting by public transportation to commuting by automobile. I argue that these two trends are closely related and self-reinforcing: automobile commuting enabled jobs to suburbanize, but once they had suburbanized, more and more jobs were accessible only by car. Third, higher-income households generally choose to live farther from the city center than lower-income households. This phenomenon was true in the past and continues to be true in U.S. cities. Since higher-income households in the United States tend to choose suburban rather than central locations in cities, their behavior reinforces the trend for cities to suburbanize. This paper documents these trends in U.S. housing development and attempts to explain them.

A few basic facts concerning U.S. cities should be noted. The downtown area, usually the historic center, of U.S. cities is referred to as the central business district, or CBD. CBDs consist of concentrated office/employment districts with few residents, which have the highest density levels in their metropolitan areas and are surrounded by residential areas. Other employment subcenters, less dense than the CBD, are scattered around the metropolitan

Michelle J. White is professor of economics at the University of Michigan.

The author is grateful to Sharon Parrott for very capable research assistance and to Charles Lave for helpful comments.

area. They are often located at major road or public transportation intersections in both the central city and suburbs. The political structure of U.S. metropolitan areas consists of a central city and many small suburban jurisdictions, each of which is a separate local government. There may be from ten to several hundred independent suburban jurisdictions. The central city and the suburban jurisdictions each provide public services such as education, police and fire protection, streets, trash collection, and some social services. In a typical metropolitan area, the central city contains one-third to one-half the entire metropolitan-area population and the suburban jurisdictions contain the rest.

Section 6.2 reviews the major economic theories of urban spatial structure and explores their implications for urban housing. Section 6.3 provides data illustrating the changes in the metropolitan housing stock in the United States during the postwar period. Section 6.4 explores the spatial pattern of employment in cities and its implications for how workers' job locations and their residences are related by the commuting journey. Section 6.5 is the conclusion.

6.2   Population Growth and Suburbanization in U.S. Cities

Economists analyzing urban housing patterns have focused on explaining three broad trends: first, how rising real incomes over time have affected the spatial pattern of housing development; second, how falling costs of commuting in cities affect the spatial pattern of housing; and third, how high- versus low-income households differ in their taste for housing consumption in cities.

Two approaches have dominated economists' thinking. The first is the Mills-Muth urban spatial model and the second is a historical model of urban growth. I also explore a variety of other factors that do not fit neatly into either model. It should be noted that most of the models described in this section assume that all jobs in cities are located at the CBD and that each household has one worker only.

6.2.1   The Mills-Muth Model of Urban Development

The Mills-Muth model, in its simplest form, assumes that all households have identical tastes and incomes and each has one worker. Households maximize utility over consumption of housing and a composite other good. Commuting to work is costly, so that a worker's income minus commuting cost must equal the household's expenditure on housing and the composite good. Locational equilibrium in the metropolitan area requires that all households achieve the same utility level living at any location in the city, since otherwise households would move to the locations where utility is highest and housing prices would readjust. Based on these assumptions, it can be shown that the per unit price of land is highest near the CBD—where land is most scarce— and falls at a diminishing rate with distance from the CBD. This is because commuting cost increases with distance, requiring that the price of land fall in order to make households indifferent to commuting farther. By itself, this effect explains why land prices fall at a constant rate with distance from the CBD. But as land prices fall relative to the cost of other goods, households shift toward consuming more land and less other goods. This shift toward greater land consumption reduces the rate of decrease of land prices—hence land prices overall fall at a diminishing rate with distance.[1] Small, high-density housing units (apartments) are built near the CBD, where the price of land is high, and large, low-density housing units (single-family houses) are built in the suburbs, where the price of land is low. Households living near the CBD consume less housing but have more money available for consumption of other goods; while households living farther away from the CBD consume more housing and less other goods.

As a summary measure characterizing the spatial pattern of housing in cities, economists have estimated density/distance functions. It is straightforward to show in the Mills-Muth model that population density, housing density, land prices, and housing prices must all decline at a decreasing rate with distance from the CBD. Since there is no reliable source of data on land prices in U.S. cities, urban economists have concentrated on estimating density/distance functions rather than land price/distance functions. The density/distance relationship is usually represented as a negative exponential function. The critical parameter of this function, referred to as the density gradient, gives the proportional rate of decrease in density per mile of increase in distance from the CBD. In the next section, I present the results of estimating population density/distance functions for a sample of U.S. cities. These have the advantage of being available over a fairly long span of time.[2]

Over time, two major trends have occurred in U.S. cities: faster modes of commuting have been introduced and household incomes have risen. Commuting costs include both time costs and out-of-pocket costs. The introduction of faster commuting modes lowers the time required to commute a mile and, since most of the cost of commuting is time cost, lowers the total cost of commuting per mile. A decline in the cost of commuting per mile causes the density/distance function to flatten, so that the density gradient approaches zero. This is because the scarce land near the CBD is no longer as valuable, since it is now cheaper to commute to the CBD from farther away. Conversely, the more plentiful land in the suburbs becomes more valuable, since it is

---

1. The price of land or housing as a function of distance from the CBD is denoted $R(x)$, where x is distance from the CBD. It can be shown that $R(x)$ must satisfy the following condition: $dR(x)/dx = -t/h(x)$, where t is the cost of commuting per mile round trip and $h(x)$ is housing demand. Since $h(x)$ rises as distance increases, $R(x)$ declines at a diminishing rate with distance.

2. The negative exponential function is $D(x) = D_o e^{-\gamma x}$ where $D(x)$ is the number of people or the number of housing units per square mile of land x miles from the CBD, D_o is the number of people or housing units per unit of land area at the CBD, and $-\gamma$ is the density gradient or the rate of decline in population or housing density per mile increase in distance from the CBD. Note that use of the negative exponential density function ignores the fact that population and housing densities are very low near the CBD, since business rather than residential land use predominates there.

cheaper to commute from the suburbs to the CBD. As a result, housing densities in the suburbs rise relative to housing densities near the CBD. Also, the city increases in size, since agricultural land at the outer periphery is converted to urban use.

An increase in household income has two offsetting effects on the density/distance function. First, as household income rises, households demand more housing and/or higher-quality housing. Land is a component of housing and is cheaper in the suburbs, so higher-income households find the suburbs relatively more attractive, since the cost of housing per unit is lower there. Second, higher income causes the value of time spent commuting to rise, which makes housing near the CBD more attractive. If the income elasticity of housing demand exceeds the income elasticity of the value of time spent commuting, then an increase in household income causes the density/distance function to flatten.[3] Assuming that this condition holds, then the two important time trends in metropolitan areas both cause the density/distance function to flatten.[4]

The model can also be extended to include more than one income class. Suppose there are two income groups and the income elasticity of housing demand exceeds the income elasticity of the value of time spent commuting. Then lower-income households will occupy housing located in an inner ring around the CBD, and higher-income households will occupy housing located in an outer ring around the low-income households. Intuitively, this means that the suburbs' low housing price attracts higher-income households more than the high cost of commuting repels them.[5] Paradoxically, low-income households occupy high-priced land, although they consume relatively little of it by living in high-density housing, while high-income households occupy lower-priced land.

6.2.2   The Historical Model of Urban Development

Now turn to the historical model of urban development, first proposed by Harrison and Kain (1974). It is based on the idea that cities originate at arbi-

---

3. Differentiating $dR(x)/dx$ with respect to income, Y, we get

$$\frac{dR^2(x)}{dxdY} = \frac{t(Y)}{h(x,Y)Y}[\varepsilon_h - \varepsilon_v],$$

where Y denotes household income, ε_h is the income elasticity of demand for housing, and ε_v is the income elasticity of the value of time spent commuting. The rent function becomes flatter as income increases if this expression is positive, which requires that $\varepsilon_h > \varepsilon_v$.

4. Whether in fact the income elasticity of housing demand exceeds the income elasticity of the value of time spent commuting is unclear. If the value of time spent commuting is a constant fraction of the hourly wage rate, as many studies have assumed (McFadden 1974), then the income elasticity of time spent commuting is unity. But Polinsky and Ellwood (1979) argue that the income elasticity of housing demand is less than unity.

5. This short summary neglects a number of extensions of the Mills-Muth model, such as a dynamic version (Wheaton 1982), version in which some households have two workers, and versions in which there are two or more taste classes. See below for discussion of the model when firms are assumed to locate outside the CBD.

trary locations determined by historical considerations—usually at a port or rail junction—and then expand outward over time from their historic centers. In the Mills-Muth model, whenever exogenous changes occur, the city's housing stock is assumed to be completely rebuilt to reflect the new conditions. In contrast, the historical model assumes that housing is infinitely durable, so that once built, it remains unchanged. Therefore cities consists of inner rings of older housing around the CBD and outer rings of newer housing in the suburbs. The newest housing is always on the periphery of the city. The gradual introduction of faster commuting modes is also an important element in the historical model, since as commuting speeds rise and commuting costs fall, workers can live farther away from the CBD without increasing their commuting costs. Therefore when a faster commuting mode is introduced, the city expands by adding a new ring of housing on the periphery, since workers are willing to live farther away from the CBD. Faster commuting thus allows cities to increase in both population and area.

Since the early nineteenth century, when the dominant mode of commuting was walking, there have been a number of changes in commuting mode. Horse-drawn wagons were the first public transportation system, followed by steam-powered vehicles, underground rail systems, electric-powered streetcars, and motorized buses running on surface roads. In general, new public transportation modes were faster than their predecessors, and each new mode led to new housing built at the periphery, which was occupied by commuters. In the postwar period, commuting by automobile has largely replaced commuting by public transportation, which has dramatically increased commuting speeds and enabled cities to increase greatly in land area.

New commuting modes tended to be faster and more expensive in terms of out-of-pocket costs than their predecessors—at least initially. This means that for high-income workers, the total cost of the new commuting mode is cheaper than the total cost of older modes of commuting, since their value of time is high. But for low-income workers, the total cost of the new commuting mode is more expensive, since their value of time is lower. Therefore, the earliest group of users of new commuting modes tends to be high-income workers. But if high-income workers shift to the new mode and low-income workers continue using the older mode, then high-income workers at least temporarily have lower commuting costs per mile than low-income workers. As a result, high-income housing is built on the periphery of the city and occupied by high-income workers who use the fast commuting mode and can therefore commute farther. Low-income workers remain in older housing closer to the CBD. Later, the fast commuting mode falls in price and is adopted by all workers, which might suggest that spatial income segregation would be eroded. But by this time, new suburban rings have already been developed with high-income housing. Thus an alternative explanation of why we observe high-income housing in the suburbs is that high-income workers adopt faster commuting modes earlier and thus have a lower marginal cost of commuting than low-income workers. This explanation suggests that a pattern of high-income households living in the suburbs and low-income households living near the CBD might be observed even if the income elasticity of housing demand were smaller than the income elasticity of the value of time spent commuting.[6]

The introduction of the automobile for commuting differs from prior mode shifts, since it replaced commuting by public transportation with commuting by private transportation. Compared to public transportation, the automobile involves a very low time cost per mile since it is much faster than commuting by bus or train. This might suggest that it would be adopted for commuting by workers of all income levels at the same time. The automobile also involves a high fixed cost, however—the cost of purchase. So high-income workers still adopted it earlier than low-income workers.

Another important aspect of the historical model is that housing units fall in quality as they age. This is both because older houses gradually wear out, which increases maintenance costs, and because older houses become economically obsolete, since they do not contain modern features such as air conditioning, insulation, multiple bathrooms, and modern kitchens. Higher-income households demand higher-quality housing than lower-income households (as well as more housing). Higher-quality housing tends to be cheaper to provide in the suburbs, where the housing stock is newer. In contrast, to provide high-quality housing near the CBD, old houses must be renovated or replaced, which is very expensive. Thus as housing ages and its quality falls, high-income households move from older housing nearer the CBD to newer housing farther out. The older housing vacated by high-income households is occupied by middle-income households, whose housing in turn is occupied by lower-income households in a process known as filtering. Thus over time, individual housing units move down the income scale. Filtering has the effect of reducing the amount of new housing built for middle- and low-income households, since any new housing built for them must compete with formerly high-quality housing that has filtered down from high-income households and has no alternative use. But because filtering does not supply housing for high-income households, most new housing is built for them. This means that the outer rings of housing in the historical model are occupied by high-income households because they contain the city's newest housing, and the intermediate rings of housing are occupied by middle-income households.

The oldest and lowest-quality housing in U.S. cities is generally located near the CBD and is occupied by the lowest-income households. Housing near the CBD is frequently abandoned by landlords, because low-income tenants' willingness to pay for rent is less than the high operating expenses for old buildings. Abandonment of buildings by landlords causes the heat and other utilities to be cut off, so tenants also move away.[7]

6. See LeRoy and Sonstelie (1983) for discussion.
7. Abandonment also increases when cities apply modern building code regulations to older buildings and when they allow assessments of old buildings to remain constant as property values

Thus the historical model develops an urban picture in which housing age declines monotonically with distance from the CBD and household income rises monotonically with distance. There are at least two ways in which this pattern might be changed. First, older houses are sometimes renovated to incorporate modern features, which delays or reverses the filtering process. But renovation of old housing is generally more expensive than construction of new housing, so that only the highest-quality or best-located old houses are renovated. Second, older housing can be demolished and new housing built to replace it. But demolishing old housing and replacing it with new housing on the same site is more expensive than building new housing on raw land at the urban periphery. So replacement of old with new housing occurs only rarely, usually when government subsidies are provided. When government subsidies are not provided, old housing is often abandoned and the land remains unused. Both renovation and demolition/replacement break the monotonic pattern of rising household incomes with distance from the CBD. Most U.S. cities have a few close-in neighborhoods with attractive older housing that has been renovated—a phenomenon referred to as "gentrification." Such neighborhoods attract high-income households. Also some abandoned housing in poor neighborhoods has been renovated with government subsidies for use by low-income households. But the number and size of these neighborhoods is quite limited.

6.2.3   Other Factors Affecting Suburbanization

In addition to the issues already considered, a number of other factors affect the pattern of housing development in U.S. cities. These have in general reinforced the tendency for metropolitan areas to become more suburbanized by reducing the attractiveness of the central city and encouraging middle- and high-income households to move to the suburbs.

One factor is that since central cities contain most of their metropolitan areas' poor families, the public services they provide tend to be specialized to the needs of the poor. Typically, central cities spend substantial amounts on public hospitals, which serve the poor, on shelters for the homeless, and on income transfer programs and other social services for the poor. These services are financed by property taxes, which all households pay for in rough proportion to the value of housing they occupy. Thus high-income households living in the central city cross-subsidize low-income households through the public sector. If these households moved to the suburbs, they would not escape paying property taxes. But suburban jurisdictions, having few poor families, provide public services oriented to the needs of their middle- or high-income residents,

---

fall, causing property taxes to rise over time as the tax rate increases. Rent control may also contribute to abandonment if it holds rents at levels below the cost of operation. See Sternlieb and Burchell (1973) and White (1986).

who are typically much more homogeneous than the residents of the central city.[8]

Central city schools are also oriented to a clientele of poor children. Most research on education suggests that quality of education depends more on the other students and their family backgrounds than on expenditures per pupil (Hanushek 1981). Thus even if central city schools spend as much on education per pupil as suburban schools, the quality of education they provide is lower. Middle- and upper-income families who demand higher-quality education than the central city provides thus face a choice between staying in the central city and paying for private schools for their children or moving to the suburbs and sending their children to public schools. Since private schools are expensive, education provides a substantial financial incentive for middle- and upper-income families to move to the suburbs.

Another change that encouraged suburbanization in U.S. metropolitan areas was the racial desegregation of schools that followed the 1954 Supreme Court decision. Central city schools were most affected by school integration, since most black families live in central cities. To avoid sending their children to racially integrated schools, many white families moved from central cities to their suburbs, where few blacks live and where desegregation had little effect. School desegregation in effect accelerated the filtering process: middle-income white households moved to the suburbs and black households occupied central city housing vacated by whites.

Crime—which is higher in central cities than in suburbs—also encourages suburbanization. Crime has always been present in U.S. cities but has become more important recently, as drug dealing and drug use have increased. Markets for drugs are usually concentrated in central city neighborhoods to take advantage of the same agglomeration economies that attract legitimate entrepreneurial activities to the central city. Also higher housing- and population-density levels in central cities cause more "aesthetic" offenses to occur there, such as noticeable air pollution, rats, noise, litter on the streets, begging, peddling, and homeless people sleeping in doorways. These reduce the quality of life in the central cities and encourage households that can afford to do so to move to the suburbs.

Finally, suburban local governments in the United States have the power to regulate land use by controlling new construction. (Central cities also have this power, but their control is less effective since most of their land is already developed.) Suburban jurisdictions often use this power to prevent low- and lower-middle-income households from moving there by not allowing apartments or small houses to be built within their boundaries. Such regulations increase the attractiveness of the suburbs to households that can afford to live in them, since the resulting suburban homogeneity prevents many central city

8. See Tiebout (1956) for a model of the effects of governmental fragmentation in metropolitan areas. See Fischel (1985) for an extension of the model to include land use regulation and Mieszkowski and Zodrow (1989) for a survey of the literature.

Table 6.1   **Characteristics of Large U.S. Metropolitan Areas**

SMSA	Population (thousands)	Proportion of Housing Built before 1940		Average Commute Time	Proportion Commuting by Car
		Central City	Suburbs		
NY/Nassau/Suffolk	11,725	.49	.27	34.8	.51
Chicago	7,103	.52	.18	28.2	.74
Detroit	4,353	.45	.15	23.3	.92
Washington, DC	3,061	.39	.073	28.5	.76
Houston	2,905	.085	.045	26.6	.92
Pittsburgh	2,264	.63	.37	23.1	.80
Minneapolis/St. Paul	2,114	.54	.12	20.1	.83
Newark	1,966	.47	.35	24.8	.82
Cleveland	1,899	.58	.21	23.4	.84
Miami	1,626	.49	.048	23.7	.87
Seattle/Everett	1,607	.39	.060	23.1	.82
Cincinnati	1,401	.46	.25	22.0	.88
Kansas City	1,327	.35	.12	21.0	.91
Buffalo	1,242	.73	.29	19.5	.85
New Orleans	1,187	.38	.058	25.5	.82
Columbus	1,093	.24	.22	20.0	.89
Rochester	971	.63	.31	19.5	.86
Providence/Pawtucket	919	.53	.37	18.1	.87
Louisville	906	.42	.10	22.2	.91
Birmingham	847	.28	.14	23.4	.94
Dayton	830	.40	.18	19.3	.92
Norfolk	807	.13	.14	21.9	.82
Average	2,370	.44	.18	23.3	.84

Source: U.S. Bureau of the Census, *U.S. Census of Population and Housing* (Washington, D.C.: U.S. Government Printing Office, 1980).

problems from taking root and allows local public services to be specialized to the needs of middle- and upper-income households. (See Hamilton [1975] and Fischel [1985].) In some metropolitan areas, suburban land use regulation tends to prevent lower-income and poor households from moving out of the central city.

6.3   Trends in U.S. Urban Development during the Postwar Period

I turn now to data on U.S. urban housing patterns and to testing some of the predictions of the models just discussed. As background, table 6.1 gives 1980 data on population, housing, and commuting for twenty-two of the fifty largest U.S. metropolitan areas.[9] The historical model predicted that the housing stock

9. The data are for alternating metropolitan areas, ranked by population, and are for SMSAs (central cities combined with counties around them that meet a minimum population density criterion). A few SMSAs have been combined when an SMSA consists mainly of suburbs of another

Table 6.2   **Density Gradients for a Sample of Eighteen U.S. Metropolitan Areas (absolute values)**

	1948	1954	1958	1963	1970	1972	1977	1980
Population	.58	.47	.42	.38	.29			.24
Manufacturing	.68	.55	.48	.42		.34	.32	
Retailing	.88	.75	.59	.44		.35	.30	
Services	.97	.81	.66	.53		.41	.38	

Sources: These data are taken from Macauley (1985). They are estimated by the two-point method developed by Mills and Ohta (1976), in which only overall data for the central city and its suburbs are used.

in the central city would be older than the housing stock in the suburbs of the same metropolitan area. The second and third columns of table 6.1 give the proportion of housing built before 1940 in the central city and suburbs of each metropolitan area. For the entire group of cities, 44 percent of central city housing and 18 percent of suburban housing was built before 1940. Thus the spatial pattern of older housing predominating in the central cities and newer housing predominating in the suburbs supports the historical model. Note that there are distinct differences between older metropolitan areas, which are predominantly located in the East and Midwest, and younger metropolitan areas, which are mainly located in the West and South. The older metropolitan areas have much higher percentages of old housing in both the central city and suburbs. As an example, compare Washington, DC, and Houston, which have similar populations. Washington has 39 percent old housing in its central city and 7.3 percent in its suburbs, while Houston has only 8.5 percent old housing in its central city and 4.5 percent in its suburbs. Thus while the pattern is the same for both, the levels differ substantially.

I turn now to measuring suburbanization. The Mills-Muth model predicts gradual suburbanization of housing in metropolitan areas, due to declining commuting costs and higher incomes. This implies that the density gradient must approach zero over time.[10] The top line of table 6.2 gives the results of estimating population density/distance functions for a sample of eighteen U.S. cities for varying years between 1948 and 1980. While the actual functions estimated are population density/distance functions rather than housing density/distance functions, the Mills-Muth model predicts that both functions

---

SMSA. Note that U.S. SMSAs vary widely in the size of the central city relative to the suburbs, because some central cities are able to expand by annexing surrounded suburbs, while others are not.

10. The historical model also predicts that density functions flatten over time, although the predicted rate of change is slower since existing housing near the CBD is not rebuilt. Therefore the flattening of the density function results solely from the building of new low-density housing at the edge of the city.

will have the same density gradient as long as household size does not vary systematically with distance from the CBD. The results show that population density decreased by .58 per mile of distance in 1948, but the rate of decrease had dropped by more than half, to .24 per mile, by 1980. Thus housing in U.S. cities has suburbanized substantially during the postwar period.

Both the Mills-Muth and the historical models predict that income levels of households living in the suburbs will be higher than income levels of households living near the CBD. Table 6.3 gives data on median family income in U.S. central cities and suburbs from 1959 to 1979 and shows that in fact suburban median income levels are higher. The last column gives the percentage difference between cities and suburbs, which has risen from 18 percent to 29 percent over the period.

Table 6.4 gives data characterizing changes in the U.S. urban housing stock since 1950. In general, rising incomes during the postwar period caused both substantial improvement in the quality of the urban housing stock and a large increase in the amount of housing space per person. The number of persons per room has decreased substantially over time, from 0.67 in 1950 to 0.46 in 1980, or a drop of 28 percent. Thus an average urban resident in the United States occupies two rooms. Since the median number of rooms per household rose by only 10 percent during the period, from 4.6 in 1950 to 5.1 in 1980, most of the drop in number of persons per room was due to decreases in average household size during the period.

The Mills-Muth model predicts that housing units will be smaller in the central city than in the suburbs. This prediction is supported by data given in table 6.4: suburban housing units on average have 10 to 15 percent more rooms than central city housing units have, and the differential has risen over time. This latter supports the historical model, since an unchanged housing stock in the inner rings remains constant in average size, but the housing stock in the suburbs increases in average size as newly built houses on the periphery get larger. During the 1960s and 1970s, suburban housing was more crowded than central city housing, probably because suburban households had more children, but this differential was eliminated by 1980.

As a housing quality measure, table 6.4 also gives the proportion of housing units lacking complete plumbing. The data show that the proportion of housing

Table 6.3   **Median Family Income in U.S. Central Cities and Suburbs, 1959–79**

	SMSA ($)	Central City ($)	Suburbs ($)	Difference (%)
1959	6,324	5,940	7,002	18
1969	10,474	9,507	11,586	22
1979	23,303	18,379	23,639	29

Source: U.S. Bureau of the Census, *Census of Population: U.S. Summary* (Washington, D.C.: U.S. Government Printing Office, 1960–80). SMSA income figures include rural populations living within SMSAs in 1959 and 1969 but not in 1979.

Table 6.4   Size, Occupancy, and Quality of U.S. Urban Housing, 1950–80

	1950	1960	1970	1980
Persons per room				
United States	.67	.60	.54	.46
SMSAs		.60	.54	.46
Central cities		.56	.51	.47
Suburbs		.63	.57	.45
Rural areas		.64	.51	.49
Median rooms per household				
United States	4.6	4.9	5.0	5.1
SMSAs		4.8	5.0	5.1
Central cities		4.6	4.7	4.7
Suburbs		5.1	5.3	5.4
Rural areas		5.0	5.1	5.3
Proportion of occupied housing units lacking complete plumbing[a]				
United States	.34	.16	.069	.027
Urban[b]	.20	.088	.033	.016
Central cities		.094	.034	.021
Suburbs		.092	.035	.009
Rural	.53	.34	.168	.059

Source: U.S. Bureau of the Census, *U.S. Census of Population and Housing* (Washington, D.C.: U.S. Government Printing Office, 1950–80).

[a]Lacking complete plumbing means that the housing unit lacked a private toilet, private bath, or hot water.

[b]In order to maintain comparability across the period, the urban figure for lacking complete plumbing refers to urbanized areas. However, the suburb figures refer to the non–central city portions of SMSAs.

units that are low quality has declined dramatically during the postwar period, from 20 percent of the urban housing stock in 1950 to only 1.6 percent in 1980. Central city–suburb differentials remained small throughout the period.

The historical model with its emphasis on filtering suggests that new housing will tend to be of higher value than existing housing, because it has been built to the tastes of present-day high-income households. Table 6.5 shows that the median price of new single-family houses in fact exceeds that of existing single-family houses and that the difference has been rising over time.[11]

Finally, there is limited evidence concerning the effect of crime and racial factors on suburbanization of U.S. metropolitan areas. A recent study by Palumbo, Sacks, and Wasylenko (1990) attempts to explain patterns of popula-

11. About 60 percent of new housing units constructed recently are single-family houses (U.S. Bureau of the Census, *Statistical Abstract of the United States* [Washington, D.C.: U.S. Government Printing Office, 1990], table 1260).

tion change between 1970 and 1980 in the central cities versus the suburbs of a cross-section of U.S. metropolitan areas. They find that a 1 percentage point increase in the proportion of the central city's population that was black in 1970 was associated with a reduction in the central city population growth rate of 0.2 percentage points. They also find that an increase in the central city's crime rate in 1970 was associated with a statistically significant drop in the central city's population growth rate and a statistically significant increase in the suburban population growth rate during the following decade.

6.4   Urban Employment and Commuting Patterns

The most important trend in urban commuting during the postwar period has been the replacement of public transportation by the automobile. In this section, I first explore the relationship between the shift to commuting by automobile and the rapid suburbanization of urban employment. Second, I explore in greater detail what we know about urban commuting generally.

6.4.1   Commuting and Employment Suburbanization

Commuting by automobile differs from commuting by public transportation because a worker traveling by automobile can go anywhere that has a paved road. In contrast, those using public transportation can travel only along fixed routes. This means that, as more workers have shifted to commuting by car, it has become more profitable for firms to move from CBD to suburban locations. Suburban locations that previously were infeasible for most firms have become desirable places to locate.

To be more precise, suppose the city has a network of radial fixed-rail transportation lines originating at the CBD and all workers commute by public transportation. A particular firm is located at the CBD and pays the going wage at the CBD, which is w^c per day. Then workers living anywhere in the city are potentially willing to work for the firm since they can travel to it from all directions, that is, the firm's commuting area is the entire metropolitan area. Now suppose the firm moves to the suburbs and locates at a station along one of the

Table 6.5   **The Value of New versus Existing Single-Family Houses, 1970–90**

	Median Sales Price ($)		
	New	Existing	Ratio
1970	23,400	23,000	1.02
1980	64,600	62,200	1.04
1986	92,000	80,300	1.15
1990	122,900	95,500	1.29

Source: U.S. Bureau of the Census, *Statistical Abstract of the United States* (Washington, D.C.: U.S. Government Printing Office, 1992), tables 1215, 1217.

radial routes. At the suburban location, the firm pays a wage equal to the wage at the CBD, w^c, minus the cost of commuting between the firm's suburban site and the CBD, $t_r x$. Here t_r is the (time plus out-of-pocket) cost of commuting a mile by rail in each direction, and x is the distance between the suburban firm and the CBD. Since the suburban firm has reduced its wage by the full cost of commuting between itself and the CBD, only workers who save this entire amount would be willing to work there. Workers who fit this condition live along the same radial transportation route as the suburban firm, but farther away from the CBD. They are indifferent between working for the suburban firm and working at the CBD, since wages net of commuting costs are equal at both job locations.[12] Thus the firm's commuting area once it moves to the suburbs becomes very restricted since it includes only workers who live along the same radial commuting line but farther from the CBD. As a result, moving to the suburbs is attractive only to very small firms.

Alternatively, the firm could move to the same suburban location but enlarge its commuting area by paying a higher wage. A higher wage would encourage workers located along the same line but closer in than x' to out-commute to the firm. For example, if the suburban firm offers to pay the CBD wage w^c, then a worker living halfway between the firm and the CBD will be just willing to out-commute to the firm. Workers living between the firm and the CBD but closer to the firm will prefer work at the firm over work at the CBD. Suppose the firm still needs more workers. It can raise its wage yet further, but eventually it will have to attract workers who live along other rail lines. These workers must commute to the firm by traveling to the CBD along one line and then traveling away from the CBD to the firm along another. This requires a change of trains at the CBD, which is time-consuming and must be compensated by a large wage increase at the suburban firm. What all this suggests is that moving to the suburbs will be attractive only to small firms. Further, firms that move to the suburbs when commuting is by rail must locate near rail stations. But land within walking distance of suburban rail stations is scarce, which makes it expensive. This implies that firms receive little benefit in the form of lower land prices when they move out of the CBD.

Now suppose the number of public transit routes increases, perhaps by adding circumferential routes in addition to the existing radial routes. Then suburban locations would become more attractive to firms, either because additional public transit stations increase the number of suburban sites for firms or because more suburban sites are located at the intersection of two transit routes. The latter increases firms' commuting areas for the same wage, since workers can commute to the firm from four rather than two directions without having to transfer. But the general picture remains that firms locating in the suburbs

---

12. Workers can be shown to maximize utility by choosing the job location that maximizes wages net of commuting costs when housing densities are assumed to be fixed (White 1990).

have relatively small commuting areas and that the cost in terms of higher wages of enlarging their commuting areas is high.

Now suppose most workers shift to commuting by car. All suburban locations are now accessible. This in itself makes moving out of the CBD more profitable, since suburban employment sites are less scarce and therefore cheaper. Also workers can commute to the firm along any road. This means that all suburban sites are in effect located at the intersection of several commuting routes, which makes them as accessible as sites located at the junction of several fixed-rail transportation lines. Also, there is never any need to compensate workers for the cost of waiting for buses or subways or for the cost of changing from one route to another. Therefore the cost to the firm in higher wages of a given expansion in its commuting area is smaller. In addition, the fact that commuting by car is faster expands the firm's commuting area for a given wage. Therefore when workers commute by car rather than by public transportation, moving to the suburbs becomes much more attractive for firms, particularly large firms (White 1988a, 1990).

Suburbanization of employment in metropolitan areas can be measured using an employment density/distance function similar to the population density/distance functions discussed above. Again the main parameter of interest is the density gradient, which measures the rate of decrease of employment density per mile of distance from the CBD. Table 6.2 also gives the results of estimating employment-density gradients for a group of U.S. cities during the postwar period. It shows that there has been rapid suburbanization of employment. The density gradient for manufacturing jobs fell from .68 in 1948 to .32 in 1977, a decrease of over 50 percent. The density gradients in retailing and services fell even more rapidly, although the decline occurred somewhat later. In general, employment was much more centralized than housing at the beginning of the postwar period, but suburbanization of employment has proceeded more rapidly during the period, so that the density gradients for housing and employment are now approaching one another.

In explaining this trend, commentators often have stressed the attractiveness of lower suburban land prices to firms. When firms rent or buy sites in the CBD, the opportunity cost of the site is use by another firm, so that land values are high, while when they rent or buy suburban sites, the opportunity cost of a site is its value used for housing, which is much lower. Suburban land has always been cheaper than land near the CBD, however; in fact it was cheaper relative to CBD land in the past than it is currently. The shift by workers from commuting by public transportation to commuting by automobile made it possible for firms to benefit from the suburbs' lower land prices.[13]

---

13. The cost of transporting inputs and outputs has also fallen, and the urban export node for most firms is no longer located at the CBD. Both of these factors have also made suburban sites more attractive to firms.

The suburbanization of housing documented in section 6.3 would necessarily have lengthened workers' commuting journeys if all firms had remained at the CBD. However, suburbanization of jobs has an offsetting effect on the length of workers' commuting journeys. Increased employment suburbanization has in turn encouraged additional housing suburbanization, because workers having jobs in the near suburbs of a metropolitan area can live in the far suburbs of the same metropolitan area, where housing prices are particularly low, and have commuting journeys that take no longer than the commute from the near suburbs to the CBD. Thus employment suburbanization has encouraged the growth of new suburban rings on the periphery of the metropolitan area. As a result, the largest U.S. metropolitan areas have grown to the point that the farthest suburbs may be located fifty miles or more from the CBD. Few workers commute as far as this, though, since most residents of the far suburbs work at jobs in nearer suburbs. As cities have grown and employment has suburbanized, jobs at the CBD have become less and less attractive, since workers who commute to the CBD from the suburbs must cross congested suburban employment subcenters along the way as well as experiencing the congestion around the CBD itself. The result is that few jobs are located at the CBD. For the fifty largest U.S. metropolitan areas, only 8 percent of jobs on average are located at the CBD.

Urban roads are undeniably congested at the peak rush hours, and the popular press often suggests that congestion has been getting worse over time. It should be noted, however, that some level of congestion is efficient. Suppose road systems were designed to minimize the total cost of travel, including drivers' time cost and the cost of constructing and maintaining roads. Then the optimal road capacity, measured in lanes, would occur where the marginal cost of increasing traffic capacity by widening the road equals the marginal cost of increasing traffic capacity by increasing the level of congestion. Since the cost of widening roads is high, the marginal cost of congestion must also be high at the optimum road width.

6.4.2   The Shift from Public Transportation to Automobile Commuting

In this section, I document the shift from public transportation to automobile commuting and other aspects of urban commuting and urban travel generally.

Table 6.6 gives data on automobile ownership since 1950. It shows that, while automobile ownership was already widespread by 1950, when 60 percent of families owned cars, it had became nearly universal by the late 1980s, when about 90 percent owned cars. More important, the average number of persons per vehicle has fallen drastically, from 3.7 in 1950 to only 1.4 in 1990. (The 1990 figure includes light trucks and vans owned by households.) Since these figures include children, the elderly, and other nondrivers, they imply that most households now have a vehicle for each driver. The increase in the number of vehicles was accompanied by an enormous increase in the total number

Table 6.6   Automobile Ownership, Miles of Travel, and Road Mileage, 1950–90

	1950	1960	1970	1980	1986	1990[a]
Proportion of families owning cars	.60	.77	.82	.87	.89	.91
Average persons per car	3.7	2.9	2.3	1.9	1.8	1.4
Miles of travel by car in urban areas (billions)	184	287	497	671	1,088	1,410
Miles traveled per mile of road in urban areas (thousands)	571	667	886	1,075	1,552	1,834
Number of passenger trips on public transportation (millions)	17.2	9.4	7.3	8.6	8.8	8.9
Number of registered cars (millions)	40.4	61.7	89.2	121.6	135.4	165
Miles of urban roads (thousands)	323	430	561	624	701	769

Sources: U.S. Bureau of the Census, *Statistical Abstract of the United States* (Washington, D.C.: U.S. Government Printing Office, various years); U.S. Bureau of the Census, *Historical Statistics of the United States* (Washington, D.C.: U.S. Government Printing Office, 1975); American Transit Association, *Transit Fact Book* (New York: American Transit Association, 1987); U.S. Department of Transportation, *Nationwide Personal Transportation Survey, 1990* (Washington, D.C.: U.S. Department of Transportation, 1991), 1990 data only.

[a]These figures are for households, and they include vans and light trucks in addition to cars.

of miles driven in urban areas, from 184 billion in 1950 to over 1,400 billion in 1990.

The increase in the amount of driving has clearly increased the average urban congestion level. Table 6.6 shows that, since 1950 the number of miles traveled in cities has increased much more quickly than the number of miles of urban roads, resulting in more than a tripling of intensity of road use as measured by miles traveled per mile of urban road.[14] Since only about one-third of total urban travel is for commuting, much of the increase in miles driven is probably due to noncommuting trips.[15] But both types of travel add to congestion.

14. This measure of congestion ignores the fact that average road width has increased during the period, and thus is biased upward.
15. U.S. Department of Transportation, *Personal Travel in the United States, 1983–84 Nationwide Personal Transportation Study* (Washington, D.C.: U.S. Department of Transportation, 1986), vol. 2, tables E-23, E-27.

Table 6.7   Relationship between Commuting Distance and Time and Speed

Distance Range (miles)	Automobile		Public Transportation	
	Time (min)	Speed[a] (mph)	Time (min)	Speed[a] (mph)
Under 5	16	9.4	28	5.4
6–10	24	20	50	9.6
11–14	30	25	57	13
15–19	32	32	59	17
20–24	36	38	67	20

Source: U.S. Department of Transportation, *Nationwide Personal Transportation Survey, 1973* (Washington, DC, 1974), 32.

[a]Speeds are evaluated at the midpoint of the distance range.

From 1950 to 1970, the number of passenger trips on public transportation dropped by 57 percent, from 17.2 million trips to 7.3 million trips. Since 1970, the number of trips has risen by 21 percent but remains much lower than in 1950. Because of decreased ridership, rail and streetcar public transportation systems have been shut down entirely in a number of U.S. cities. Most U.S. cities now have only bus service, with a few large cities also having subways. Even the public transportation that remains is lightly used except at rush hours. Because of reduced ridership, many public transportation systems operate infrequently outside of the rush hours and provide poor service. This raises waiting time and encourages the remaining few riders to shift to automobiles.

What do we know about urban commuting trips? First, the average one-way commuting trip in U.S. metropolitan areas is about 20–25 minutes and ten miles. More precisely, for the fifty largest U.S. metropolitan areas, the average commuting journey length was 23 minutes in 1980, while for urban workers generally it was 21.5 minutes. In distance terms, the average one-way commute was about nine miles for workers living in central cities versus eleven miles for workers living in suburbs.[16] Table 6.1 gives the average one-way commuting journey length for twenty-two large U.S. metropolitan areas. The range is from 35 minutes in New York to 19 minutes in Dayton, which has only 7 percent of New York's population.

Second, when the commuting trip is longer, speed is greater. Table 6.7 shows that speed by both car and public transportation increases by a factor of four when the length of the commuting journey increases from less than five miles to twenty to twenty-four miles. For car commuters, speed increases because a longer commuting trip justifies using freeways rather than local streets. For

16. The data on commuting times are from U.S. Bureau of the Census, *U.S. Census of Population 1980: U.S. Summary* (Washington, D.C.: U.S. Government Printing Office), and the data on commuting distances are from U.S. Department of Transportation, *Nationwide Personal Transportation Survey* (1986), vol. 2.

Table 6.8   **Urban Commuting Journey Length, Speed, and Distance, 1969**

	Distance (miles)	Time (min)	Speed (mph)
Automobile	9.3	21	27
Public transportation	6.8	37	11

Source: U.S. Department of Transportation, *Nationwide Personal Transportation Survey, 1973* (Washington, DC, 1974), 26, 34.

public transportation commuters, speed probably increases because of mode shifts: shorter trips are made by bus, and longer trips are made by subway or train. This means that when workers commute farther by car, commuting cost at the margin falls substantially. But the cost of commuting by public transportation is probably constant as long as there is no mode shift. Further, the speed of commuting by car is nearly twice as fast as the speed of commuting by public transportation, regardless of the length of the trip.

Third, workers commuting by public transportation travel shorter distances but still spend more time commuting. Table 6.8 shows that the average commuting trip by car is 9.3 miles compared to 6.8 miles by public transportation. But the typical commuter by car spends 21 minutes traveling, while the typical commuter by public transportation spends 37 minutes.

Fourth, few workers commute by public transportation except in the largest U.S. cities. Table 6.1 shows that in only three cities, New York, Chicago, and Washington, DC, do less than 80 percent of workers use automobiles for commuting.

Fifth, another important aspect of urban commuting trips is that, over time, more urban commuters are women. The labor force participation rate of women in the United States has increased from 31.5 percent in 1950 to 52.4 percent in 1976.[17] Most of the increase for women generally is due to higher rates of labor force participation for married women, particularly those with children. Married women workers are more likely to work part-time and typically have shorter commuting journeys than male workers; that is, they work closer to home (Madden 1981; Juster and Stafford 1991). Also they frequently combine commuting with shopping and dropping off or picking up children. The income that working wives earn makes two-worker households more likely to live in the suburbs rather than in the central city. But since public transportation is often not available at off-peak hours and in the suburbs, married women workers generally commute by car. Thus the increase in women's labor force participation rate is probably an important cause, although not the only one, of the increase in the number of cars in cities and the amount of commuting by car.

Finally, have commuting journeys been getting longer or shorter over time?

17. U.S. Bureau of the Census, *Statistical Abstract of the United States* (1990), Table 608.

Two offsetting trends are operating here: by itself, the increased suburbanization of housing in cities tends to cause commuting journeys to become longer,
but the increased suburbanization of jobs has an offsetting effect as long as it
does not result in long circumferential commuting journeys. Recent data from
the U.S. Census of Population suggest that overall average commuting time
remained about the same over the decade of the 1980s—it was 21.7 minutes
in 1980 and 22.4 minutes in 1990. Data covering a longer period from the
Nationwide Personal Transportation Survey suggest, however, that average
commuting distance has risen by 11 percent over the last two decades, while
average commuting time has fallen by 10 percent over the same period. (See
table 6.9.) For all commuting trips, average distance rose from 9.9 miles in
1969 to 10.6 miles in 1990, and average time fell from 22 minutes in 1969 to
19.7 minutes in 1990. Together, these two trends imply that average commuting speed has risen from 27 to 32 miles per hour. These trends probably reflect
the fact that more commuting was by car in 1990 than in 1969 and that more
commuting journeys were within the suburbs, where roads are less congested
than near the CBD. The rising speed of commuting does not support popular
accounts of increased congestion.

I have argued that the shift from public transportation to automobile commuting occurred for a combination of reasons, including that it saves time and
that increased suburbanization of both jobs and houses has made commuting
by public transportation infeasible for many workers. This explanation differs
from the popular one, that "Americans are in love with the automobile." In fact,
given the suburbanization of jobs and housing and the increased proportion of
married women working, most American workers probably would have shifted
to commuting by automobile even if they hated driving.

6.4.3   A Cross-city Regression Model of Urban Commuting

A regression model using a cross-section sample of U.S. metropolitan areas
can help to disentangle some of the factors affecting commuting journey
length. The sample consists of the fifty largest metropolitan areas in the United

Table 6.9   Commuting Journey Length, 1969–90

	1969	1977	1983	1990	% Change, 1969–90
Distance (miles)					
Automobile	9.4	9.2	9.9	10.4	11
Truck	14.2	10.6	11.4	13.0	−8
Bus	8.7	7.2	8.6	9.3	7
Total	9.9	9.2	9.9	10.6	7
Total time spent	22	20.4	20.4	19.7	−10

Source: U.S. Department of Transportation, *Summary of Travel Trends: 1990 NPTS Nationwide
Personal Transportation Survey,* FHWA-PL-92-027, (Washington, DC, 1992).

States in 1980. The dependent variable is average time spent commuting, in minutes. Measuring commuting journey length in terms of time rather than distance is preferable, since the major resource cost of commuting is its time cost rather than its out-of-pocket cost. Average commuting journey length is hypothesized to depend on population of the metropolitan area (*POP*), median income per person in the metropolitan area (*MEDINC*), the proportion of workers in the metropolitan area who are black (*BLACK*), the proportion of workers in the metropolitan area who use public transportation (*PUBTRAN*), the proportion of jobs in the metropolitan area located at the CBD (*CBDJOBS*), the proportion of households in the metropolitan area who have moved within the last five years (*MOVER*), and the proportion of households in which both the husband and wife work (*2WHH*).

Higher urban population is expected to raise the average commuting journey length, since larger cities tend to be more spread out. However, while population suburbanization increases average commuting journey length, employment suburbanization tends to have an offsetting effect. The proportion of jobs located at the CBD is a measure, albeit quite crude, of employment centralization, so that its coefficient is expected to be positive. Higher household income is expected to be associated with higher average commuting journey length, since higher-income households tend to prefer suburban housing. Cities having greater use of public transportation are expected to have longer commuting times, since commuting by public transportation is slower than commuting by car. Cities with more black workers are expected to have higher average commuting journey length. This is because black workers are likely to live near the CBD, while many jobs have moved to the suburbs. This means that black workers often have long out-commuting journeys that are slow. The variable *MOVER* could have either sign. Workers may change residential locations in order to be closer to their jobs, which would make the sign of *MOVER* negative. But workers may also move because their incomes have risen, in which case they are likely to locate farther out, making the sign of *MOVER* positive. Which effect predominates is an empirical question. Since married women workers have shorter commuting journeys than other workers, an increase in the proportion of two-worker households is expected to reduce the average commuting journey length.

The results are shown in table 6.10. The constant term is 10 minutes, indicating a significant fixed time component to commuting, regardless of mode. The population variable (*POP*) is positive and significant, but small. An increase in the metropolitan area population of one million people increases the average commuting journey length by only 0.4 minutes. This suggests that employment suburbanization in large cities has almost, but not fully, offset the effect of population suburbanization in raising commuting journey length. The percentage of jobs at the CBD has the expected positive sign but is insignificant. Use of public transportation for commuting carries a large time disadvantage: if all of a city's workers commuted by public transportation rather than by car, the

Table 6.10   Regression Results Explaining Average Commuting Time for the
Fifty Largest U.S. Metropolitan Areas, 1980

	Mean Value	Coefficient
POP (millions)	2.15	0.383
		(0.102)
PUBTRAN	.068	20.2
		(5.78)
BLACK	.11	18.0
		(2.42)
MEDINC	8.84	0.662
		(0.205)
CBDJOBS	.081	4.96
		(6.56)
MOVER	.52	6.57
		(2.95)
2WHH	.42	−3.00
		(1.75)
Intercept		9.73
		(2.14)
R^2		.86
N		50

Sources: 1980 Census of Population, Characteristics of the Population: General Social and Economic Characteristics, PC80-1-C, (Washington, D.C.: U.S. Bureau of the Census), tables 118 (for commuting time, number of workers, public transportation use, and population), 117 (number of one- and two-worker households), and 133 (number of black workers); 1980 Census of Population, Subject Reports: Geographic Mobility for Metropolitan Area, PC80-2-2C (Washington, D.C.: U.S. Bureau of the Census), table 10 (number of mover households and income data); 1980 Census of Population, Subject Reports, Journey to Work: Metropolitan Commuting Flows (Washington, D.C.: U.S. Bureau of the Census), PC80-2-6C, table 3 (number of workers working in the CBD).
Note: Standard errors are in parentheses.

average commuting journey would be 20 minutes longer. Black workers commute 18 minutes more than white workers, even after taking account of the time penalty associated with public transportation. Both variables are statistically significant. Workers' average commuting journey length increases by 0.66 minute for each increase of $1,000 in income. The MOVER variable is positive and significant. It indicates that a recent move is associated with an increase of 6.5 minutes in commuting journey length. Finally, the percentage of households having two workers has the expected negative sign but is short of statistical significance. It indicates that, if all of a city's workers lived in two-worker households, the average commuting journey length would be 3 minutes shorter.

6.4.4   Do Urban Workers Commute Too Much?

The data discussed so far indicate that American households live in cities that have become very suburbanized and that American workers commute approximately ten miles or twenty minutes each way by car on increasingly congested roads, regardless of whether they live in large or small cities. Does this suggest that urban workers in the United States commute too much?

One reason to think that urban workers commute too much is that automobile travel is underpriced generally and the underpricing is more severe on congested urban roads used by commuters. While drivers pay for the cost of purchasing and operating automobiles, they do not pay the full cost of building and maintaining highways (although they do pay excise taxes on gasoline, which in turn pay for part of the cost of roads). In addition, urban drivers do not bear the costs of congestion and air pollution that extra driving produces. In a recent paper (White 1990), I quantified this externality and found that central city rush hour driving is underpriced by around 44 percent and suburban rush hour driving by around 18 percent. The lower suburban figure results from lower congestion levels in the suburbs. This underpricing of urban driving gives workers an incentive to commute too much. The obvious policy measure to deal with the underpricing of urban driving would be congestion tolls collected only on congested roads during rush hours. But no U.S. jurisdiction has ever tried this approach.[18]

Hamilton (1982) first raised the question of whether urban commuting is "wasteful" in the sense that the aggregate amount of commuting could be reduced, without changing the spatial pattern of jobs and housing, by pairs of workers trading jobs or houses. The efficient amount of commuting is the minimum necessary to connect the metropolitan area's existing houses with its existing jobs. Any commuting in excess of this amount is wasteful.[19] Note that the question as posed assumes that the dispersed land use pattern in U.S. cities is efficient, both for jobs and housing. It thus ignores any distortions in the land use pattern that might be caused by such factors as the underpricing of road use or of gasoline.

Efficient commuting includes both radial and circumferential commuting. Circumferential commuting is efficient when a group of firms or a single large firm locates at a particular point in the suburbs, presumably to take advantage of agglomeration economies or economies of scale. This makes it necessary for workers to commute to these firms from around the metropolitan area, since more jobs are offered than there are workers living along the same ray from the CBD. Thus a nonuniform distribution of suburban jobs in different directions around the CBD implies that some amount of circumferential commuting must be efficient.

White (1988b) developed an approach by which actual commuting could be separated into efficient versus wasteful commuting, using an assignment

18. The city of Singapore levies a toll on drivers who enter the CBD during the day.

19. Not all "wasteful" commuting would be considered to be inefficient in an economic model. For example, if a household chooses to live in a particular neighborhood that requires its worker to make a long out-commuting trip, then the trip would be wasteful according to the definition given here, but would not be economically inefficient unless the household's choice were distorted by some factor such as rent control, zoning, or transportation subsidies.

model.[20] For each city analyzed, I used data consisting of the number of jobs in each geographical subdivision of the metropolitan area, the number of houses in each subdivision of the metropolitan area, a matrix of actual commuting times to get from each subdivision to every other subdivision, and a matrix of the number of workers that live in each subdivision and work in every other subdivision (actual commuting flows). Using the two matrices of actual commuting flows and actual commuting times, the average actual commuting journey length can be calculated. Then an assignment model was used to determine a new, optimal matrix of commuting flows that minimizes total time spent commuting for all workers in the metropolitan areas, taking as given the actual number of jobs and houses in each subdivision. From the matrix of optimal commuting flows, the average efficient commuting journey can be computed. The difference between efficient commuting and actual commuting is the amount of wasteful commuting.[21]

I found that wasteful commuting constituted only around 10 percent of total urban commuting—a surprisingly low figure. The results of the assignment model typically resulted in an efficient commuting pattern in which most workers work in the same jurisdiction in which they live or in the neighboring jurisdiction, and excess suburban workers commute to the CBD. Out-commuting and circumferential commuting journeys were eliminated by trading.

The result that only a small fraction of urban commuting in the United States is wasteful is subject to two major criticisms. First, the assignment model treats all workers and all jobs in the metropolitan area as identical. Obviously in the real world, workers and jobs are not homogeneous, so that many such trades would not be possible. In particular, the model ignores the special commuting circumstances faced by black workers and by working couples. Black workers may live near the CBD because housing discrimination reduces opportunities to live anywhere else, but they may make long out-commuting journeys because most job opportunities are in the suburbs. The assignment model treats these trips as wasteful and eliminates them by trading jobs or residences. Similarly, workers in two-worker households may make circumferential or out-commuting journeys because they choose to live halfway between their two jobs. The assignment model separates couples so as to reduce commuting by assigning each worker separately. Further, households often are attached to their neighborhoods and their jobs and prefer to commute more in order to avoid change. These two latter factors tend to bias my wasteful commuting results upward.

On the other hand, I used census data for my study, and this means that

---

20. Hamilton (1982) also developed a methodology to separate commuting into efficient versus wasteful commuting, but his methodology was flawed since it assumed that all circumferential commuting was wasteful. See also Hamilton (1990).

21. Note that census data are available only for commuting time, not commuting distance.

data were available for only a relatively small number of subdivisions in each metropolitan area. But the assignment model implicitly assumes that any commuting journeys by workers who both live and work in the same subdivision are efficient. It therefore ignores any wasteful commuting that could be identified if the unit of analysis were smaller. In particular, census data treat the central cities of most SMSAs as one subdivision, although the CBD is a separate unit. More recent research using the same approach has taken advantage of transportation surveys for particular cities that identify a much larger number of subdivisions. Thus, for example, Clopper and Gordon (1991) estimated an assignment model for Baltimore with data that identified five hundred subdivisions and found that about half the amount of commuting, measured in terms of distance, was wasteful. This suggests that while urban models—which predict that workers themselves will tend to minimize commuting given the spatial pattern of jobs and housing—do a reasonably good job of explaining commuting behavior, the relatively low cost of travel in the United States allows workers to trade off longer commuting trips against many other objectives.

6.5   What Lies Ahead?

The historical model discussed above suggests that suburban housing, like central city housing, will decay as it ages, causing central city problems to appear in the suburbs. Such a pattern has been observed in some suburban areas, mainly where the suburbs of metropolitan areas surround subcenters that are in effect small central cities. The city of Yonkers in Westchester County, NY, is an example. Otherwise, most housing in suburban areas has seemed to grow old without decaying, and close-in suburbs in many metropolitan areas have appeared to benefit from their high accessibility to jobs. Part of the reason for this may be that suburban jurisdictions are inherently more stable than central cities because of their aggressive use of land use controls to regulate new development and keep out problems. This suggests that the decline in the quality of the housing stock in central cities may have occurred, not so much because of aging, but because of proximity to central city problems.

Continuing suburbanization suggests that metropolitan areas in the future will be even more spread out than today. They will also be less compact than in the past, with more vacant areas within the developed margin. The vacant areas may be either places where housing has been abandoned or areas that are subject to overly restrictive land use controls and have been skipped over. Metropolitan areas are likely to consist of widely scattered employment subcenters and scattered residential neighborhoods. If the price of gasoline rose drastically—either because of new taxes or a new oil crisis—jobs and residences would become more spatially integrated, but the trend toward amorphous cities would probably continue.

Employment will also continue to suburbanize. Greater use of computers and new forms of telecommunications are likely to reduce agglomeration economies, because there is less need for face-to-face contact and because parties can communicate and exchange documents quickly without being physically close to each other. This change seems likely to further erode the attractiveness of CBDs as employment locations.

What about urban congestion? The data discussed here suggest that urban congestion has been getting better rather than worse, so it is not surprising that local government officials appear to be unconcerned about it. Ironically, the only serious proposals to do anything about urban congestion have come from the Environmental Protection Agency—the U.S. government agency responsible for enforcing clean air laws. The EPA has proposed a number of drastic measures designed to clean up the air by reducing driving. In Los Angeles, it has proposed that a regional clean air authority be given power to shorten commuting journeys by directing new job growth to suburban areas where most new housing is currently being built and directing new housing growth to more central areas along the coast where most jobs in the Los Angeles region are located. The latter is likely to be resisted by local officials, since high land costs on the coast make only high-density housing economically feasible, but apartments are barred by local zoning rules. The former is more feasible, since employment is suburbanizing rapidly anyway. Although jobs are likely to become more suburbanized and jobs and housing to become more balanced, however, commuting trips are likely to remain about the same length as they are now, regardless of what the EPA or other government agencies might try to do.

References

Clopper, M., and P. Gordon. 1991. Wasteful Commuting: A Reexamination. *Journal of Urban Economics* 29:2–13.

Fischel, W. 1985. *The Economics of Zoning Laws.* Baltimore: Johns Hopkins University Press.

Hamilton, B. 1975. Zoning and Property Taxation in a System of Local Governments. *Urban Studies* 12:205–11.

———. 1982. Wasteful Commuting. *Journal of Political Economy* 90:1035–53.

———. 1990. Wasteful Commuting Again. *Journal of Political Economy* 97:1497–1504.

Hanushek, E. 1981. Throwing Money at Schools. *Journal of Policy Analysis and Management* 1:19–41.

Harrison, D., and J. Kain. 1974. Cumulative Urban Growth and Urban Density Functions. *Journal of Urban Economics* 1:61–98.

Juster, T., and F. Stafford. 1991. The Allocation of Time: Empirical Findings, Behavioral Models, and Problems of Measurement. *Journal of Economic Literature* 29:471–522.

LeRoy, S., and J. Sonstelie. 1983. Paradise Lost and Regained: Transportation Innovation, Income, and Residential Location. *Journal of Urban Economics* 13:67–89.

Macaulay, M. 1985. Estimation and Recent Behavior of Urban Population and Employment Density Gradients. *Journal of Urban Economics* 18:251–60.

McFadden, D. 1974. The Measurement of Urban Travel Demand. *Journal of Public Economics* 3:303–28.

Madden, J. 1981. Why Women Work Closer to Home. *Urban Studies* 18:181–94.

Mieszkowski, P., and G. Zodrow. 1989. Taxation and the Tiebout Model: The Differential Effects of Head Taxes, Taxes on Land Rents, and Property Taxes. *Journal of Economic Literature* 27:1098–1146.

Mills, E. 1972. *Studies in the Structure of the Urban Economy.* Baltimore: Johns Hopkins University Press.

Mills, E., and K. Ohta. 1976. Urbanization and Urban Problems. In *Asia's New Giant: How the Japanese Economy Works,* ed. H. Patrick and H. Rosovsky. Washington, D.C.: Brookings Institution.

Muth, R. 1969. *Cities and Housing.* Chicago: University of Chicago Press.

Palumbo, G., S. Sacks, and M. Wasylenko. 1990. Population Decentralization within Metropolitan Areas: 1970–1980. *Journal of Urban Economics* 27:151–67.

Polinsky, A. M., and D. Ellwood. 1979. An Empirical Reconciliation of Micro and Grouped Estimates of the Demand for Housing. *Review of Economics and Statistics* 61:199–205.

Sternlieb, G., and R. Burchell. 1973. *Residential Abandonment: The Tenement Landlord Revisited.* New Brunswick, N.J.: Rutgers University Press.

Tiebout, C. 1956. A Pure Theory of Local Expenditures. *Journal of Political Economy* 54:416–24.

Wheaton, W. 1982. Urban Residential Growth under Perfect Foresight. *Journal of Urban Economics* 12:1–21.

White, M. 1986. Property Taxes and Urban Housing Abandonment. *Journal of Urban Economics* 20:312–30.

———. 1988a. Location Choice and Commuting Behavior in Cities with Decentralized Employment. *Journal of Urban Economics* 24:129–52.

———. 1988b. Urban Commuting Is Not 'Wasteful.' *Journal of Political Economy* 96:1097–1110.

———. 1990. Commuting and Congestion: A Simulation Model of a Decentralized Metropolitan Area. *Journal of the American Real Estate and Urban Economics Association* 18:335–68.

7   Housing and Saving in Japan

Toshiaki Tachibanaki

7.1   Introduction

The consensus has been that the savings rate in Japan was considerably higher than in other industrialized countries. Japanese and non-Japanese economists have investigated the reasons why the savings rate was so high. Some doubts were cast on this consensus quite recently, however, proposing that the Japanese savings rate would not be markedly higher than that in other countries, if the measurement of savings were made properly. Another widely held belief was that savings related to potential housing purchase were very important. Some say that this is no longer true. The purpose of this paper is to examine these subjects, namely, the proper measurement of savings, and housing-related savings. Since a housing purchase normally implies a housing loan, special attention is paid to the contribution of repayment to debt. The influence of gifts and inheritances on the savings rate is also investigated, because a house and land are the typical goods of intergenerational transfers. Finally, wealth distribution is briefly analyzed.

7.2   Saving Motives and Objects

It has been widely believed that four saving motives and objects are important in Japan: for uncertainties such as illness or disaster; for consumption during old age; for purchase, construction, expansion, or renovation of land and houses (called housing-related saving for short); and for children's educa-

Toshiaki Tachibanaki is professor of economics at Kyoto University.

The author is grateful to Charles Horioka, Takatoshi Ito, Yukio Noguchi, James Poterba, and Michelle White for their useful comments. He is responsible for any errors and opinions in this paper.

Table 7.1   The Three Most Important Motives for Saving (%)

	Precautionary Saving for Illness or Disaster	Children's Education and Marriage Expenses	Housing-Related	Consumption during Old Age	Consumer Durables	Travel and Leisure	Tax Payment	No Specific Aims	Other
1974	81.5	54.4	32.3	37.3	7.4	8.2	3.9	27.3	1.6
1975	83.2	55.3	30.2	38.1	7.5	9.0	3.9	27.1	1.7
1976	82.2	53.9	30.1	41.8	8.0	9.3	3.5	26.3	1.6
1977	79.6	54.2	32.0	38.5	8.6	10.7	2.9	30.2	1.4
1978	77.9	50.5	32.2	40.2	8.7	10.1	3.9	27.6	1.3
1979	76.6	53.0	33.9	39.8	8.2	9.9	3.8	27.2	1.2
1980	79.1	53.5	32.0	38.4	7.8	10.0	4.8	27.2	1.2
1981	76.9	50.9	31.4	36.4	8.7	11.4	4.1	26.5	1.2
1982	78.5	52.7	27.1	42.1	7.9	9.9	4.6	25.8	1.2
1983	75.4	53.0	28.6	41.0	8.7	10.4	4.9	27.1	1.1
1984	75.0	59.2	26.3	42.1	7.5	9.7	5.2	25.7	1.2
1985	77.2	60.1	19.8	42.5	10.5	4.8	5.4	26.4	1.6
1986	75.0	60.0	20.5	42.5	10.8	5.2	5.5	25.3	1.4
1987	76.4	57.5	20.4	46.1	9.4	6.1	4.7	26.1	1.4
1988	77.1	64.4	19.2	50.2	10.5	6.3	5.0	28.0	2.9
1989	80.5	58.2	17.7	51.5	11.1	7.0	5.7	28.7	3.7

Source: Central Council for Saving Promotion, *Public Opinion Survey on Saving* (in Japanese) (various issues).

tion and marriage expenses. It would be useful to confirm these motives by looking at some recent surveys.

Tables 7.1 and 7.2 show the most popular and widely cited survey, *Objects for Savings,* conducted by the Central Council for Savings Promotion, an institute affiliated with the Bank of Japan, from 1974 to 1989. Figures in table 7.1 are the percentages of respondents who gave the top three motives for saving, while figures in table 7.2 are the percentages of respondents who gave the top motive for saving. Although there is a subtle difference between table 7.1 and table 7.2 because of differing relative weights on the evaluation, the data confirm that the four motives mentioned above are very important.

Another survey on motives for saving is the *Survey on Consciousness and Objects of Savings,* conducted by a research group at the Department of Sociology of the University of Tokyo. The results are in table 7.3. The survey was conducted in 1977, 1981, and 1985. The first part of the survey asks saving motives and consciousness without necessarily specifying objects of savings, while the second part asks for specific saving objects. The second part, namely specific objects, is roughly equivalent to table 7.2.

These three tables show, not the amount of savings for particular objects, but how people evaluate important saving motives and objects. For example, the most important object in table 7.2 (1989) is precautionary saving for illness and disaster, 34.2 percent. This number merely shows that 34.2 percent of respondents regard precautionary saving for illness and disaster as the most important object; it does not necessarily imply that the amount of saving for precautionary reasons is the largest. The tables suggest that motivation to save for children's education and marriage expenses is very high. As Horioka (1985, 1987) points out, however, the amount of saving for children's educational expenses and marriage expenses is quite marginal. I present later the amount of savings for housing.

The tables suggest that the importance of housing-related motive and object, namely purchase, construction, expansion, or renovation of land and house, has declined constantly over the past fifteen years. Table 7.1 shows that it is only the fifth most important, namely, 17.7 percent in 1989. It is the fourth most important (7.1 percent) in table 7.2. These percentages were 33.9 in 1979 and 17.3 in 1978, respectively. These are remarkable declines. It is possible to conclude that housing-related saving is no longer an important motive. We have to verify whether this is true for the amount of housing-related savings in addition to the housing-related motive and object, and to find the causes for this trend if it is true.

The two surveys have a serious drawback: neither asks about the bequest motive for and object of saving. As Hayashi (1986), Hayashi, Ando, and Ferris (1988), Hayashi, Ito, and Slemrod (1988), and Tachibanaki and Shimono (1986, 1991) pointed out, the life-cycle saving hypothesis with a bequest motive is quite plausible for Japan. An exception is Horioka (1990). Since the surveys do not touch on the bequest motive, we have to take account of the

Table 7.2   The Most Important Motive for Saving (%)

	Precautionary for Illness or Disaster	Children's Education and Marriage Expenses	Housing-Related	Consumption during Old Age	Consumer Durables	Travel and Leisure	Tax Payment	No Specific Aims	Other
1974	39.2	16.2	14.0	13.9	0.9	0.3	0.3	7.4	0.7
1975	42.2	16.4	13.9	13.0	0.8	0.3	0.3	7.7	0.9
1976	39.0	15.8	15.2	14.4	0.9	0.4	0.4	7.4	0.9
1977	32.9	20.4	16.9	14.8	0.8	0.7	0.3	6.9	0.9
1978	34.5	17.6	17.3	13.2	1.1	0.9	0.4	6.9	0.8
1979	34.4	18.1	16.9	13.9	0.9	0.8	0.7	6.4	0.6
1980	36.1	18.3	15.4	11.3	0.9	0.8	0.8	5.9	0.7
1981	39.0	17.9	16.2	13.4	1.4	1.1	0.8	7.6	0.7
1982	38.7	19.5	13.2	15.3	1.4	1.1	0.7	7.0	0.7
1983	36.1	20.7	14.3	15.4	1.3	0.9	1.0	7.0	0.7
1984	34.4	18.3	12.3	15.5	1.1	1.0	0.9	6.5	0.7
1985	31.4	18.1	9.0	16.6	0.9	0.5	0.7	6.6	1.0
1986	31.6	17.6	9.9	15.9	0.8	0.3	0.5	7.1	0.9
1987	33.0	16.2	9.0	19.2	0.9	0.6	0.9	6.4	0.7
1988	39.3	18.5	8.6	21.3	1.3	0.4	0.9	7.4	0.7
1989	34.2	16.8	7.1	23.7	0.9	0.4	0.6	6.7	0.9

Source: Central Council for Saving Promotion, *Public Opinion Survey on Saving* (in Japanese) (various issues).

Table 7.3   **Motives and Objects for Saving (%)**

	1977	1981	1985
Motives			
Consumption during old age	39.5	42.3	45.9
Precautionary for illness and disaster	75.0	73.1	71.5
Particular objects and purposes	42.3	40.1	38.1
Raising revenue	5.9	5.4	6.6
Nonspecific	10.3	3.1	2.9
Objects			
Children's educational expenses	56.8	57.3	59.1
Marriage expenses (own and			
children's)	30.3	31.2	32.9
Housing-related	57.9	52.0	42.3
Opening independent business	8.0	5.9	5.2
Working capital of business	11.8	11.1	11.5
Durable goods such as car and			
furniture	18.4	21.5	23.6
Travel and leisure	22.2	28.4	33.0
Other	2.8	2.5	3.3

Source: Department of Sociology, University of Tokyo, *Survey on Consciousness and Objects of Savings* (in Japanese).

contribution of this motive in judging the relative importance of saving motives. It is likely that the relationship between housing and bequests is crucial. Also, the surveys do not deal with repayment of loans, which is one of the important components of savings, as will be argued later. In other words, they do not cover all components of savings.

It is interesting to inquire into the effect of age on saving motives and objects. Figure 7.1 shows the percentages of objects by age class. This figure was drawn using the same source as table 7.1 (i.e., the top three important objects). Several interesting observations are possible based on this figure. First, uncertain expenditure for illness and disaster is the highest over all age classes. The Japanese are risk-averse regardless of age. Second, consumption during old age increases directly with age. Third, children's educational expenses decline fairly drastically as people become older. These two are fairly natural outcomes of the life stages. Finally, the housing-related saving object decreases gradually with age from 30 percent in the twenties to 8.4 percent in the seventies.

In summary, life stages are crucial to determine the importance of saving motives and objects. With respect to housing-related savings, younger ages (say ages 20–40) give a heavier weight to housing motives than middle or older ages. This does not necessarily imply, however, that younger people save more for housing. As will be shown later, middle-aged and sometimes older people save a lot if we take account of repayment of housing loans.

I have examined how people in Japan assess saving motives and objects. The

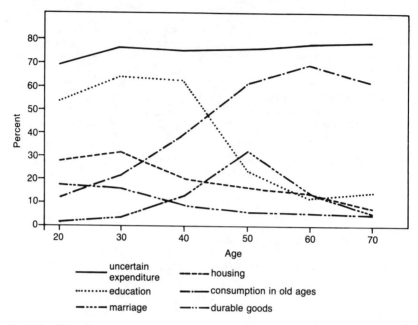

Fig. 7.1   The effects of age on saving motives and objects
Source: Central Council for Saving Promotion, *Public Opinion Survey on Saving* (1987).

next task is to investigate the extent to which people prepare to achieve these motives and objects. Table 7.4 suggests that the ratio of "considerably insufficient" and "utterly insufficient," totaling 49.0 percent, is not so high for housing-related saving motive in comparison with savings for life during old age, totaling 74.8 percent, or for illness and hospitalization, totaling 65.6 percent. Therefore, the Japanese attempt to prepare a fairly sufficient amount of savings for housing purposes, and they worry a lot about their insufficient amount of savings for life after retirement and for health problems. This table again shows that saving for housing is no longer a major motive.

7.3   Housing Purchase and Living Conditions

This section examines the issues that indicate the relationship between savings and housing. It must be emphasized that all households do not buy houses. Some prefer rental houses to owner-occupied houses, and never buy a house during their lives. Also, some hold multiple homes, used as second homes or villas at vacation areas or rented as homes or rooms. These second homes and rental homes are not my major concern; only 1.7 percent of the population hold second homes or villas currently. Since housing statistics do not provide useful information on the number of houses or rooms rented out by individuals or on the amount of rents, I ignore these issues. An important issue is that housing quality in Japan is generally poorer than that in other industrialized countries, although no evidence is provided here. This may imply that the Japanese have to continue their high saving rates in order to improve the quality of their housing stock.

One remark must be added with respect to the quality of homes in Japan. Owner-occupied homes and rental homes are not close substitutes because the two categories are very different in the number of rooms per home and in the floor area. In general, owner-occupied homes have a larger number of rooms and larger areas than rental homes. This reflects largely the difference in the number of family members. Single-person households or married couples without children tend to live in rental homes with a smaller number of rooms when they are young, while older married households with children, and parents in some cases (called a merged family), tend to live in owner-occupied homes with a larger number of rooms. Thus, getting married and having children are important incentives to switch from rental homes to owner-occupied homes. Also, it is often suggested that the lack of qualified rental homes caused by the Land Lease Law and Building Lease Law is serious. These facts suggest that, because rental homes and owner-occupied homes are demanded by different households, they are not close substitutes.

Figure 7.2 shows that the lack of close substitution is verified by the data. Two peaks of total area per home are distinguished for rental homes and owner-occupied homes. The distinction is more apparent for national levels than for urban, condensed areas. Yoshikawa and Ohtake (1989) made an important contribution to the study of saving and labor-supply behavior, by taking account of this separation.

Since age was crucial for the determination of the saving motive for housing, it is useful to know at what age households obtain their own homes. Table 7.5 shows the percentage of households who have their own homes for various age classes and various years. First, more than 50 percent of households in 1988 have their own homes at ages 35–39, and more than 70 percent at ages over 45. Second, the majority of households obtain their homes when they are

Table 7.4   The Extent of Preparations for Each Saving Motive (%)

	Sufficient	Considerably Insufficient	Utterly Insufficient	No Need to Prepare	No Answer
Consumption during old age	19.6	34.1	40.7	4.6	1.0
Illness and hospitalization	28.2	37.6	28.0	4.3	1.9
Housing-related	18.1	18.1	30.9	29.7	3.2
Children's education	20.6	28.2	14.5	31.0	5.7
Children's marriage	12.4	17.6	34.2	31.2	4.6
Own marriage	14.6	28.1	29.2	23.8	4.3

Source: Economic Planning Agency, *Survey on Life Preference* (in Japanese) (1985).

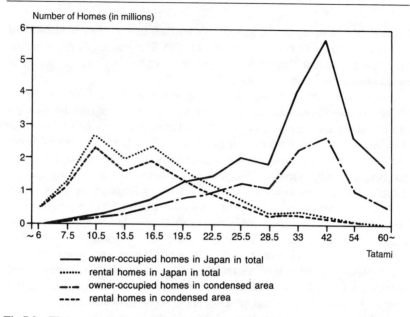

Number of Homes (in millions)

owner-occupied homes in Japan in total
rental homes in Japan in total
owner-occupied homes in condensed area
rental homes in condensed area

Fig 7.2   The number of tatami mats and housing status
Source: Maki 1988, based on Management and Coordination Agency, *Housing Survey* (1963).

Table 7.5	The Rate of Owner-Occupied Homes by Age Class (%)				
	1968	1973	1978	1983	1988
Total	59.1	58.4	59.0	62.0	61.1
Less than 25	16.5	11.4	9.9	7.6	5.0
25–29	27.9	26.0	27.9	24.8	17.8
30–34	} 48.9	} 48.2	44.4	45.5	38.6
35–39			58.0	59.8	56.2
40–44	} 67.4	} 68.7	66.8	68.2	65.8
45–49			73.4	73.1	72.5
50–54	} 74.9	} 76.6	77.1	77.0	74.7
55–59			79.0	80.1	78.9
60–64	} 79.8	} 78.9	77.9	78.3	80.2
65 and over			75.9	76.1	77.0

Source: Management and Coordination Agency, *Survey on Housing* (in Japanese) (various years).

Table 7.6   **The Relationship between Housing Loan and Owner-Occupied Homes** (%)

	Total	Owners	Renters
Prefer owner-occupied home despite heavy housing loan	53.9	62.9	30.7
Prefer rental home because of heavy housing loan	31.9	20.8	60.3
Do not know	14.2	16.2	9.0

Source: Management and Coordination Agency, *Survey on Housing in Large Urban Areas* (in Japanese) (1986).

between ages 30 and 49, and in particular between 35 and 44 in 1988. This is important to understanding the relationship between housing and saving. Third, about 20 percent of households never own their homes throughout their lives. Fourth, when we look at ages younger than 25 and 25–29, ownership rates have declined constantly and significantly. This is true also for middle-aged generations, say, 30–44 from 1983 to 1988, although the rate of decrease is less significant than that for younger generations. The decrease in the rates of owner-occupied homes might be explained by a drastic increase in land prices in urban areas and a change in tastes (i.e., some people prefer rental homes to owner-occupied homes, for convenience and avoiding the heavy financial burdens caused by housing loans).

Surveys of people who live in the two largest urban areas, Tokyo and Keihanshin, confirm that the above reasons are valid. The rate of housing purchase plans among renters has declined drastically (32.5 percent in 1977, 27.4 in 1982, and 15.2 in 1986). On the basis of table 7.6, about two-thirds of renters do not want to commit to the heavy financial burdens of a housing loan and prefer living in rental homes, when we exclude households who did not answer the question.

I must emphasize that favoring rental homes is, at this stage, restricted to households who are in large urban areas. Table 7.7 gives the percentage of those renters who plan to obtain owner-occupied homes in various regions. The rate of housing purchase plans is considerably higher in rural areas than in urban areas. Also, the rate decreases as the size of urban areas increases. This reflects the much higher increase in land prices in large urban areas than in rural areas. Some people in urban areas are obliged to abandon their housing purchase plans unless they receive extra revenues, such as bequests.

A recent survey conducted by the Ministry of Post and Telecommunication, *Survey on Financial Asset Choices of Households,* gave the reasons for not wanting to obtain owner-occupied homes (table 7.8). Among renters, 40.6 percent of households responded that the prices of land and a home are too high to buy, and 37.0 percent responded that it is difficult to find financial sources for housing. A total of 77.6 percent of households replied that they cannot

Table 7.7   Housing Purchase Plan among Renters, by Location (%)

			Have a Plan				
	Total	12 Largest Cities	Medium-sized Cities	Small Cities	Rural Areas	No Plan for a While	No Plan at All
1985	46.4	42.6	40.7	52.4	57.1	33.2	13.2
1986	49.6	49.2	46.8	53.2	51.5	31.2	12.6
1987	51.0	45.0	52.6	53.9	58.5	28.2	14.6
1988	45.1	35.3	45.9	53.6	54.6	32.1	14.6
1989	46.5	42.0	45.7	48.4	53.9	29.9	16.2

Source: Central Council for Saving Promotion, *Public Opinion Survey on Saving* (in Japanese) (various years).

Table 7.8   Reasons for Not Wanting to Own Home (%)

Reason	Total	Owners	Renters
Prices of land and house too high	16.5	8.6	40.6
Rental home preferred	3.8	0.2	14.5
Financial sources difficult to find	16.4	9.6	37.0
Owner-occupied home just obtained	12.5	15.8	1.9
Satisfaction with current home	55.4	68.1	17.4
Uncertainty about future	19.6	14.4	35.5
Other	3.7	2.7	7.6

Source: Ministry of Post and Telecommunication, *Survey on Financial Asset Choices of Households* (in Japanese) (1990).

afford to buy a home. If the prices of land and a home were low enough, households would be able to buy homes even if finding financial resources were difficult. In other words, a cause for lack of financial resources is that housing and land prices are too high. Therefore, it is concluded that the fundamental reason for the inability to buy homes is their extremely high prices.

The above conclusion is in particular applicable to large urban areas such as Tokyo and Keihanshin. Nihon Keizai Shinbunsha (1988) initiated a timely and valuable survey right after the period of sky-rocketing land prices in the Tokyo metropolitan area, *Survey on the Effect of Land and Housing Prices on Consumption.* The survey was given exclusively to people who live in the Tokyo metropolitan area. The survey provides us with several interesting observations. First, nearly 70 percent of renters and about 60 percent of homeowners say that they have to give up on obtaining their ideal homes because the cost is too high. "Ideal" in Japan means a moderately spacious house with a garden in a good neighborhood. Second, a very high proportion (about 50 percent) of households switch from ideal houses to "collective homes, i.e., condominiums" as secondary targets. Third, about 30 percent of renters believe that they would enjoy their lives (spending money on other items) without owning their homes and worrying about paying off housing loans. The majority of people in the Tokyo metropolitan area have abandoned the idea of having owner-occupied houses and will have to buy collective homes if they want to own a home.

In what way have households lost their incentive for buying homes? The *White Paper on Households' Living Conditions* (*Kokumin Seikatsu Hakusho*), published by the Economic Planning Agency (1989), calculated the degree of ability to buy homes for several representative cases (table 7.9), using the formula

$$\text{Ability} = \frac{\text{Attainable housing loan and financial assets}}{\text{Housing price (land and housing construction)}} \times 100,$$

where the attainable housing loan was calculated assuming that the annual repayment is 25 percent of annual income. The maximum amount is borrowed from the public housing loan program (to get a cheaper rate of interest), and the rest is from private banks. Households borrow for the maximum duration allowed legally. Annual incomes are for various locations, and the price of land and a house are from various sources.

Table 7.9 shows severe conditions for housing purchases. In 1988, the price of a house (detached) in Tokyo was over 80 million yen, and the price of a collective home was over 60 million yen. The price of a house in smaller cities was 26 million yen. The average in Tokyo is 167 square meters of land and 89 square meters of floor area, and in smaller cities the average is 247 square meters of land and 101 square meters of floor area. (Incidentally, the average

Table 7.9　　　**Housing Prices and Ability to Buy**

	Tokyo, House		Tokyo, Collective Home		Region House	
	Price (million yen)	Ability (%)	Price (million yen)	Ability (%)	Price (million yen)	Ability (%)
1979	25.52	64.2	24.75	70.3	14.50	89.7
1980	29.99	60.3	31.82	60.0	18.91	85.1
1981	34.23	56.6	33.35	61.2	20.79	82.7
1982	39.04	52.8	32.86	65.8	23.08	80.8
1983	39.93	55.6	32.93	70.7	23.51	85.0
1984	40.73	59.2	32.62	77.3	23.89	90.1
1985	43.22	60.2	34.65	78.3	24.14	97.0
1986	56.98	48.3	33.99	85.8	24.35	102.8
1987	85.31	35.5	45.64	69.3	25.04	113.3
1988	83.61	38.6	56.33	61.7	26.01	113.4

Source: Economic Planning Agency, *White Paper on Households' Living Conditions* (1989).

floor area of the collective home in Tokyo is 78 square meters.) The ability to buy a house is 38.6 percent for a (detached) house and 61.7 percent for a collective home in Tokyo, and 113.4 percent for a house in smaller cities. Average households in Tokyo are unable to afford owner-occupied homes, while average households in smaller cities can afford them with a considerable margin.

More important, the ability to buy a house or even a collective home in Tokyo has declined constantly. The decrease in the former is more apparent than that in the later. Also, the decrease is more serious in recent years, due largely to the drastic increases in the price of land in 1986–1988 in the Tokyo metropolitan area. The increase in land prices spread to Osaka and Nagoya in 1988 and 1989. The current housing price/annual income ratio in Tokyo is about seven to nine, and it is about four to six in rural areas. It is difficult to buy a house at the Tokyo ratio.

I do not discuss here the reasons for this drastic increase in land prices in urban areas. I merely point out that only two strategies remain for younger people buying homes: move to rural areas or pray for windfall income (receiving a bequest or marrying a son or a daughter of the extremely rich).

7.4 Bequests and Housing

This section examines whether the joke about windfall income has roots in reality. I have pointed out a fairly solid consensus of strong bequest motives among the Japanese. It is interesting and useful to investigate the relationship between bequests (and gifts) and housing, and the effect of bequests (and gifts) on savings. Invaluable data on bequests became available quite recently.

First, I examine the effect of bequests and gifts on the extent of owner-occupied homes. Table 7.10 shows the ratio of owner-occupied homes, and the motive for owning homes (i.e., whether households bought a home or obtained it through a bequest or gift) by region, age, occupation, and income class.

First, about 30 percent of homeowners obtained their homes through bequests and gifts. This figure is fairly low, for two reasons: the number of children was large in the past, and thus some children have not received any bequests; second, regional mobility of the labor force was quite high, so many children sell inherited houses. For 70 percent of households, some may have bought their homes by using all or part of the financial resources that were left them by their parents or by selling the parents' home. The latter is likely to occur when children move away from their parents' place of residence. Therefore, 30 percent should be understood as a minimum rate that signifies the importance of bequests and gifts in housing purchases. In reality, more than 30 percent should be assigned to the influence of bequests and gifts when we assess housing purchases. Also, many households anticipate that they will receive bequests in the future. These households are not covered in this survey.

Second, there is considerable variation both by region and by city size in the importance of bequeathed homes. Tokyo, Kanto, Kinki, Chugoku, and Hok-

Table 7.10   **The Ratio of Owner-Occupied Homes and the Motives for Homeowning by Region, Age, Occupation, and Income Class (%)**

	Owner-Occupied (A)	Bought (B)	Bequest and Gift (C)	C/A
Total	68.5	48.4	20.1	29.3
Region				
Tokyo	54.3	37.9	16.4	30.2
Kanto	70.1	53.4	16.7	23.8
Shinetsu	83.7	53.2	30.5	36.4
Tokai	71.0	47.6	23.5	33.1
Hokuriku	77.3	45.5	31.8	41.1
Kinki	69.3	49.5	19.8	28.6
Chugoku	63.7	48.2	15.5	24.3
Shikoku	62.0	35.5	26.4	42.6
Kyushu	67.6	47.3	20.4	30.2
Tohoku	77.5	48.9	28.7	37.0
Hokkaido	68.1	58.4	9.7	14.2
City size				
Tokyo (23 districts)	53.2	34.0	19.1	35.9
Ten largest cities	58.9	47.0	11.9	20.2
More than 150 thousand	66.3	49.7	16.5	24.9
More than 50 thousand	71.3	53.8	17.9	25.1
Less than 50 thousand	74.3	50.2	24.1	32.4
Rural area	77.7	47.0	30.8	39.6
Age				
Less than 29	17.5	10.9	6.6	37.7
30–39	45.1	31.6	13.5	29.9
40–49	71.2	51.9	19.3	27.1
50–59	80.4	56.9	23.5	29.2
60–69	86.0	60.4	25.7	29.9
70–79	78.0	48.9	29.1	37.3
Occupation				
Farmers	81.2	27.3	53.9	66.4
Self-employed	74.2	51.4	22.8	30.7
Employees	62.3	46.1	16.2	26.0
Managers	77.4	61.0	16.4	21.2
Professional	61.5	47.1	14.4	23.4
None	82.7	56.5	26.2	31.7
Other	57.7	33.8	23.9	41.4
Income (millions of yen)				
Less than 2	71.2	39.8	31.4	44.1
2–3	64.0	43.2	20.8	32.5
3–4	54.8	37.5	17.3	31.6
4–5	58.9	39.1	19.9	33.8
5–7	69.1	51.4	17.7	25.6
7–10	77.8	56.0	21.8	28.0
10–15	83.6	66.8	16.8	20.1
15 or more	85.4	68.0	17.5	20.5
No answer	67.8	47.0	20.8	30.7

Source: Ministry of Post and Telecommunication, *Survey on Financial Asset Choices of Households* (in Japanese) (1989).

kaido have relatively lower rates of bequests. Urban areas except for Tokyo (twenty-three districts only) also show lower rates, while rural areas and smaller cities show higher rates. These observations suggest that children who continued to live near their parents and did not move to larger urban areas tend to receive bequests. (Hokkaido is a special case because it is a frontier.)

Third, the timing of a transfer is universally distributed, although a somewhat higher rate is observed at ages under twenty-nine and over seventy. More important, occupation of children does matter in the determination of bequests. Farmers have a very high rate, 66.4 percent. "No occupation," "other occupations," and self-employed follow. The cases of farmers and self-employed are very natural; the other two categories may be associated with female heads of household after their husband's death. Employees, managers, and free professions show lower rates. It is likely that they moved to larger urban areas in order to find jobs and that most of them are second or third sons.

Fourth, income does not have a strong influence on the importance of bequests. The highest rate of bequests is observed among households whose incomes are less than 2 million yen. Most of those households would be retired or female heads. An interesting observation is that the rate decreases as income levels increase.

Table 7.10 demonstrates the effect of bequests on housing. One difficulty with the data, however, is that it does not identify the case in which children moved away from a parent's place of residence. (I call them changers for short.) Table 7.11 takes account of changers in city, town, or village. The table suggests, first, that the distinction between changers and nonchangers is crucial with respect to the effect of inheritance on the rate of landholding. Much higher rates of inheritance are observed among nonchangers, while most of the changers obtained land with their own financial resources. Incidentally, the rate of inheritance for self-employed people is higher than that for employees. Second, contribution of gifts is not negligible, but fairly important for employees. A gift is normally transferred before the parent's death. Third, although it was anticipated that many households would use all or part of an inheritance or a gift to buy new land, they did not. An exception is changers and employees. However, the rate is just over 10 percent. Inheritances and gifts were transferred largely to first sons (in most cases), and other sons and daughters (in some cases). This is responsible for explaining the above observations. In return for gifts, children are expected to live with their aging parents or to give financial aid and other help. This is a Japanese form of the so-called strategic (gift-exchange) bequest.

So far I have been concerned with bequests and gifts that have been received. To forecast what will happen, in particular the bequests and gifts that will be left, gives us information to predict the relationship between housing and the savings rate. We will look now at the current generations, who will leave bequests and gifts to their heirs.

The survey conducted by the Ministry of Post and Telecommunication, ex-

Table 7.11   **How Households Obtained Land**

	No Changers, Self-employed	Changers, Self-employed	No Changers, Employed	Changers, Employed
Inheritance	62.0	19.5	36.5	11.9
Inherited present home totally	56.8	11.7	34.8	7.8
Used inheritance as financial resource to buy new land	3.1	3.9	0.9	3.0
Used inheritance as part of financial resource to buy new land	2.1	3.9	0.9	1.1
Gift	7.4	3.9	12.1	14.1
Gifted totally	5.3	2.9	7.8	3.3
Used part of gift	2.1	1.0	4.3	10.8
Own financial resources	23.2	68.9	41.7	68.8
Not available	7.4	9.7	9.6	5.2

Source: Keizai-Seisaku Kenkyusho, *Bequest and Its Effect* (in Japanese) (1989).
Notes: For males aged 55–64 in the Tokyo metropolitan area. Changers include locational changes in prefecture or city, town, and village.

amined above, provides us with valuable information. According to the survey, among households whose ages are over sixty, 64.0 percent want to leave some form of bequest, on average 65.96 million yen. I find this a strong bequest motive, and the average amount that they plan to leave is considerably higher. With respect to forms of bequests and gifts, 57.0 percent of households plan to give "through land and house," and 24.2 percent "through financial assets." The majority regard land and a house as vehicles for intergenerational transfer, and financial assets play only a limited role. (See Barthold and Ito [1992], who estimated the amount of intergenerational transfers based on tax data and confirm this statement.)

It is possible to present a table showing the effect of region, city size, occupation, and income class on the choice between land/house and financial assets as inheritance vehicles. Since I observe no significant difference from table 7.10, I do not present it here. The only difference is the effect of income. The degree of desire to bequeath land, house, and financial assets, as well as the amount that households plan to leave, increases as income level increases. This is not surprising in view of the fact that the quality and quantity of bequests and gifts are largely determined by the desires of households who leave them.

Horioka (1990) proposed that no strong bequest motive is observed in the *Public Opinion Survey on Saving* used in this study. In his interpretation of the survey, 33 percent of Japanese households are not planning to leave a bequest to their children, and 22 percent plan to leave a bequest as part of an intrafamily implicit annuity contract. He concludes that no strong bequest motive exists in Japan, since the total of these two figures, 55 percent, is high. First, I find that 33 percent are talking about only an *intended* bequest. Although it is not possible to provide figures for *unintended* bequests, the percentage of households who leave bequests would be much higher if both *intended* and *unintended* bequests were included. Second, the reason for leaving bequests does not matter when we investigate the contribution of intergenerational transfers. Whatever the reason (e.g., an intrafamily gift exchange), intergenerational transfer happened. I consider, therefore, that a bequest is an important source of intergenerational transfer.

Strong bequest motives (including unintended bequests) of people who may soon die have an important implication for the future course of the savings rate in Japan, because the majority of future generations will feel no need to save. Future generations anticipate that they will inherit great wealth (principally land and a house) sometime in the future. Therefore, they are unlikely to have a strong incentive to save, and it may be that the savings rate will decline considerably.

Two supplementary reasons explain why the above projection is likely. First, Japan faces a serious aging trend. The proportion of younger generations will decline, while the proportion of older generations will increase for the coming twenty or thirty years. This implies a decrease in the number of children who can receive bequests, and an increase in the number of parents who can bequeath. Thus, not only the probability of receiving bequests but also the amount of bequest per inheritance will increase under demographic changes (i.e., an aging trend).

Muramoto (1989) performed an interesting simulation to show that the above story is plausible for Japan. Table 7.12 gives various simulation results for households in their thirties. The average number of children decreases from 5.1 in 1965 to 2.3 in 1995, a vivid sign of the aging trend. The recently available data report this more strongly. Also, the proportion of unmarried people has increased. These demographic changes have an important effect on the probability of receiving bequests and the number of owner-occupied homes acquired through inheritance.

Table 7.12 shows the probability of receiving a bequest is above 80 percent in 1995, and more important, the probability of homeowning through inheritance is above 60 percent. The majority are able to own their homes through inheritance and are not obliged to take the trouble to save for housing purchase.

A large number of the elderly (not all of them) hold a relatively high level of wealth (both physical assets and monetary wealth), as will be shown. This supports the view that the amount of bequest per household head will be relatively high, and current younger generations predict that they will receive a high amount of inheritance in the near future. This depresses a motive for saving.

7.5   Housing Purchase, Housing Loan, and Saving

This section discusses the amount of saving (flow basis) and of financial assets (stock basis) for the particular purpose (i.e., housing). I examine whether

Table 7.12   Households Who Are Able to Obtain Owner-Occupied Homes through Inheritances

	Average Number of Children	Unmarried (%)	Probability of Receiving Bequest		Rate of Homeowning by Parents (%)	Probability of Homeowning through Inheritance		Households who Can Own Home through Inheritance	
			Model I (%)	Model II (%)		Model I (%)	Model II (%)	Model I (millions)	Model II (millions)
1965	5.1	4.3	39.2	38.4	82.3	32.3	31.6	2.54	2.49
1975	4.6	5.4	43.5	42.3	79.9	34.8	33.8	3.07	2.99
1985	3.1	9.2	64.5	61.5	77.6	50.1	47.7	4.96	4.72
1995	2.3	10.4	87.0	82.4	77.6	67.5	63.9	5.37	5.08

Source: Muramoto 1989, using sources such as the census, *Demographic Changes,* and the *Housing Survey.*

Notes: Model I assumes that everybody gets married, while Model II includes some unmarried. The expected probability of receiving a bequest is calculated from the expected amount of a bequest and the number of children. The probabilities and the number of households are for people in their thirties.

the amount of saving differs between owner-occupied homeowners and renters. I also examine the relationship between housing loans and saving.

It is not an easy task to estimate the amount of saving and financial assets for particular purposes, say housing or preparing for unexpected events, although statistics on motives of saving for particular purposes are available. Individuals and households are unable to identify exactly the amount for a particular purpose except in a few cases, such as education and marriage. Horie (1985) adopted a skillful method and simplifying assumptions. Briefly, he used a combination of two sources, the stock level of monetary assets or the consumption level for each purpose, and the annual change in motives of saving for each purpose. The second source is the same as the public opinion survey on saving motives that was examined before. Of course, we have to accept significant measurement errors. Nevertheless, his attempt is a valuable contribution.

Table 7.13 presents the component of saving (flow basis) and of monetary assets (stock basis) for four major purposes: (1) future consumption except for durable goods and rents, (2) future consumption of durable goods, (3) buying land and a house, and (4) consumption in old age and unexpected events.

The following equations were used to estimate figures in table 7.13.

$$\frac{\Delta A_1}{\Delta A_0} = \frac{CG \times a_1 \times p_1}{T} \qquad \frac{\Delta A_2}{\Delta A_0} = \frac{CDK \times a_2 \times p_2}{T}$$

$$\frac{\Delta A_3}{\Delta A_0} = \frac{IHLK \times a_3 \times p_3}{T} \qquad \frac{\Delta A_4}{\Delta A_0} = \frac{PREC \times a_4 \times p_4}{T}$$

CG is consumption expenditure at constant price, excluding durable goods and rents; CDK is stock value of durable goods; $IHLK$ is asset value of land and house; $PREC$ is asset value for precautionary saving motive; $a_i(i = 1, 2, 3, 4)$ is the share of importance for each motive; and $p_i(i = 1, 2, 3, 4)$ is the price level of each item. T is defined by

$$T = (CG \times a_1 \times p_1) + (CDK \times a_2 \times p_2) + (IHLK \times a_3 \times p_3) + (PREC \times a_4 \times p_4).$$

The most important component is consumption in old age and unexpected events, and is around 50 percent according to Horie's study. The next most important is buying land and a house, which is our major concern. Its importance, however, is lower in most years (except for 1973) than consumption in old age and unexpected events. Nevertheless, it is impressive that the sum of the two components is about 80 percent.

With respect to saving for buying land and a house, I base two observations on table 7.13. The share of A_3 on the flow basis gave an increasing trend (with a minor fluctuation) until 1979, and showed a slight decrease in 1982. The share on the stock basis (i.e., the share in total monetary assets) gave a continuously increasing trend. I therefore conclude that the amount of savings for buying land and a house has increased gradually until recently. This is due

Table 7.13   **Component of Saving for Four Major Purposes (%)**

	Flow Basis				Stock Basis			
	$\Delta A_1/\Delta A_0$	$\Delta A_2/\Delta A_0$	$\Delta A_3/\Delta A_0$	$\Delta A_4/\Delta A_0$	A_1/A_0	A_2/A_0	A_3/A_0	A_4A_0
1964	16.8	1.6	23.6	58.0	16.5	1.8	21.9	59.8
1967	15.2	1.2	29.9	53.7	16.2	1.6	24.6	57.6
1970	13.2	1.2	37.0	48.6	15.2	1.4	28.5	54.9
1973	12.4	0.7	43.4	43.5	14.2	1.2	33.4	51.3
1976	14.1	0.5	35.3	50.1	14.0	0.9	35.0	50.1
1979	13.7	0.5	39.3	46.5	14.0	0.8	35.8	49.4
1982	14.1	0.4	36.4	49.1	14.0	0.7	36.4	49.0

Source: Horie 1985.

Notes: A_1 = future consumption except for durable goods and rents; A_2 = future consumption of durable goods; A_3 = buying land and house; A_4 = consumption in old age and unexpected events.

largely to the increase in housing prices, according to Horie (1985). I find an interesting contrast between the motives for saving and the amount of savings with respect to housing-related savings, because the former shows a decreasing trend, while the latter shows a minor increasing trend.

Horie also calculated the household savings rate by adding the annual payment for purchasing land and a house to the previous saving amount and dividing the sum by disposable income. He found that about 60 percent of the household savings rate was for land and a house. This is an overestimation of the saving rate. It is desirable to adjust it by subtracting the amount of depreciation for the house, as Horioka (1988) pointed out. Horioka found that housing-related saving was less important than was popularly believed.

It would be interesting to inquire into the effect of housing purchase plans and the difference in the amount of monetary assets and of debt. *Family Saving Survey* and *National Survey of Family Income and Expenditure* provide us with useful information on these issues. Since these data have been examined by various authors such as Maki (1988) and Horioka (1988), I avoid detailed interpretations and make only brief comments.

Table 7.14 shows statistics from *Family Saving Survey*. First, financial conditions such as yearly income, monetary assets, and net monetary assets (i.e., monetary assets minus debt) are considerably better for owner-occupied householders than for renters. Based on this table, age and the number of earners per household are not the variables that differentiate earning capacity between homeowners and renters. Therefore, it should be understood that the genuine earning capacity of homeowners is higher than that of renters. These capabilities may be higher education, working at larger firms, and so forth.

One important aspect of the higher amount of monetary and net monetary assets of homeowners is the influence of initial wealth. As discussed above, a nonnegligible proportion of homeowners obtained their houses through inheritance. Therefore, they did not have to make a down payment or commit to a

Table 7.14   **Housing Purchase Plan and Economic Conditions (in millions of yen)**

	Average	30–34	35–39	40–44	45–49
Owners of Homes					
Households planning to buy within 3 years					
Earners per household	1.81	1.37	1.55	1.52	1.98
Yearly income	9.54	4.95	9.12	10.76	10.15
Monetary asset	34.35	7.90	11.42	21.15	28.61
Debt outstanding for purchase of house/	14.52	4.04	7.73	31.04	21.06
land	13.85	3.14	7.20	30.68	21.02
Net monetary asset	19.83	3.86	3.69	−8.99	7.55
Households planning to buy at 3 years or later					
Earners per household	1.86	1.53	1.46	1.56	1.89
Yearly income	8.60	7.57	6.04	9.51	10.78
Monetary asset	18.37	13.06	9.19	13.32	20.21
Debt outstanding for purchase of house/	4.83	9.90	5.54	7.43	3.88
land	3.93	8.90	4.24	5.00	1.58
Net monetary asset	13.54	3.16	3.65	5.89	16.33
Households without plans to buy					
Earners per household	1.62	1.39	1.47	1.59	1.80
Yearly income	6.72	5.41	5.93	6.72	7.63
Monetary asset	14.39	5.57	7.79	9.13	11.88
Debt outstanding for purchase of house/	4.37	7.06	6.24	6.81	5.86
land	3.82	6.62	5.62	6.29	5.09
Net monetary asset	10.02	−1.49	1.55	2.32	6.02
Renters					
Households planning to buy within 3 years					
Earners per household	1.43	1.40	1.25	1.45	1.65
Yearly income	6.80	5.21	6.23	7.47	8.02
Monetary asset	14.71	7.23	12.59	15.03	11.37
Debt outstanding for purchase of house/	1.59	2.00	0.73	0.48	0.98
land	1.36	1.95	0.54	0.27	0.11
Net monetary asset	13.12	5.23	11.86	14.55	10.39
Households planning to buy at 3 years or later					
Earners per household	1.36	1.29	1.30	1.56	1.50
Yearly income	5.97	4.84	5.88	6.54	8.64
Monetary asset	9.32	5.11	9.83	8.70	19.32
Debt outstanding for purchase of house/	1.65	0.72	2.79	2.58	1.06
land	1.29	0.39	2.74	2.36	0.96
Net monetary asset	7.67	4.39	7.04	6.12	18.26
Households without plans to buy					
Earners per household	1.35	1.25	1.19	1.40	1.60
Yearly income	4.96	4.39	4.94	5.24	6.06
Monetary asset	6.31	4.09	5.95	6.00	7.16
Debt outstanding for purchase of house/	0.81	0.50	0.63	1.14	1.06
land	0.52	0.25	0.34	0.85	0.66
Net monetary asset	5.50	3.59	5.32	4.86	6.10

Source: Management and Coordination Agency, *Family Saving Survey* (1989).

housing loan. It implies that their monetary wealth accumulation had an advantage from the beginning. Unfortunately, neither *Family Saving Survey* nor *National Survey of Family Income and Expenditure* has relevant statistics to confirm this implication. However, my previous examination of bequests and inheritances supports this.

Second, households who plan to buy or build homes show higher amounts of yearly income and particularly monetary assets, regardless of the home status, than do households who have no plans. One interesting observation is that the amount of monetary assets among renters jumps considerably between age 30–34 and 35–39, because this age class corresponds to the highest rate of obtaining homes, and a large down payment is required.

Third, households in owner-occupied homes have relatively high amounts of debt. Consequently, their net monetary wealth is smaller and occasionally negative. Also, 80–90 percent of total debt outstanding is due to housing loans. This supports a view that households have to rely on housing loans when they have no other sources such as bequests and gifts, and the amount of housing loans is necessarily very high.

Fourth, as noted previously, some households gave up buying and building homes, saying that the financial burden is too severe. Yoshikawa and Ohtake (1989) took up this issue and found in their econometric study that a 20 percent increase in the price of housing would lower the renters' initial savings rate of 20 percent by about 0.25 percent. They attribute the decrease in the personal savings rate since 1974 to this factor. However, they examined only renters. Households in owner-occupied homes are influenced to a lesser extent. Excess consumption is also reported in other studies, implying that households who have not committed to housing loans have extra resources for consumption. Related to this, the effect of capital gains due to an increase in housing prices on consumption has been considerable recently.

National Survey of Family Income and Expenditure shows the rate of saving for each category of housing status. In 1984, the household saving rate (ages 30–49) was 16 percent for homeowners, 11 percent for renters who plan to buy homes within five years, and 7 percent for renters who have no plans. These numbers are reported in Maki (1988). The higher saving rate of homeowners is caused by the fact that their repayment of housing loans is one form of savings (flow basis), and the lower rate of saving of renters is caused by the fact that their payment of rent is counted as consumption, which reduces saving unavoidably.

It would be useful to examine the role of housing loans in housing purchase and in the relationship between consumption and saving. As emphasized previously, a lot of households rely on housing loans, and repayment of them implies saving. Table 7.15 presents the incidence of housing loans and their amounts for various housing conditions, incomes, and ages. Owners of collective homes show a rate of loan commitment almost twice as high as that for owner-occupied (detached) houses. Also, the amount of debt is almost double,

Table 7.15   Outstanding Debt by Housing Status, Income, and Age

	1981		1985	
	Rate (%)	Debt (millions of yen)	Rate (%)	Debt (millions of yen)
Housing status				
Owner-occupied detached house	32.3	2.54	33.9	2.49
Owner-occupied collective home	63.1	5.03	60.5	5.04
Renter of private detached house	5.7	0.44	5.2	0.52
Renter of private collective home	2.1	0.41	3.2	0.43
Renter of public home	2.2	0.28	4.0	0.37
Home or room owned by organization	10.2	0.68	8.8	0.70
Annual household income (in millions of yen)				
Less than 2.5	13.3	0.90	15.0	1.14
2.5–3.5	15.9	1.09	15.5	0.93
3.5–4.5	26.8	2.02	24.1	1.64
4.5–6.0	34.9	2.54	31.7	2.47
6.0 and over	38.3	4.25	40.3	4.27
Household head's age				
10–29	8.8	0.74	7.0	0.52
30–39	27.7	2.19	28.0	2.18
40–49	30.2	2.46	40.3	3.14
50–59	24.7	1.87	26.1	1.73
60 and over	12.5	1.22	12.3	1.00

Source: Department of Sociology, University of Tokyo, *Survey on Consciousness and Objects of Savings* (in Japanese).

for two reasons. On the one hand, the price of collective homes is on average higher than the price of (detached) houses partly because collective homes are constructed mainly in urban areas, while houses are constructed in both urban and rural areas. On the other hand, households, who prefer houses to collective homes, are likely to have had higher income and/or monetary assets and so do not require higher amounts of housing loans. It is also possible that many households inherited their houses from parents. We should not forget that construction of collective homes is a recent phenomenon (for about twenty or at most thirty years) in Japan, which does limit the number of inheritances at this stage.

Further, both the rate and the amount of housing loans increase as the household income level increases. This is because high-income households normally buy more expensive homes and are less likely to face liquidity (i.e., borrowing) constraints than low-income households.

Finally, households in their forties have the highest rate and amount of housing loans. Those in their thirties and fifties follow, and those in their twenties and sixties commit to housing loans very marginally. This observation is consistent with the statement that households attempt to buy and build homes if necessary when they reach their thirties with mostly housing loans, and terminate their repayments in their late forties or fifties. This is one of the typical life courses of the Japanese. I emphasize that the existence of inheritance alters such courses considerably.

How heavy is the burden of housing loans, particularly repayment? Since repayment of housing loans is one of the components of savings, it is worthwhile to examine a time-series change. Figure 7.3 shows the historical change in the ratio of debt outstanding (and debt for housing) to annual income. This ratio clearly shows a gradual but steady increase. Currently, it reaches over 40 percent. It is quite natural that some households feel too heavy a burden from housing debt and give up purchasing homes.

The most important consequence of housing loans is its "contractual, committed, or forced saving." (I call it forced saving for short.) Normally, a housing loan contract is kept for over twenty years. Households have to repay its interest and principal until the end of a contract. During the period, forced saving continues. According to Muramoto (1989), the average monthly repayment is 69,500 yen for houses with the public-housing loan program, and 94,240 yen for houses with pension-program housing loans.

The two major types of forced saving are repayment of loans (mostly housing and sometimes durable goods) and contribution to life and casualty insurance and pensions. Obviously, the repayment of housing loans and contribution to life insurance are the most important. Tachibanaki and Shimono (1988) found that forced saving had increased continuously in Japan. Incidentally, over 50 percent of saving in Japan is forced saving, and the repayment of housing loans is responsible for this higher rate, based on the monthly amount of repayment.

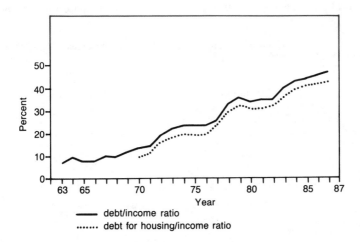

Fig. 7.3   The ratio of debt outstanding (and housing loan) to annual income (%)
Source: Management and Coordination Agency, *Family Saving Survey* (various years).

This high rate of forced saving has several economic implications. First, since households have difficulty in modifying the amount of forced saving, the degree of fluctuation in the saving rate in Japan is necessarily lowered nowadays. Second, a higher rate of forced saving is observed among households whose ages are between thirty-five and fifty-five years, because they show the highest rate and the largest amount of housing loans. I emphasize that, historically speaking, the highest rate of forced saving is in the 1980s and 1990s, since these generations are a large share of the population. The importance of forced saving will decline in the twenty-first century, partly because Japan will face an aging society that does not have large housing loans, and partly because households will rely on housing loans less and less in anticipation of obtaining homes relatively easily through inheritances (see Tachibanaki 1991).

Unlike the scenario above, a large number of households are currently obliged to bear a heavy burden of repayment of housing loans. Households who have lower annual incomes have to bear a heavier burden, about 25 percent of annual income for the first quintile income class and 21 percent for the second one, than those who have higher annual incomes, 16.3 percent for the fourth quintile class and 14.0 percent for the fifth one. These are the ratios of the annual repayment to annual income estimated by the Public Housing Loan Agency. In other words, the poor are obliged to accept a higher rate of forced saving than the rich. It is not surprising that a considerable number of poor households give up homes because of a heavy repayment burden.

It is useful to investigate the extent to which households are obliged to abandon the idea of housing purchase plans because of the heavy repayment burden. Maki (1988) performed an interesting simulation study, investigating the difference between an increase in housing prices and an increase in interest rates for housing loans. Table 7.16 shows the results, obtained under several behavioral assumptions of consumption and housing purchase for households

Table 7.16   Simulation of Housing Purchase by Housing Price and Interest Rate

	Housing Price (millions of yen)	Real Interest Rate of Deposit (%)	Real Interest Rate of Loan (%)	Retirement Age	Rate of purchase by Age (%) 32	37	42	47	Accumulated Purchase Rate (%)
Actual					4	26	15	4	49
Simulated									
1	30	3	5	60	5	13	16	14	48
2	27	3	5	60	9	18	23	19	69
3	33	3	5	60	2	8	10	10	30
4	30	3	6	60	4	13	16	11	44
5	30	3	5	60	5	16	19	18	58

Source: Maki 1988.

and income distribution. Rows 1, 2, and 3 give the effect of a change in housing prices, while rows 1, 4, and 5 give the effect of a change in interest rates for housing loans. The simulation suggests that the effect of housing prices is more important than that of interest rates with respect to the rate of housing purchases. Increasing the housing price from 30 million yen to 33 million yen lowers the purchase rate from 48 percent to 30 percent, and decreasing the price to 27 million yen raises the rate to 69 percent. Increasing the interest rate from 5 percent to 6 percent lowers the purchase rate from 48 percent to 44 percent, and decreasing interest to 3 percent raises the rate to 58 percent. An increase in housing prices is a more serious obstacle than an increase in interest rates, so long as we are concerned only with a rational and economic calculation.

However, there are at least two reasons for proposing that the effect of interest rates for housing loans is equally crucial. First, the previous simulation pays no attention to differences among income classes. As we saw, lower-income classes bear a heavier burden caused by housing loans than higher-income classes. Consequently, a higher proportion of the lower-income classes is obliged to give up house buying, because of the heavy repayment burden. Second, the rational and economic calculation is not the sole criterion to buy homes. Some households may dislike the psychological burden of repayment of housing loans and lose incentive to buy a home, even if they have enough financial resources. They may also like to spend their financial resources on items other than housing.

7.6 Housing and Wealth Accumulation

This section evaluates the relationship between housing and wealth accumulation. Land and a house are important sources of real (or physical) assets, and they have market values that can be assessed by both the current price and the historical price. One's gross asset or wealth value is the sum of physical assets and monetary assets, and net wealth is this sum minus debt. I am concerned with both gross wealth and net wealth and examine the effect of housing purchase on the course of wealth accumulation and distribution. Therefore, land and a house are analyzed in the framework of asset choices, and the return to physical wealth is examined.

Which group would increase their wealth more, homeowners or renters who never obtained homes? Homeowners' wealth increases by both physical and financial assets (sometimes including debt), while renters' wealth increases only in financial assets. The difference in the rates of return of physical assets and financial assets plays a crucial role.

Several studies have estimated the difference in wealth accumulation between homeowners and renters by using cohort data and cross-sectional data. Cohort data are certainly preferable for investigating wealth accumulation but are unavailable for Japan except indirectly. I examine several studies briefly.

Tachibanaki and Shimono (1986) examined transformed cohort data and found that the lifetime balance (i.e., bequest) is positive for a household who bought a home in the past. The longer a household owned its home, the higher the lifetime balance is. Most lifelong renters are unable to have a positive life balance and thus to leave any bequest. These results imply that households who bought homes even with housing loans could accumulate considerably more wealth than households who kept only financial assets and lived at rental homes. This study did not consider regional differences but took account of income classes and demographic differences.

Sanwa Soken (1990) also estimated cohort data, proposing that a household in a large urban area that buys a home with a housing loan will accumulate after thirty years wealth that is about 5.4 times higher than a household that rents and keep its initial financial asset for thirty years. In a rural area the difference is much smaller. This study assumes the recent rate of increase in land prices will continue for the next thirty years. This assumption is over-simplified.

The *White Paper on Household Living Conditions* in 1987 calculated the difference in wealth increase between homeowning and holding only financial assets. Figure 7.4 shows the average annual increases in wealth values. The year in the figure indicates that a choice among the four alternatives was made in that year, and the terminal year is 1986. Case I is choosing an owner-occupied house in Tokyo and repaying a housing loan; case II is choosing an owner-occupied house in cities other than Tokyo and repaying a housing loan; case III is choosing a rental home and paying rent that is half as much as

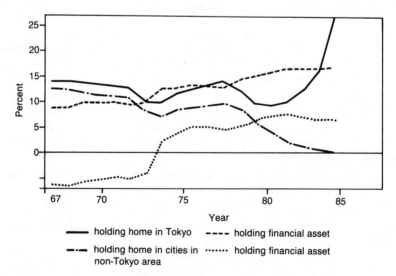

Fig. 7.4   Profitability of holding financial assets versus homeowning
Source: Economic Planning Agency, *White Paper on National Life Standard* (1987).

repaying a housing loan; and case IV is choosing a rental home and paying rent that is as much as repaying a housing loan. It is assumed that rent increases at the rate for the price of consumer goods, and that people decide to save or not, depending on whether they rent or they commit to a housing loan.

This study found a considerable fluctuation of the rate of increase in asset values among renters and homeowners. The above is true for all cities. The rate of increase for households in owner-occupied homes in the non-Tokyo area was higher in the past and has declined constantly. Holding only financial assets (i.e., renters) shows a higher rate of increase in asset values than homeowning currently. Homeowners in Tokyo had a higher rate of increase in asset values than renters in several years, but the order was reversed in other years. Currently, owner-occupied homes are considerably more advantageous in Tokyo. The difference between case III and case IV is very big. In other words, the amount of rent paid is crucial for the determination of the wealth increase. A renter who lives in an expensive home has to sacrifice an increase in wealth.

The above results suggest a need to examine whether households make a portfolio choice between physical assets and financial assets in a systematic way, to maximize the amount of their wealth. The rate of returns on physical assets and financial assets are key variables in the systematic demand theory. Tanigawa and Tachibanaki (1991) estimated a portfolio choice function for one real asset, namely land and a house, and four different financial assets by adopting a standard demand theory with a qualitative response econometric approach. They concluded that holding real assets could not be explained by such a standard portfolio demand theory. Therefore, it is possible that a household makes a decision about holding real assets not on the basis only of the rates of return on real assets and financial assets, but on the basis of various factors.

We can derive the following implications from the above studies. First, the difference between large urban areas (Tokyo and Kansai) and nonurban areas is important for the determination of total wealth accumulation and physical assets versus financial assets. Households in large urban areas accumulated wealth thanks to the recent increase in land prices. Takayama et al. (1990) estimated that the amount of total assets (both physical and financial) per household in Japan had increased from 20.8 million yen in 1984 to 34.3 million yen in 1987, while the total assets in Tokyo had increased from 42.7 million yen to 124.1 million yen during the same period. Households in Tokyo benefited greatly by obtaining their own homes for the purpose of wealth maximization.

Second, it is not certain yet whether households in rural areas should buy homes with housing loans to maximize wealth. If they do buy a house, however, it is certainly preferable to buy it at younger ages rather than older ages to maximize wealth.

Third, the above studies all ignored the contribution of inheritances. In other words, the condition of initial wealth holding was not taken into account. If it was considered, the course of wealth accumulation would be quite different. I have already examined it to a certain extent in this paper. As Tachibanaki and Shimono (1991) pointed out, households who may receive larger amounts of bequests would be able to have higher rates of wealth accumulation than households who could receive smaller or no bequests.

Noguchi (1990) confirmed the above implication. According to the survey conducted by his group, the average current physical asset value of households who inherited land is about 200 million yen in the Tokyo area, while the average asset value of households who bought land with their own financial resources is about 86 million yen. The asset value of households who inherited in Saitama prefecture is three times higher than the asset value of households who bought land with their own financial resources.

Wealth distribution became a serious problem in contemporary Japan for the obvious reasons described above. Both owning land and a house in urban areas and inheriting land and a house are the important factors in Japan's unequal wealth distribution. This inequality is a serious and devastating problem, in my opinion. It may destroy the institutional socioeconomic background that led Japan to perform relatively well. See Tachibanaki (1989) for a more extensive argument on the subject.

7.7 Conclusion

This chapter gave an overview of the relationship between housing and saving in Japan. Various issues such as (1) saving motives and purposes, (2) housing purchase and housing conditions, (3) bequests and housing, (4) housing purchase, housing loan, and saving, and (5) housing and wealth distribution were examined. These interrelated issues determine the level of saving behavior.

References

Barthold, T. A., and T. Ito. 1992. Bequest Taxes and Accumulation of Household Wealth: U.S.-Japan Comparison. In *The Political Economy of Tax Reform,* ed. T. Ito and A. O. Krueger, 235–92. Chicago: University of Chicago Press.

Hayashi, F. 1986. Why Is Japan's Saving Rate So Apparently High? In *NBER Macroeconomics Annual,* ed. S. Fischer, 1: 147–210.

Hayashi, F., A. Ando, and R. Ferris. 1988. Life Cycle and Bequest Savings: A Study of Japanese and U.S. Households Based on Data from the 1984 NSFIE and the 1983 Survey of Consumer Finance. *Journal of the Japanese and International Economies* 2 (2): 450–91.

Hayashi, F, T. Ito, and J. Slemrod. 1988. Housing Finance Imperfections, Taxation, and Private Saving: A Comparative Simulation Analysis of the United States and Japan. *Journal of the Japanese and International Economies* 2 (3): 215–38.

Horie, Y. 1985. Research on the Contemporary Japanese Economy: An Empirical Analysis of Household Saving and Consumption Behavior (in Japanese). Tokyo: Toyo Keizai Shinposha.

Horioka, C. Y. 1985. The Importance of Saving for Education in Japan. *Kyoto University Economic Review* 55 (1): 47–58.

————. 1987. The Cost of Marriages and Marriage-Related Saving in Japan. *Kyoto University Economic Review* 57 (1): 47–58.

————. 1988. Saving for Housing Purchase in Japan. *Journal of the Japanese and International Economies* 2 (3): 351–84.

————. 1990. The Importance of Life Cycle Saving in Japan: A Novel Reestimation Method. *ISER Discussion Paper* 225.

Maki, A. 1988. Saving and Financial Asset Choice of Households in Japan (in Japanese). In *Money and Richness,* ed. Center for Saving Economy, 137–76. Tokyo: Gyosei.

Muramoto, T. 1989. Saving and Debt (in Japanese). In *Saving and Life in Affluent Ages,* ed. Center for Saving Economy, 183–228. Tokyo: Gyosei.

Noguchi, Y. 1990. The Role of Intergenerational Transfer in the Formation of Household Asset (in Japanese). *JILI Forum* (1): 6–17.

Sanwa Soken. 1990. *Future Course of Wealth Accumulation* (in Japanese). Report of the Sanwa Soken.

Tachibanaki, T. 1989. Volatility of Asset Prices and Inequality in Wealth Distribution (in Japanese). *JCER Economic Journal* 18: 79–93. English version: Japan's New Policy Agenda: Coping with Unequal Asset Distribution. *Journal of Japanese Studies* (Summer 1989): 345–69.

————. 1990. Life Cycle and Asset Choice (in Japanese). In *Aging Trend, Saving, and Asset Choice,* ed. Center for Saving Economy, 71–98. Tokyo: Gyosei.

————. 1991. An Analysis of Savings: Contracted or Discretionary, and for Real Asset Holding or for Financial Asset Holding (in Japanese)? *The Quarterly of Social Security Research* 27: 245–64.

Tachibanaki, T., and K. Shimono. 1986. Saving and the Life-Cycle. *Journal of Public Economics* 31: 1–24.

————. 1988. Household Saving, Life Insurance, and Public Pension (in Japanese). *Bunken Journal* 82: 23–58.

————. 1990. Wealth Accumulation Process by Income Class. *Journal of the Japanese and International Economies* 5 (3): 239–60.

Takayama, N., et al. 1990. Household Asset and Saving Rate in Japan (in Japanese). *Keizai Bunseki* 116.

Tanigawa, Y., and T. Tachibanaki. 1991. Cross-section Analysis of Household Portfolio: A Simultaneous Equation Approach (in Japanese). In *Economic Analysis of Monetary Function,* ed. K. Matsuura and T. Tachibanaki. Tokyo: Toyo Keizai Shinposha.

Yoshikawa, H., and F. Ohtake. 1989. An Analysis of Female Labor Supply, Housing Demand, and the Saving Rate in Japan. *European Economic Review* 33 (5): 997–1022.

8 Housing and Saving in the United States

Jonathan Skinner

8.1 Introduction

Between 1955 and 1970, the share of owner-occupied housing in total household net wealth hovered around 21 percent. In the nine years between 1970 and 1979, housing wealth climbed to 30 percent of net wealth (Board of Governors 1991).[1] During the 1970s, the increased value of owner-occupied housing delivered a $700 billion windfall (in 1986 dollars) to homeowners. While the share of housing has since fallen to 28 percent, it is likely that consumption and saving decisions by American households have been affected by this fundamental shift in the size and composition of U.S. household wealth.

How has this shift in housing prices affected aggregate capital accumulation? Will the combination of higher long-term inflation rates and higher real housing prices since the 1970s depress future nonresidential saving? The first goal of this paper is to survey the growing literature on life-cycle housing decisions to shed light on these issues. Such empirical and theoretical studies have examined the "tilting" of real mortgage payments during periods of high inflation, the down-payment constraint, the introduction of home equity loans, mobility decisions of the elderly, and the impact of uncertainty in asset returns—including housing assets—on household portfolios. The implication of these studies appears to be that both higher real housing prices and higher inflation rates should have only a small impact on aggregate capital accumulation in the long run.

Jonathan Skinner is professor of economics at the University of Virginia and a research associate of the National Bureau of Economic Research.

The author is especially grateful to Jonathan Feinstein, Don Fullerton, Patric Hendershott, Charles Horioka, Martin Feldstein, James Poterba, and conference participants for insightful suggestions, and to Daniel Feenberg and Marjorie Flavin for assistance with data sources.

1. Wolf (1989) calculated that owner-occupied equity as a fraction of total wealth in 1980 was at its highest level in this century.

Most of the theoretical work has been couched in terms of steady-state comparisons between equilibrium solutions. In the theoretical models, shifts in the underlying structure of the model are anticipated, and the economy has time to adjust to the new regime. For those who rode the tide of higher housing prices in the 1970s and parts of the 1980s, the shift in housing wealth was largely unanticipated and the economy's response largely short-run in nature. The second goal of this paper is to examine how the *unexpected* wealth increase in the 1970s affected both individual portfolios and aggregate saving behavior in the short run.

The standard life-cycle model predicts that an unanticipated increase in housing wealth should have a much larger impact on aggregate saving in the shortterm. Homeowners are predicted to increase consumption in response to the windfall. Indeed, some economists have attributed the low saving rate in the 1980s to the consumption behavior of homeowners unlocking their housing capital gains with home equity loans or by drawing down other assets. When the life-cycle model is expanded to include a bequest motive, however, the answer is less clear. In 1988, the Economist conjectured that "most of those who inherit their parents' home . . . will regard the proceeds of their parents' thrift as an insurance against poverty in their old age. So, for the time being, they will save, converting their parents' physical assets into financial equity of their own." (April 9, 1988, 13).

That is, the question of whether housing windfalls are spent or passed along to future generations is crucial to understanding how the housing windfall has affected aggregate saving. As is shown below, the evidence is not entirely clear on this question; aggregate data appear to support the notion that housing wealth is spent, but microeconomic data suggest that the housing wealth is saved.

The converse of this unexpected wealth enjoyed by existing homeowners is the unexpected high housing prices faced by potential house buyers. The third goal of the paper is to examine how higher housing prices affects current renters. In comparing saving behavior across metropolitan areas, Sheiner (1990) found that higher housing prices encourage saving for the now larger down payment. That is, the shift in housing prices—particularly in urban areas—could have indirectly spurred overall wealth accumulation by the young.

The final goal is to measure how the fundamental change in housing values has affected the riskiness of household portfolios. Are current younger households facing greater economic uncertainty as a result of overleveraged houses? I use the *Survey of Consumer Finances* from 1969 and 1986 to show that the ratio of mortgage principal to housing value actually declined during the period, suggesting that households are not at appreciably greater risk from highly leveraged housing. If families are not more leveraged, then are they at greater risk from volatile housing prices? Evidence from the *Panel Study of Income Dynamics* (PSID) suggests that housing prices were only slightly more variable in the late 1970s than they were in the late 1960s.

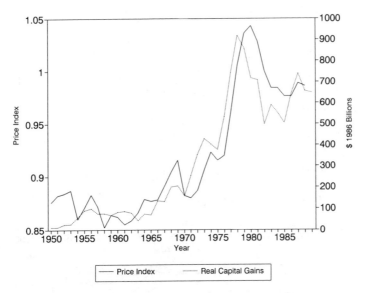

Fig. 8.1   Housing prices and housing real capital gains, 1950–89
Sources: McFadden 1992; Federal Reserve System, various years.

The next section documents the broad-based change in the housing wealth of the United States during the 1970s. First, the dramatic capital gains in housing wealth during the 1970s are documented using aggregate data from the Federal Reserve Bank's balance sheets. Second, microeconomic evidence from the *Survey of Consumer Finances* in 1969 and 1986 is used to establish two empirical regularities: housing equity makes up a majority of total wealth for the median household, and housing equity grew relatively uniformly between 1969 and 1986 across both age and income groups. That is, changes in housing value during the 1970s had a major impact on the asset positions of a large fraction of U.S. households.[2]

8.2   An Overview of Housing Wealth

Figure 8.1 shows the real index of housing prices between 1950 and 1989 based on the Commerce Department deflators for housing prices and quality indices (McFadden 1992). Following gradual stagnation of housing prices in the 1950s and 1960s, prices turned up sharply by 18 percent in the 1970s before a decline in the 1980s.

These price shifts led to substantial changes in wealth holdings. Figure 8.1

---

2. By contrast, changes in the value of financial wealth such as stocks affect consumption and saving decisions of only the 28 percent of families that own any stocks at all (Mankiw and Zeldes 1991).

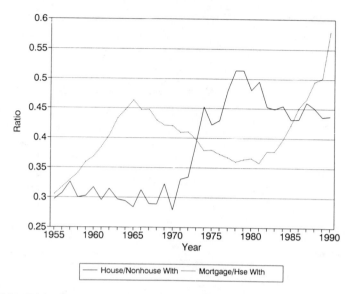

Fig. 8.2   Ratio of housing to nonhousing wealth, and mortgage to housing wealth, 1955–90
Sources: Federal Reserve System, various years.

documents the magnitude of capital gains—or wealth appreciation net of new investment—in the housing market. Using 1950 as the benchmark, Federal Reserve Board data on housing and landholdings are used to calculate accumulated real capital gains in owner-occupied housing.[3] By the end of the 1970s, accumulated capital gains in housing neared $1 trillion. To express this in another way, average capital gains in housing between 1970 and 1978 was 42 percent of average real personal saving.[4]

Housing has become a more important element in the aggregate wealth portfolio. Figure 8.2 graphs the ratio of owner-occupied housing assets to net nonhousing wealth between 1955 and 1990.[5] This ratio has grown from 0.31 in the 1960s to a high of 0.49 in 1979, when housing was at a high and stock markets at a low, before declining through the 1980s. Even in 1990, this ratio was 15 percentage points higher than in 1965.

The ratio of mortgage debt to total housing wealth, reported in figure 8.2, is a good measure of the degree of leverage in housing markets. Not surprisingly, the ratio of mortgages to housing wealth fell during the 1970s to a low of 0.35

3. As McFadden (1990) notes, his price index excludes changes in land prices. However, his index matches the pattern of wealth changes quite closely, and those wealth changes include land.
4. Personal saving does not include capital appreciation in housing.
5. Note that this aggregate measure includes nonhousing wealth of renters as well as homeowners. Net nonhousing wealth is calculated as net wealth less durables less owner-occupied housing and land. Unfortunately, assets of trust and nonprofit organizations are included with these household figures. See Board of Governors (1991).

Table 8.1   **Housing Equity and Tenure, 1986**

Age	Homeowner (%)	Equity/ Net Worth	Median Equity/ Net Worth
Under 31	40.4	.480	.597
31–40	57.5	.443	.604
41–50	70.5	.354	.563
51–60	78.3	.287	.613
61–70	70.9	.239	.545
Over 71	65.0	.264	.611

Source: Survey of Consumer Finances, 1986.

in 1979—mortgages tend to be fixed nominally and adjust slowly over time, while the value of housing changes more rapidly. What is more surprising is that even during the mixed housing markets of the 1980s, the leverage ratio has more than rebounded from its previous low level. By 1990, the ratio was 58 percent, 23 percentage points higher than the equivalent ratio in 1965. Some part of the increase was caused by the relatively tax-favored status of housing mortgages following the Tax Reform Act of 1986.

Aggregate household wealth measures are useful for assessing changes in the overall capital stock, but given the skewed distribution of wealth, they provide less information about the extent to which households are affected by the changes in asset value. For example, one might expect that changes in the stock market might affect the consumption of households that own stock, but 72 percent of households own no stocks at all (Mankiw and Zeldes 1991). To measure the extent to which housing price changes might affect consumption choice across households, I use microeconomic data from the 1969 and 1986 *Survey of Consumer Finances.* While they share the same name, the 1969 survey was administered by the Michigan Survey Research Center and focused largely on durable and automobile purchases, so the wealth data are less complete than for the 1986 survey.[6]

Table 8.1 presents summary statistics on home ownership and the share of housing wealth to total wealth for the 1986 sample only, with families weighted to be representative of the total population.[7] The first column tabulates the percentage of families in that age group who own a house. The percentage who own houses rises from 40 percent under age 31 to a peak of 78.3 percent for ages 51–60.

Focusing on the importance of housing in the wealth portfolio for homeown-

6. The unit of observation is neither the family or the individual, but the automobile. Hence a family with three cars would appear in the sample three times. The subsequent analysis has corrected for this unusual weighting scheme.

7. Observations were deleted if income was below $2,000 or if—for homeowners—either the house market value was less than $2,000 or if mortgage payments were not made on a monthly basis. A total of 2,726 observations remained, of which 2,148 represented homeowners.

Table 8.2   Housing Equity and Income by Age, 1969 and 1986

Age	Housing Equity, 1986	Change in Equity, 1969–86 (%)	Family Income, 1986	Change in Income, 1969–86 (%)
Under 31	27,494	50.13	32,241	1.84
31–40	40,396	32.89	38,709	2.92
41–50	69,411	75.08	50,035	24.22
51–60	74,560	42.15	40,714	15.59
61–70	76,397	67.68	31,020	61.38
Over 71	60,490	64.78	25,206	44.17

Source: Survey of Consumer Finances 1969, 1986.

ers, table 8.1 details the aggregate share of housing equity to total net wealth for each age group. Aggregate housing equity accounts for less than half of total net wealth, with the fraction falling to roughly one-quarter at ages above 51. These fractions are not representative of the typical family, however, because of the highly skewed distribution of nonhousing wealth. A better measure of the importance of housing is the (weighted) median ratio of housing equity to net household wealth, again broken down by age. Table 8.1 suggests no age trend in this ratio; the *median* homeowner holds slightly more than half of his wealth in housing equity regardless of age. That is, at least in the 1986 cross-section, housing equity and nonhousing wealth is accumulated at roughly the same rate as homeowners age.

Were the aggregate increases in housing wealth concentrated within a few age groups or income groups? Table 8.2 details the changes, for homeowners, in housing equity and income in constant 1986 dollars. There is a consistent rise in the real value of home equity across age groups, with the largest increase, 75 percent, for those aged 41–50.[8] In part, these increases may be a consequence of the overall rise in family income during the same period. But as table 8.2 shows, the average increase in real income was at most half of the percentage increase in home equity, at least for those under the age of 61.

The increase in home equity across income groups was not as evenly distributed. For homeowners only, table 8.3 presents a comparison of housing equity in 1969 and 1986 by income decile, once again expressed in 1986 dollars.[9] For most deciles, real housing equity rose by roughly 50 percent over the period. Not every group experienced an increase in housing equity; decile 3 registered

8. These are not comparisons among "synthetic cohorts"; a homeowner who was 28 in 1969 would have been in the "<31" category in that year but in the "51–60" category in 1986.

9. The income deciles were created by the *Survey of Consumer Finances* for the entire sample. Hence the subsample of homeowners is likely to be underrepresented in the lower deciles.

a 13 percent decline. By contrast, housing equity for the highest income decile more than doubled.

In summary, despite its relatively small share of total national wealth, housing is a dominant asset for the majority of American households that own homes. The dramatic changes in housing wealth during the past two decades were widely distributed across many groups, although middle-aged and higher-income families appeared to have experienced the greatest growth in housing equity between 1969 and 1986. Section 8.3 addresses a much harder issue, which is how this broad-based change in wealth might be expected to affect long-term capital accumulation.

8.3   Housing in the Life-Cycle Model

The life-cycle model of consumption is the standard workhorse for analyzing housing and saving decisions. This section reviews the basic results arising from the theoretical models, and asks how well these models explain the observed changes discussed in section 8.2. I restrict the analysis to owner-occupied housing.

It is easiest to begin with a partial equilibrium life-cycle model under complete certainty. If moving costs were negligible, financing considerations ignored, housing perfectly divisible (either rented or owner-occupied), and capital markets perfect, then the life-cycle model would predict that housing consumption would be chosen continuously in conjunction with other types of consumption. Housing investment could then be chosen according to an optimal portfolio rule, but it would not necessarily be equal to optimal housing consumption.

Table 8.3   **Housing Equity and Income by Decile, 1969 and 1986**

Decile	Housing Equity, 1986	Change in Equity, 1969–86 (%)	Family Income, 1986	Change in Income, 1969–86 (%)
1	35,249	52.55	3,985	0.61
2	35,782	6.53	7,613	−0.65
3	40,234	−12.94	11,660	−4.70
4	47,809	73.39	15,480	−6.90
5	40,811	57.73	19,993	−5.15
6	47,035	45.57	25,149	−0.83
7	51,265	44.34	30,891	2.70
8	52,274	58.96	38,379	8.81
9	67,972	65.77	49,019	14.46
10	128,898	101.04	108,054	47.59

Source: Survey of Consumer Finances 1969, 1986.

A number of authors have pointed out the implausibility of such a model and have introduced a variety of factors to make the analysis of housing more realistic. They have focused on (1) a down-payment constraint, (2) equality between housing held for consumption and housing held for investment, (3) moving costs, and (4) high initial real mortgage payments during an inflationary period, or "tilt."

Restrictions by banks on borrowing lead to minimum requirements not only for current income, but also for current liquid wealth. Hence high lifetime-income but low current-wealth families could be constrained by higher housing prices either to defer home ownership or to begin with a smaller ("starter") house at early ages. Jones (1990), for example, found that the presence of liquid assets was a very strong positive predictor of home ownership, holding current earnings constant, in a sample of young Canadians. Liquid wealth may have a weaker impact on housing demand in the United States; in Canada, mortgages neither allow tax-deductible interest payments nor twenty–thirty-year loan periods.

The second complication in typical housing markets is that the consumption of owner-occupied housing is typically limited by the amount invested (Henderson and Ioannides 1983). This constraint, coupled with a minimum house size, implies not only that households must balance consumption demand for housing with optimal investment choices, but that the lumpy nature of housing may leave their wealth portfolio highly undiversified for moderate lengths of time.

Moving costs introduces a third element of rigidity (or "stickiness") to housing choices. Grossman and Laroque (1990) develop an elegant generalized model of durable purchases and show that small moving costs may lead to considerable rigidity in durable (or housing) consumption. This result suggests that changes in the timing of housing consumption over the life cycle have relatively little impact on lifetime utility. The intuition is as follows: Suppose that without adjustment costs a family would move six times during the life cycle. With the introduction of a small adjustment cost, the family moves only four times. Hence the utility loss (in dollar terms) of the existence of adjustment costs is bounded from above by only twice the small adjustment cost.[10]

Finally, high persistent inflation rates coupled with fixed nominal mortgage interest payments leads to a "tilting" of real mortgage payments (Kearl 1979; Schwab 1983). Inflation raises the nominal interest rate and thereby increases the fixed nominal mortgage interest payment. This in turn tilts the real mortgage interest flows toward earlier payments. While the nominal payment is fixed for the life of the mortgage, the real payment gradually declines over time. For example, Schwab (1983) considers two thirty-year mortgages of $20,000, each with a real interest rate of 3 percent (and ignoring tax issues). In the first case, inflation is zero, and real (and nominal) annual payments are

10. In practice, of course, adjustment costs may be substantial.

$1,020. In the second case, the inflation rate is 8 percent and the nominal rate 11 percent. Real mortgage payments vary from $2,130 in the first year to only $229 in the final year.

Suppose that the increase in housing prices during the 1970s was a permanent change. According to the theoretical model, housing purchases are likely to be deferred because of down-payment constraints and the restrictions on borrowing. The equality of housing investments and housing consumption may further discourage purchases of housing, since a larger expenditure share would also imply a larger and less balanced portfolio share of housing. Mobility may also rise as households must closely match housing size with their current (rather than future) income.[11] The consequent rise in adjustment costs from more frequent moves might further reduce the demand for housing.

How would housing prices affect overall saving? Obviously, a higher house price implies fewer nonhousing assets. To the extent that families defer house purchases, overall (nonhousing) saving may be increased. For example, Krumm and Kelly (1989) present evidence that saving rises prior to the house purchase to meet the down payment, and after the house purchase to rebuild liquid assets. Still it is unlikely in the aggregate that changes in the time path or in the composition of housing and nonhousing consumption will have a large impact on aggregate capital accumulation. Hayashi, Ito, and Slemrod (1988) developed a life-cycle model to test how higher housing prices would affect aggregate saving. They applied the model to the Japanese economy and suggested that the higher Japanese housing prices relative to the United States account for only a small fraction of the overall differences in saving rates between the two countries.

Inflation is predicted to have an ambiguous impact on housing demand. The tilt effect tends to encourage the deferral of housing purchases and to reduce the total quantity of housing (Schwab 1983; Kearl 1979). Because the tilt effect increases real mortgage payments when the house is purchased (from $1,020 to $2,130 in the example above), prospective home buyers may find that limitations on mortgage payments as a fraction of current income require them to come up with a larger down payment. Hence inflation could render the minimum down-payment constraint superfluous.

Offsetting this effect is the potential tax advantage of home ownership in an inflationary world. The nominal appreciation of owner-occupied housing is essentially untaxed.[12] Hence when inflation and the nominal interest rate both rise in tandem (the orthodox Fisher effect), both the real return on alternative

11. That is, suppose that anticipated earnings in the future are large. A family might choose to purchase a larger house now to avoid the transactions costs of moving in the future. With more expensive housing prices (and a tilt in mortgage payments), families are less able to anticipate future housing demand because of down-payment or mortgage constraints.

12. The effective tax rate on housing wealth gains is very low because of the $125,000 allowance for capital gains of housing for owners over age fifty-five and the stepped-up basis at death.

nonhousing investment and the real cost of mortgage financing fall, conferring a greater advantage to home ownership over other forms of wealth.

Housing would not benefit from inflation in the presence of taxation if nominal interest rates rose by a sufficient amount to keep the after-tax real return unchanged.[13] The intuition is that the after-tax rate of return on alternative, nonhousing assets is unchanged in the presence of heightened inflation, so the asset value of housing is similarly unchanged. There is little evidence to support this modified Fisher effect; empirical evidence suggests that nominal interest rates rise by at most the change in inflation (Tanzi 1980; Melvin 1982). Goodwin (1986) finds that the tax-inflation benefits and the tilt effect roughly cancel each other out, implying that anticipated inflation has a neutral impact on housing demand in the long term.

How might inflation affect the degree of leverage in the house? On the one hand, households may seek to increase their initial leverage rate because of the shortened real duration of their mortgage.[14] On the other hand, bank requirements restricting the ratio of nominal mortgage payments to nominal income would restrict leverage, forcing new home buyers to provide larger down payments. As is shown in section 8.7, the empirical result that leverage rates have not changed dramatically between 1969 and 1986 lends some credence to the view that these two effects also offset one another.

One potential solution to the tilt problem currently being considered by the U.S. government is to offer inflation-adjusted mortgage policies. Under this plan, households would pay only the real interest rate (nominal interest minus inflation), with the inflation premium rolled back into the mortgage principal. Kearl (1979) suggested that such a plan would increase the demand for housing substantially. Of course, by stimulating demand for an asset that already enjoys tax advantages, the net impact on nonresidential saving and government revenue might be negative.

The orthodox life-cycle model has strong predictions about the housing decisions of the elderly—they should be dipping into home equity and possibly downsizing their home. Section 8.4 examines in more detail the empirical support for these predictions.

8.4   Housing Demand by the Elderly

Housing is both a consumption good and an investment good. While the life-cycle model may have little to say about consumption by the elderly, it does imply that retired households should gradually spend down both housing and nonhousing wealth. A number of recent studies, however, have found little

---

13. That is, the nominal interest rate would rise by $1/(1 - t)$ points for every point increase in the inflation rate, leaving the real after-tax return on nonhousing equity unchanged (Darby 1975). Berkovec and Fullerton (1989) address this issue in a general equilibrium setting.

14. That is, the inflation tilt loads real mortgage payments in earlier years, thereby reducing the effective length of the loan.

evidence of the gradual downsizing of home equity implied by the life-cycle model (Merrill 1984; Venti and Wise 1989, 1990; Feinstein and McFadden 1989). In fact, these studies have found that retired households on average are as likely to increase their housing equity as to decrease it. Merrill (1984) reports that more retired households switch from *renters* to *owners* than from owners to renters, not a transition normally associated with life-cycle "downscaling." Additional evidence comes from Feinstein and McFadden (1989), who suggest that more than one-third of elderly households reside in dwellings with at least three more rooms than the number of inhabitants, and are hence "overconsuming" housing services.

Despite the apparent inability of the life-cycle model to explain such phenomena, it cannot yet be discarded as a model of retirement housing demand for a number of reasons. First, the life-cycle model places no restrictions on the housing consumption choice of the elderly (see also Ioannides 1989a). Absent evidence that housing choices of the elderly violate restrictions on utility, the demand for housing services may simply be stronger at older ages (e.g., Venti and Wise 1990). Alternatively, the decline in the user cost of housing for older families (Ai et al. 1990) could induce relative price effects for housing as well.

Furthermore, Sheiner and Weil (1992) present persuasive evidence that elderly households do reduce their housing services, although the reduction generally occurs later in the life cycle and is often precipitated by widowhood.[15] For example, the home-ownership rates of all women aged 65–69 is 77 percent; by ages 80—85, the percentage drops to 59, with less than half owning their own house after age 85. They also report that for widows, home ownership falls by 12 percentage points and median home equity by roughly 30 percent, in the four years after the husband's death. Based on comparisons of home ownership for high- and low-income households, they suggest that these changes in housing tenure are a consequence of taste changes rather than financial necessity.[16]

Suppose that retired households are consuming housing optimally. A portfolio model of the life cycle might still predict that households should attempt to spend down their home equity.[17] But as Merrill (1984), Venti and Wise (1989), and others have shown, housing equity for the elderly generally increased during the period of analysis. How can this finding be reconciled with the life-cycle model?

There are at least two possible explanations. The first is that the size of home equity is not large, so that the gains to tapping into home equity through re-

---

15. Venti and Wise (1989) and Feinstein and McFadden (1989) earlier noted the strong impact of events such as widowhood, children's moving, or divorce on mobility decisions, but did not directly test the impact of such changes on ownership patterns.

16. Feinstein and McFadden (1989), however, suggest that families with both low incomes and low levels of liquid wealth are more likely to switch from owner-occupied to rental property conditional on moving.

17. Alternatively, individuals could spend down other types of assets but leave housing equity unchanged. However, such a strategy would lead to an unbalanced portfolio.

verse mortgages is light.[18] For example, Venti and Wise (1991) suggest that the reverse mortgage would supplement income for the median retired families by between 4 and 10 percent of their existing income. In short, the transactions costs of reaching the home equity may not be worth the minimal extra income.

A different explanation for why home equity was observed to increase for elderly families is that the period of time covered by the *Retirement History Survey*—the predominant source of data on elderly housing—was also a period during which housing prices rose substantially. So increases in home equity may not have been a conscious life-cycle plan by retired households, but rather the outcome of housing windfalls.

McFadden (1992) has developed a model of housing demand and supply to predict the future trends in housing prices based on projected income and demographic changes. His preliminary results suggest that the capital appreciation in housing enjoyed by earlier cohorts will nearly evaporate for later cohorts, with real returns on housing dropping from an annual average of 3 percent (for cohorts born between 1880 and 1900) to roughly 0.5 percent for the baby boom generation. While McFadden's estimates are not as pessimistic as those of Mankiw and Weil (1989), they suggest that future patterns of home equity could display earlier and more pronounced downsizing by retired households.

To this point, much of the theory has been largely in terms of steady-state or at least stationary equilibrium. I next turn to a consideration of how both existing and prospective homeowners were affected by the largely unanticipated shift in housing wealth after the 1970s.

8.5 Housing Price Appreciation and Saving by Current Homeowners

The saving slowdown of the 1980s has spawned many explanations. One explanation is that housing wealth windfalls have stimulated consumption. Because capital gains from housing and land are not included in national income and product accounts, a rise in the price of housing will have no impact on measured income but could cause consumption to rise. Thus the declining saving rate (as conventionally measured) may be a consequence of increased consumption by homeowners flush with windfall capital gains.

Such a view gains support from the simple life-cycle model. Because housing is often held by older families, the aggregate marginal propensity to consume out of housing wealth tends to be high. Suppose that an exogenous change in tax policy (Poterba 1984) causes the price of housing and land to increase.[19] Calculations from a life-cycle simulation model with fifty-five overlapping generations suggest that a 10 percent increase in the real price of hous-

18. One version of a reverse mortgage annuity would involve a bank paying the household a fixed stream of income until death, at which point the bank takes title to the house.
19. Assume that land is in fixed supply so that despite new investment in housing, overall housing prices still rise.

ing (such as that during the past two decades) causes a short-term decline of 3 percentage points in saving (Skinner 1989). Ultimately, as the spendthrift generations die out and the new generations save more for the now more expensive housing, aggregate saving rates and the capital stock (per worker) are predicted to rebound to near their previous levels.

The theoretical implication that housing capital appreciation depresses non-housing saving depends on at least three assumptions: capital markets allow older families to spend their housing wealth, homeowners treat housing wealth similarly to other types of wealth, and there is no bequest motive. Violating any of these assumptions implies an attenuated effect of housing capital gains on consumption.

The 1980s saw the rapid growth of one popular method of freeing housing capital gains: the home equity loan. As Manchester and Poterba (1989) have documented, second mortgages as a fraction of total mortgages have increased from 3.2 percent of all home mortgages in 1980 to 10.8 percent in 1987. Their results using survey data suggest that, of each dollar from a home equity loan taken out subsequent to purchasing the house, other assets are reduced by 60–70 cents. One interpretation of this finding is that homeowners are successful at spending their windfall home equity gains. Alternatively, as the authors note, the result could also reflect differences in the population between those with home equity loans and those without. For example, unexpected medical expenses could lead both to a home equity loan and to a decline in other forms of assets. However, the cumulative balance of $100 billion in home equity loans is not large. Even starting from a zero balance in 1986, the average net increase in loans would have been only $20 billion annually, or less than 0.5 percent of current national income.

A further explanation for why housing wealth might not affect consumption and saving has been proposed by Thaler (1990). In his view of economic psychology, individuals control their spending impulses by creating "nonfungible" mental accounts that restrict certain forms of assets from being spent. If housing is nonfungible, then windfalls from housing prices would not be spent.

The final possibility is that the bequest motive will cause homeowners to save the accumulated wealth to assist their children in purchasing the now more expensive housing. Two pieces of evidence point against this intergenerational altruism hypothesis in the United States. First, one might expect that families with children should save more of their housing windfall than those without children. There was no evidence for such differences in the panel regressions by Skinner (1989).

Second, the altruism hypothesis would suggest that first-time home buyers might turn to parents or other relatives to help with more expensive housing. Some evidence on this proposition is provided by survey data from the Chicago Title and Trust Company (1991) on first-time home buyers. The real median house price for first-time buyers increased by 22 percent between 1976 and 1990. During the same period, median monthly housing payments as a fraction of income, again for first-time buyers, rose from 23 percent to 36 percent. Yet the share of the down payment provided by relatives actually fell, from 10.8 percent in 1976 to 10.2 percent in 1990.

The question of whether housing wealth windfalls affect saving and consumption is empirical. There are three approaches to testing the hypothesis. First, aggregate linear time-series consumption functions have been estimated, using housing wealth as an independent variable. Bhatia (1987) and Hendershott and Peek (1989), for example, found that consumption rose between 4 and 5 cents per dollar of housing (or housing plus durable) equity. One shortcoming of these time-series regressions is the lack of a utility function underlying the estimating equation. Another problem is the potential for spurious correlation between consumption expenditures on the left-hand side of the equation that includes an imputed flow of services from owner-occupied housing, and the market value of housing wealth on the right-hand side of the equation.

A second approach is to estimate Euler equation regressions using aggregate time-series data. For example, Skinner (1993) used aggregate data between 1950 and 1989 to estimate that the marginal propensity to consume (MPC) was roughly 0.03 percent per one percentage point increase in housing wealth, although the coefficient was not significant at conventional levels. (Note that nondurables exclude housing services and make up only one-third of total consumption expenditures.) The estimated long-term impact of housing windfalls on consumption, however, was essentially zero.

The third approach is to use microeconomic panel data. An important study by Bosworth, Burtless, and Sabelhaus (1991) documented the dramatic decline in household saving during the 1980s, using both the *Survey of Consumer Finances* (SCF) and the *Consumer Expenditure Survey* (CES). They found that much of the observed decline in saving rates between 1963 and the 1980s (in the case of the SCF) and between 1972–73 and the 1980s (in the case of the CES) occurred among homeowners. For example, using the SCF, the saving rate declined by 6.29 percent for homeowners between 1963 and 1983–85 but by only 0.49 percent for renters. These tabulations suggest that homeowners spending their windfalls were behind the saving decline in the 1980s. Surprisingly, the same pattern was not repeated in Canada. They calculated that, in Canada between 1978 and 1986, saving rates fell by 1.3 percent for homeowners and by 3.1 percent for renters.

Another example of the microeconomic approach is by Skinner (1989), who used the panel aspect of the PSID to construct family-specific measures of consumption and housing value over time. Consumption is not directly available from the PSID, although there are multiple indicators of consumption reported, such as food consumption, restaurant consumption, utility payments, and number of automobiles. By weighting these components using regression coefficients from the CES, overall consumption was imputed for each family in each year. Regressions of the change in housing prices for nonmovers on changes in consumption (essentially the microeconomic counterpart of the macro-Euler equations) suggested that housing price shifts had no effect on consumption.[20] In short, the empirical evidence about the effects of housing wealth on consumption are mixed.

Are the upper ranges of empirical estimates—say, an MPC out of housing wealth equal to 4 cents per dollar—large or small by the standards of the life-cycle model? A life-cycle household enjoying a $100,000 permanent windfall in its housing price would not consider itself $100,000 wealthier, since the cost of housing services in the area has likely risen. The "true" windfall is the present value of the $100,000 capital gain *when (or if) the family sells the house.* So if the windfall occurred in 1979 and the family planned to move in 2009 to an area with no real gain in housing prices, the present value of the windfall in 1979 would have been only $100,000/(1 + r)^{30}, or $41,198, assuming a real discount rate of 3 percent.[21] In this case, an estimated MPC out of housing wealth of 0.0412 would imply a true MPC out of the present value of housing wealth equal to 0.10.

The aggregate impact of housing wealth on consumption is a weighted average across all age groups, with older households exhibiting a higher MPC out of housing windfalls. Calculations using a life-cycle model with fifty-five generations suggest a short-run MPC from housing wealth of roughly 3 percent (Skinner 1989), well within the upper range of empirically estimated coefficients. Using this 3 percent MPC and assuming a housing windfall of $700 billion during the 1970s (see figure 8.1), the implied increase in consumption is $21 billion annually, or only 0.6 percent of GNP in 1986. Housing prices by themselves are unlikely to have explained the decline in saving during the 1980s.

8.6   Housing Price Appreciation and Saving by Potential Homeowners

To this point, I have focused on how the unexpected housing price increase affected existing homeowners. Price appreciation should also affect saving by renters who hope to purchase housing in the future.[22] Wealth appreciation enjoyed by current homeowners on their fixed assets are matched dollar for dollar by a wealth loss for future generations who must pay more for the existing housing stock.

Sheiner (1990) has estimated that younger families in areas with high housing prices also tend to save more, conditional on factors such as income, rental

20. Pooled cross-section and time-series regressions, however, did suggest that housing wealth affects consumption. These pooled regressions may be tainted by the problem that spendthrifts are likely both to buy large houses and to spend a high fraction of income on other consumption goods.

21. This calculation assumes no further real price appreciation in housing. If current capital gains are projected to increase in the future, the MPC out of housing wealth would be larger.

22. Rental payments might also be expected to change, although such effects are ignored in this paper.

payments, and other demographic variables. She finds that variation among states in housing prices are sufficiently large to account for a large fraction of wealth differences among renters. For example, a renter in California, the state with the highest housing prices, is predicted to hold $2,406 more in wealth than a renter in Kentucky, the state with the lowest housing price. This difference is larger than the *average* wealth holdings of the sample.[23]

As Sheiner reports, her results may suggest that higher housing prices actually encourage, rather than discourage, aggregate saving. If homeowners treat housing wealth as nonfungible and do not spend it, but renters save for the more expensive housing, then housing prices could paradoxically *increase* aggregate saving rates.

There is some evidence that, beyond some threshold in housing prices, renters give up hope of ever affording owner-occupied housing and as a consequence reduce their saving. In response to a survey asking "How has the recent increase in land and housing prices affected your plans to save for housing purchase?" only 5 percent of Japanese respondents replied that they would increase their planned purchase price, cut back on consumption, and increase saving. Thirty-two percent answered that they had abandoned their housing purchase plans entirely (Central Council 1990).[24] In short, if housing prices grow to the point where prospective buyers drop from the market, saving among renters could decline rather than increase.

8.7   Housing and Uncertainty

Models that assume perfect foresight over the life cycle ignore the important role of risk in housing wealth and the impact of this risk on consumption decisions. The lumpy nature of housing, as well as the typical equality between housing consumption and housing investment, means that portfolio decisions about housing investments cannot be derived in isolation from consumption decisions (Bossons 1978).

Berkovec and Fullerton (1992) and Hendershott and Won (1992) have recently developed complex simulation models reflecting this interdependence between housing consumption and investment. In their models, households face uncertain returns both on housing and nonhousing assets, and changes in the tax regime are shown to affect overall wealth both through the traditional incentive effect and through changes in the after-tax variance of the returns. In particular, Berkovec and Fullerton highlight the importance of financial risk in housing when they find that full taxation of owner-occupied housing has only small effects on the total quantity of housing. The disincentive effect of a tax

---

23. While net worth of less than $2,000 may seem low, the sample is restricted to renters, and the very wealthy are excluded.

24. I am grateful to Charles Horioka for pointing out this survey to me.

on housing is nearly offset by the reduction in the variance of housing returns as a consequence of the tax.

The Berkovec and Fullerton and Hendershott and Won models focus on the "hedging" demand for housing assets, in the sense that housing increases the risk of the entire family portfolio. Goodwin (1986) focuses additionally on the "speculative" demand for housing portfolio. That is, when there is uncertainty about the (nominal or real) price of future housing, owning a house provides excellent insurance against future (regional or local) price shifts. Hence under this view, purchasing housing can reduce, rather than increase, the total amount of uncertainty. Goodwin finds limited evidence that either the speculative or the hedging affects are large, although his results may be an artifact of using aggregate data.

To what extent are household portfolios disrupted by the purchase of a house? Ioannides (1989b) finds that the portfolio decisions of recent movers do appear constrained by mortgage lending requirements. That is, recent movers with lower earnings (holding nonhousing wealth constant) show higher ratios of equity to housing value, suggesting that they are constrained from leveraging their house by bank lending restrictions tied to current earnings. This disequilibrium holds only for recent movers; portfolio decisions for nonmovers appear unrelated to current earnings.

The sharp changes in housing prices during the past few decades might be expected to have two effects. The first is an increase in the volatility of housing prices, so that owning a house induces more risk to family wealth. The second is higher leverage rates (i.e., the ratio of mortgage principal to housing value) for first-time buyers. Both a higher leverage ratio and greater price volatility would increase the riskiness of the household portfolio and hence reduce the demand for housing by risk-averse households. Could these two effects have explained in part the sluggishness in housing prices during the 1980s? To address this issue, I first test whether housing prices have become more volatile and then measure the changes in leverage ratios between 1969 and 1986.

The PSID has followed five thousand families (and their dependents) since 1968. In each year, the respondent was asked the market value of his or her house. Each of the sample families yielded a maximum of nineteen observations on housing price changes (from 1968–69 to 1986–87). An observation was deleted if during the current or previous year the family had moved or experienced a major compositional change, or did not own a house, or if the real (1986) value of the house was less than $2,000. Nearly fifty-six thousand observations remained.

Figure 8.3 graphs the year-to-year real annual change in housing prices, as well as its standard deviation, from 1968–69 through 1986–87. (Log changes in excess of the absolute value of 1.0 were truncated at either 1 or −1.) As a rough measure of the accuracy of such subjective housing value measures, the log average annual rates of change were compared in figure 8.3 with the objec-

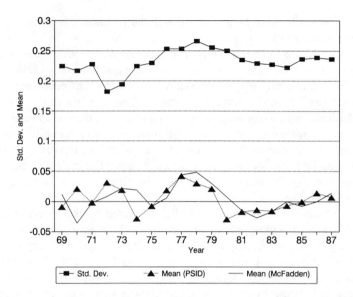

Fig. 8.3   Annual (log) change in housing prices: mean and standard deviation, 1969–87
Sources: Panel Study of Income Dynamics; McFadden 1992.

tive Commerce Department measures (McFadden 1992). The two series are quite close in mapping housing price changes over the 1970s and 1980s and diverge only in the late 1960s.

Figure 8.3 traces the standard deviation of real annual changes in housing prices. Despite the sharp run-up in housing prices during the 1970s (shown in figure 8.1), the change in the standard deviation of housing prices is relatively modest compared to the underlying pattern of uncertainty. That is, housing prices since 1969 have always been volatile, with a standard deviation in excess of 0.18 in log terms (or roughly speaking, 18 percentage points). Hence one cannot conclude that homeowners have been exposed to a significant increase in overall housing price risk in the last few decades.[25]

Household portfolios are at greater risk when they are highly leveraged.[26] Data from the Chicago Title and Trust (1991) suggest a larger fraction of home buyers with high leverage rates; the fraction of families buying a house with less than 10 percent down payment rose from .27 in 1976 to .40 in 1989.

To test this view that average homeowners have become more exposed to

25. It should be cautioned that these housing figures are subjective rather than objective appraisals. They tend to change in jumps—say, a house is reported worth $25,000 in 1968 and 1969 and then rises in 1970 to $30,000—leading to perhaps some overstatement of the true market volatility. Still, to the extent that housing demand and saving behavior reflects the subjective assessment of the household's net wealth, these measures are the appropriate ones to use.

26. For example, suppose there are two homeowners, one with a leverage ratio of 50 percent, the other with a ratio of 90 percent. A one-percentage-point shift in house prices causes a 2 percent revaluation of equity for the first homeowner, but a 10 percent revaluation for the second.

Table 8.4   **Leverage of Housing by Age, 1969 and 1986**

Age	Median Leverage, 1969	75th Percentile, 1969	Median Leverage, 1986	75th Percentile, 1986
Under 31	.690	.859	.563	.771
31–40	.531	.707	.485	.691
41–50	.308	.567	.249	.486
51–60	.000	.339	.034	.250
61–70	.000	.038	.000	.073
Over 71	.000	.000	.000	.000

Source: Survey of Consumer Finances 1969, 1986.

housing price risk, data from the SCF on leverage ratios were compiled in table 8.4. Median and seventy-fifth-percentile leverage ratios (mortgage principal remaining divided by house market value) were calculated for both 1969 and 1986. Median leverage ratios decline with age, so that the representative home-owner had nearly full equity in a house by age 51–60. The comparison between leverage rates in 1969 and 1986 suggests there has been no overall increase in the leverage ratios of households. If anything, the leverage rates have *declined* since the late 1960s; for ages under 31, the median leverage rate fell from 69 percent to 56 percent. As is also noted in table 8.4, this result holds not just for the median household, but for those "high exposure" families who are in the seventy-fifth percentile of leverage ratios.

One way to reconcile the Chicago Title and Trust data with the SCF data is to note that equity is built up more rapidly in the presence of inflation. Taking a snapshot of homeowners in 1990 would include some who may have purchased a house with very little down payment in, say, 1984, but subsequently experienced rapid equity buildup caused by inflation.[27] Note finally that, since 1986, the leverage ratio for housing wealth rose substantially owing to the tax advantages of home equity lines of credit. However, such shifting may not imply greater overall leverage if accompanied by a reduction in revolving taxable credit.[28]

It might be argued that the leverage ratio is not relevant to household risk, and that a more relevant risk is whether the household can meet the mortgage payments. In this view, a rise in the ratio of mortgage payments to total income might indicate greater riskiness of home ownership. To test for this, table 8.5 compares the ratio of mortgage payments to income in 1969 and 1986, broken down by age group. Table 8.5 shows a modest increase in the ratio of mortgage

27. Note also that the *average* down payment for first-time buyers fell from 18 percent in 1976 to 16 percent in 1990 (Chicago Title and Trust 1991).
28. For example, Skinner and Feenberg (1990) found that housing mortgage interest payments increased by 60–80 cents for every dollar reduction in nondeductible interest payments following the 1986 tax reform. That is, households shifted nonhousing debt into tax-preferred housing debt.

Table 8.5   Mortgage Payments as a Percentage of Family Income, 1969 and 1986

Age	Median Payment, 1969	90th Percentile, 1969	Median Payment, 1986	90th Percentile, 1986
Under 31	11.70	19.96	12.85	25.51
31–40	10.50	17.33	11.73	24.78
41–50	7.49	16.59	7.00	19.80
51–60	0.00	16.92	2.08	17.64
61–70	0.00	11.99	0.00	14.28
Over 71	0.00	0.00	0.00	2.24

Source: Survey of Consumer Finances 1969, 1986.

payments to income between 1969 to 1986. Families in the ninetieth percentile of mortgage payments (as a ratio to income) show a somewhat larger increase in the burden of mortgage payments. Still, the overall impact of changes in the riskiness of home ownership are likely to be quite modest for housing demand.

8.8   Conclusion

The sharp rise in housing prices during the 1970s has had an important impact on the financial health of many homeowners. During the entire decade of the 1970s, capital gains in housing alone approached $700 billion (in 1986 dollars) and amounted to nearly half of all personal saving during the decade. During this same period, average inflation rates increased substantially; even ignoring the 1970s, inflation rates doubled from an average annual rate of 2.4 percent in the 1960s to 5.0 percent in the 1980s.

How might these two fundamental shifts be expected to affect the level and composition of long-term aggregate saving? The life-cycle model suggests that homeowners should respond to a long-term rise in housing prices by a reduction in housing services. While families may wait longer before purchasing a house, theoretical studies do not suggest that the higher housing prices should depress aggregate capital accumulation in the long term. By the same token, inflation affects the tilt of nominal housing mortgages and the tax advantage of housing, but the overall impact of inflation on housing markets is also likely to be small.

The *temporary* effect of housing price windfalls may have had a larger effect on saving patterns in the United States. There is some evidence that homeowners have partially spent down their housing windfalls, although the evidence is not conclusive. Whether this accumulated housing wealth is being gradually spent down, saved for bequests, or saved because homeowners find it difficult to extract the home equity is an unresolved question.

The life-cycle model also implies that potential homeowners currently renting should save more as a consequence of higher housing prices. The study by Sheiner (1990) supports this view; variations in housing prices across cities are found to explain a large fraction of financial wealth holdings of renters. Still, if housing prices are out of the reach of renters, they may respond by giving up entirely on home ownership and by saving less.

Finally, how did the fundamental changes in housing prices and inflation affect the riskiness of household portfolios? The empirical evidence suggests little change over time, either in the housing leverage rates, or in the volatility of housing prices. We can therefore exclude increased housing risk as an explanation for laggard housing demand in the 1980s.

This paper has ignored one key piece in explaining the puzzle of housing prices—why the structural shift in housing prices during the 1970s? Some authors have pointed to the interaction between inflation and the tax code—allowing nominal mortgage interest payments to be deducted implied an often negative real after-tax cost of borrowing during the 1970s (Poterba 1984). Others have stressed demographic changes in the age structure of the population as driving housing prices—the baby boom coming of age accounted for the housing price rise and its subsequent decline (Mankiw and Weil 1989; see also Hendershott 1991). It may be difficult to pinpoint how housing prices should affect saving rates without identifying what caused the dramatic shift in housing prices in the first place.

References

Ai, Chunrong, Jonathan Feinstein, Daniel McFadden, and Henry Pollakowski. 1990. The Dynamics of Housing Demand by the Elderly: User Cost Effects. In David A. Wise, ed., *Issues in the Economics of Aging.* Chicago: University of Chicago Press.

Berkovec, James, and Don Fullerton. 1989. The General Equilibrium Effects of Inflation on Housing Consumption and Investment. *American Economic Review* 79 (May): 277–82.

———. 1992. A General Equilibrum Model of Housing, Taxes, and Portfolio Choice. *Journal of Politcal Economy* 100 (April): 390–429.

Bhatia, Kul B. 1987. Real Estate Assets and Consumer Spending. *Quarterly Journal of Economics* 102 (May): 437–43.

Bossons, John. 1978. Housing Demand and Household Wealth: Evidence for Home Owners. In Larry S. Bourne and John R. Hitchcock, eds. *Urban Housing Markets: Recent Directions in Research and Policy.* Toronto: University of Toronto Press.

Bosworth, Barry, Gary Burtless, and John Sabelhaus. 1991. The Decline in Saving: Evidence from Household Surveys. *Brookings Papers on Economic Activities* 1: 183–256.

Central Council. 1990. Public Opinion Survey on Saving. Central Council for Saving Information (Japan).

Chicago Title and Trust Company. 1991. *Who's Buying Houses in America?* Chicago, February.

Darby, Michael. 1975. The Financial and Tax Effects of Monetary Policy on Interest Rates. *Economic Inquiry* 13 (June): 266–76.

Federal Reserve System Board of Governors. 1991. Balance Sheets for the U.S. Economy, 1945–1990. Publication C-9. Washington, DC: Federal Reserve System, September.

Feinstein, Jonathan, and Daniel McFadden. 1989. The Dynamics of Housing Demand by the Elderly: Wealth, Cash Flow, and Demographic Effects. In David A. Wise, ed., *The Economics of Aging*. Chicago: University of Chicago Press.

Goodwin, Thomas H. 1986. Inflation, Risk, Taxes, and the Demand for Owner-Occupied Housing. *Review of Economics and Statistics* 68 (May): 197–206.

Grossman, Sanford J., and Guy Laroque. 1990. Asset Pricing and Optimal Portfolio Choice in the Presence of Illiquid Durable Consumption Goods. *Econometrica* 58 (January): 25–51.

Hayashi, Fumio, Takatoshi Ito, and Joel Slemrod. 1988. Housing Finance Imperfections and Private Saving. *Journal of Japanese and International Economics* 2 (3): 215–38.

Hendershott, Patric H. 1991. Are Real Prices Likely to Decline by 47 Percent?" *Regional Science and Urban Economics* (December).

Hendershott, Patric H., and Joe Peek. 1989. Aggregate U.S. Private Saving: Conceptual Measures and Empirical Tests. In Robert E. Lipsey and Helen Stone Tice, eds., *The Measurement of Saving, Investment, and Wealth*. Chicago: University of Chicago Press.

Hendershott, Patric H., and Yunhi Won. 1992. Introducing Risky Housing and Endogenous Tenure Choice into Portfolio-Based General Equilibrium Models. *Journal of Public Economics* 48 (August): 293–316.

Henderson, J. V., and Yannis Ioannides. 1983. A Model of Housing Tenure Choice. *American Economic Review* 73 (March): 98–113.

Ioannides, Yannis M. 1989a. Comment. In David A. Wise, ed., *The Economics of Aging*. Chicago: University of Chicago Press.

———. 1989b. Housing, Other Real Estate, and Wealth Portfolios. *Regional Science and Urban Economics* 19 (May): 259–80.

Jones, Lawrence D. 1990. Current Wealth Constraints on the Housing Demand of Young Owners. *Review of Economics and Statistics* 72 (August): 424–32.

Kearl, J. R. 1979. Inflation, Mortgages, and Housing. *Journal of Political Economy* 87 (October): 1115–38.

Krumm, Ronald, and Austin Kelly. 1989. Effects of Homeownership on Household Savings. *Journal of Urban Economics* 26 (November): 281–94.

McFadden, Daniel, 1992. Demographics, the Housing Market, and the Welfare of the Elderly. University of California, Berkeley. Mimeo.

Manchester, Joyce M., and James M. Poterba. 1989. Second Mortgages and Household Saving. *Regional Science and Urban Economics* 19 (May): 325–46.

Mankiw, N. Gregory, and David N. Weil. 1989. The Baby Boom, the Baby Bust, and the Housing Market. *Regional Science and Urban Eocnomics* 19 (May): 235–58.

Mankiw, N. Gregory, and Stephen P. Zeldes. 1991. The Consumption of Stockholders and Nonstockholders. *Journal of Financial Economics* 29: 97–112.

Melvin, Michael. 1982. Expected Inflation, Taxation, and Interest Rates: The Delusion of Fiscal Illusion. *American Economic Review* 72 (September): 841–45.

Merrill, Sally R. 1984. Home Equity and the Elderly. In Henry J. Aaron and Gary Burtless, eds., *Retirement and Economic Behavior*. Washington, DC: Brookings Institution.

Poterba, James 1984. Tax Subsidies to Owner-Occupied Housing: An Asset-Market Approach. *Quarterly Journal of Economics* 99 (November): 729–52.

Schwab, Robert M. 1983. Real and Nominal Interest Rates and the Demand for Housing. *Journal of Urban Economics* 13 (March): 181–95.

Sheiner, Louise M. 1990. Housing Prices and the Savings of Renters. Mimeo. Joint Committee on Taxation, Washington, DC, November.

Sheiner, Louise M., and David Weil. 1992. The Housing Wealth of the Aged. NBER Working Paper no. 4115. July.

Skinner, Jonathan. 1989. Housing Wealth and Aggregate Saving. *Regional Science and Urban Economics* 19 (May): 305–24.

———. 1993. Is Housing Wealth a Sideshow? University of Virginia, Charlottesville. Mimeo.

Skinner, Jonathan, and Daniel Feenberg. 1990. The Impact of the 1986 Tax Reform on Personal Saving. In Joel Slemrod, ed., *Do Taxes Matter? The Impact of the Tax Reform Act of 1986*. Cambridge, MA: MIT Press.

Tanzi, Vito. 1980. Inflationary Expectations, Economic Activity, Taxes, and Interest Rates. *American Economic Review* 70 (March): 12–21.

Thaler, Richard H. 1990. Anomalies: Saving, Fungibility, and Mental Accounts. *Journal of Economic Perspectives* 4 (Winter): 193–206.

Venti, Steven F., and David A. Wise. 1989. Aging, Moving, and Housing Wealth. In David A. Wise, ed., *The Economics of Aging*. Chicago: University of Chicago Press.

———. 1990. But They Don't Want to Reduce Housing Equity. In David A. Wise, ed., *Issues in the Economics of Aging*. Chicago: University of Chicago Press.

———. 1991. Aging and the Income Value of Housing Wealth. *Journal of Public Economics* 44: 371–97.

Wolf, Edward N. 1989. Trend in Aggregate Household Wealth in the U.S., 1900–1983. *Review of Income and Wealth* 34 (March): 1–29.

9   Public Policy and Housing in Japan

Takatoshi Ito

9.1 Introduction

In this paper, I examine effects of various land-related taxes and regulations in Japan. A sharp increase in land prices in the second half of the 1980s drew criticism from employees who felt their dreams of owning a house or moving into a bigger house had disappeared. By the time that policy measures, such as a limit on land-related lendings from banks and a land-holding tax, were introduced, the land price had more or less peaked.

I examine intentions and results of public policy. The traditional view is that the heart of the problem is land prices that are too high. Hence, any measure to lower land prices is good. This justified, for example, the introduction of the price monitoring system: the price of land transactions has to be approved by the municipal government prior to sale. A national landholding tax was proposed, because the local property (real estate) tax was not enough. Deductions for capital gains in the case of house replacement were abolished. There have also been proposals to raise the capital gains tax on properties held for the long term.

This paper distinguishes itself from the conventional view, which has dominated the political discussions in recent years, by emphasizing the importance of efficient use of the land rather than lowering land prices. The conventional view implicitly assumes that a sharp increase in land prices, or at least its major portion, comes from speculative investment. In order to correct a situation, a heavier burden on land-related taxes would work. In particular it has been

Takatoshi Ito is professor of economics at Hitotsubashi University, visiting professor of economics at Harvard University, and a research associate of the National Bureau of Economic Research.
The author is grateful to Martin Feldstein, Tatsuo Hatta, Patric Hendershott, Charles Horioka, Yukio Noguchi, and James Poterba for their comments.

recommended to increase tax rates on landholding and on capital gains, and to make assessments of land values closer to market values.

This paper emphasizes analyses of effects and distortions that are implied by various land-related and housing-related taxes and regulations in Japan. The conventional wisdom is that there is enough owner-occupied housing, but I show that household formation in Japan is discouraged, probably because of high housing costs.

Both the number of houses and quality of housing were not adequate in Japan. In the past, the emphasis of public policy was on public housing, maximizing the number of housing units. However, the emphasis seems to be shifting to quality.

The Japanese system of taxes on land acquisition, landownership, and housing is examined. In particular, the system of capital gains tax and property tax is discussed from the viewpoint of lock-in effects. Conventional wisdom is that the cost of landholding (property tax) is relatively low, so that speculative investment in real estate has been encouraged. Based on this conventional wisdom, raising the real estate assessment by prefectural government and creating a national landholding tax are often recommended. In addition, capital gains taxes are raised (especially for the short-term holding) to "prevent" speculative demand. This paper cautiously recommends the use of capital gains tax for this purpose.

Second, the bequest tax is shown to have caused distortions. Assessment of land and structures for bequest tax is much lower than the market value. The Japanese bequeathed assets consist mostly of real estate, in contrast to the United States. In fact, the Japanese elderly who plan to bequeath some assets have a strong incentive (1) to hold on to their principal residence, no matter how mismatched for their needs in retirement years, and (2) to borrow to buy more real estate. The latter feature is an effective tax-saving strategy, since real estate is assessed at less than market value and the mortgage liability is deducted from an estate in full. It is suspected that this tax distortion also causes a lock-in effect until the uncertain timing of death.

The paper further examines the taxes and regulations relevant to the own-rent tenure choice. There are two salient features on this point. First, interest payments for loans used to buy owner-occupied housing give only a partial tax benefit (in the form of a tax credit) in Japan. This works as less incentive for owning a house in Japan. (This, in combination with a large down-payment burden, works to delay the first-house purchase in one's life cycle.) Second, the Building Lease Law in Japan protects tenants so much that no landlords would want to put high-quality housing on the rental market. (Note that the horizon of a lease is virtually indefinite. It is almost impossible to ask tenants to leave upon the expiration of the lease.) The result is that, as children are born and the family size grows, it is necessary to purchase a house instead of relocating to larger rental housing.

Another peculiar aspect of the Japanese housing market is the existence of company housing (*shataku*) and public-servant housing (*komuin shukusha*), both of which are heavily subsidized in rents. Costs of operating company housing can be deducted as operating expenses of the corporation, while the subsidized part of rents (fringe benefits) is not taxable in employees' income. This tax wedge is part of the reason for the prevalence of company housing. Public-servant housing is generally low quality but heavily subsidized in rents. This fringe benefit is also nontaxable in government employee's income tax. These distortions may partly be responsible for not developing high-quality housing.

As a philosophy (a principle beyond allocative efficiency) of public policy regarding land and housing, "protection of the underprivileged" is most frequently mentioned in Japan. A close examination, however, reveals that taxes and regulations that are meant to protect the underprivileged often have the opposite effect. For example, the tenant law that "overly" protects the tenant discourages the supply of high-quality rental housing, so that potential tenants for that market are hurt. (There is an analogy to rent control in the United States.) Low assessments for real estate taxes and bequest taxes are often defended by the same argument. It is against the philosophy of protecting the underprivileged if they are assessed in full when land prices are skyrocketing. It is a pity if a long-term resident has to sell a home and move due to real estate taxes. However, reducing the assessment encourages the underuse of land, with owners putting off capital gains or leaving a bequest. Heavily subsidized corporate and government employee housing also works against development of high-quality housing.

9.2   Overview

9.2.1   Land Value in Japan

The high cost of housing in Japan is well known. The price of a typical new home is about two to three times annual income in the United States and about five to eight times annual income in Japan. (See Noguchi's paper, ch. 1 in this volume.) This relative disadvantage persists although the average area of new housing in Japan is 84.4 square meters, compared to 134.8 square meters in the United States. Moreover, there are 0.7 residents per room in Japan, compared to 0.5 in the United States. Since most of a typical new house's price is the cost of land, the land problem is synonymous with the housing problem.

The situation of high land prices in recent years can be highlighted by comparing the total valuation of the land area of Japan and the United States (in the balance sheet of the nations). At the end of 1988, the national land wealth of Japan was 1,892 trillion yen, equivalent to $14.6 trillion (at 130 yen/dollar), quadrupling the U.S. land value of $3.6 trillion. Since the total area of Japan is about one-twenty-fifth of the United States, the unit cost of land in Japan is about one hundred times that in the United States.

The high cost and low quality of Japanese housing prompts complaints from its citizens. High housing prices arouse the concerns of those who cannot expect to inherit a house, but must work to purchase one. Episodes of rising housing prices, especially in 1973–75 and 1986–87, have created a sense of widening inequality between those who already have a house and those who do not. Such sentiments signal difficult political problems, and the housing/land problem has reached top priority in public policy in the past five years. The seriousness of the problem has been acknowledged in government reports and long-term plans in the second half of the 1980s: the Maekawa report,[1] the so-called new Maekawa report, and the Economic Planning Agency's five-year plan.[2]

9.2.2 Housing/Land Problem in Japan

To better understand the housing situation in Japan, it is helpful to review briefly some key facts in both time-series and cross-section perspectives. (See Noguchi's introduction to this volume and Ito [1992, ch. 14] for details.) First, the quantity, quality, and costs of housing Japan are examined. Second, government policies regarding housing are reviewed.

Is there enough housing? In the 1960s and 1970s, Japan made large public and private investments in housing. In fact, the number of housing units has been increasing so much that officials at the Ministry of Construction wrote

1. Prime Minister Nakasone formed a commission headed by Maekawa, the former governor of the Bank of Japan. The task of the Maekawa commission was to recommend a strategy for the structural adjustment of the Japanese economy to reduce current account surpluses and to improve the standard of living (quality of life). The Maekawa commission reported in April 1986, and another report (the so-called new Maekawa report) by the Economic Council (Keizai Shingikai) was delivered to the prime minister in May 1987. The progress in implementing measures recommended in the report is being monitored (a progress report was released in January 1988).

It was understood from the beginning that the economic structure of Japan would have to be transformed from export-dependent to domestic demand–oriented. It was also recognized that one key component of domestic demand is housing. The Maekawa report specifically recommended the following items: (1) domestic demand stimulation, aiming at improving the quality of life; (2) transforming industrial structures to encourage imports; (3) improving access of the Japanese markets by foreign companies; (4) aligning the exchange rate to the level consistent with fundamentals; and, (5) promoting international policy coordinations. Among the five pillars, the first addresses the land/housing problem. High land price is recognized as the stumbling block to achieving a high standard of living. A main purpose of the second item is to reduce the size of the external surplus to avoid criticism from abroad. However, redirecting resources from export industries to domestic sectors will encourage, in general, a better quality in residences. More imports, the aim of the third item, will lower domestic prices and contribute to higher real income of consumers. Hence, the main purpose of the Maekawa report is arguably to increase the quality of life.

2. The Economic Planning Agency prepared the five-year plan called "Japan, coexisting with the world" (Sekai to Tomoni Ikiru Nihon) in May 1988. In this report, three major planning objectives are mentioned: raising affluence of life, smoothing changes in industrial structure and balanced growth of regions other than Tokyo, and correcting external balances and contribution to the rest of the world. In the "affluent life" section, solving the land/housing problem is listed as the first priority. However, the plan does not give any details on how to achieve better housing. There seems to be a consensus among policymakers that the land/housing problem needs immediate attention.

that the housing problem is quality and not the number of units. In the housing survey done every five years, housing units have outnumbered households nationwide since 1968. See Noguchi's introduction to this volume.) In 1988, the number of housing units was 11 percent more than the number of households. Moreover, the "ownership ratio," that is, the ratio of owner-occupied units to total housing units, in Japan is comparable to that of the United States. (See table 9.1.) These facts are frequently quoted by policymakers in Japan, who argue that the focus of housing policy should be shifted toward seeking improvements in the quality of housing.

These statistics, however, are deceptive. If the formation of households is "endogenous," the adequacy of housing may not be inferred from the fact that the ratio of housing to households is more than one. Table 9.1 rows g and h show that the number of houses per eligible member of the population in Japan still lags behind the United States. In fact, the statistics suggest that the shortage of affordable housing discourages the early formation of households. Unmarried men and women in Japan tend to live with their parents, when they attend school or work in the same town or city. Moreover, the elderly in Japan tend to live in the household of their children. However, the ratio of independent households among the elderly appears to rise with household wealth in both time-series and cross-section analyses. Many surveys also have suggested that the elderly in Japan wish to maintain an independent household, though in close proximity to their children.

The ownership ratio is just a ratio of owner-occupied housing to the entire housing stock. In Japan, the numbers of both rental and owner-occupied housing units lag behind counterparts in other advanced countries. This fact is not picked up by the ownership ratio. A better measure would be a ratio of people owning homes to the population of that cohort.

Another aspect of the housing problem is the quality of housing. The Japanese house is typically smaller than the American house: fewer rooms per

Table 9.1   **Ownership Ratio and Housing per Capita**

	United States 1987	Japan 1988
(a) Occupied units	90,888,000	37,413,000
(b) Owner-occupied	58,164,000	22,948,000
(c) Rented	32,724,000	14,015,000
(d) Ownership ratio (b)/(a)	64.0%	61.3%
(e) Population	243,942,000	122,783,000
(f) Population, 20 years and older	173,031,000	88,908,000
(g) = (a)/(e)	37.3%	30.5%
(h) = (a)/(f)	51.5%	42.1%

Sources: Japan: *1988 Housing Survey of Japan.* United States: *Statistical Abstract of the United States,* 13, 726.

Note: Japan's *b* and *c* do not add up to *a*, because some units cannot be classified as *b* or *c*.

house, more people per room, and fewer square meters per house. Moreover, the quality of facilities in a house is below international standards. (See Noguchi's introduction to this volume.)

Various studies, for example Hayashi, Ito, and Slemrod (1988) and Horioka (1988), suggest that housing in Japan is much more expensive than that in the United States. Hence, a large down payment is required to purchase a house. Hayashi, Ito, and Slemrod (1988) report that the age by which half of a generational cohort has purchased a house is about thirty in the United States and about 40 in Japan. Due to practices in financial markets, about 25 percent, on average, of the house price is paid as a down payment in the United States, compared with 35 percent in Japan. A typical mortgage maturity is thirty years in the United States, compared with twenty years in Japan. In sum, housing in Japan is certainly expensive in relative terms, which leads Japanese to purchase a house later in the life cycle than Americans.

9.2.3 Land Price Movement

Land prices have increased much faster than the consumer price index (CPI) over the entire postwar period. Table 9.2 compares land prices, defined as the average price of urban land, with the CPI index and the economic growth rate in five-year intervals.

Figure 9.1 plots the change in the real land prices measured by the log of land price minus the log of the wholesale price index (WPI). Table 9.2 and figure 9.1 confirm that land prices rose much faster from the late 1950s to the early 1970s than since then. Because real GNP grew more than twice as rapidly between 1955 and 1970 than between 1970 and 1985, we might hypothesize that real land price increases correlate with the real GNP growth rate.

Figure 9.2 shows the average nationwide land inflation rate versus the land inflation rate of the six major metropolitan areas. The price increase in the six largest cities has far outpaced that of the rest of the country after 1984. This is unusual in that the price increase in those cities has been more or less equal to the rest of the country over the long run.

Figure 9.3 shows the land inflation rates for industrial, residential, and commercial uses. The price of industrial land outpaced other land in 1961–62, the price of residential land outpaced others in 1973–74, and commercial land was the leader in 1986–87. The evidence presented in figures 9.2 and 9.3 confirms

Table 9.2   **Five-Year Inflation and Growth Rates**

	1955–60	1960–65	1965–70	1970–75	1975–80	1980–85	1985–90
Land	180.0	174.3	81.6	92.9	20.1	29.3	46.4
CPI	10.3	35.1	8.7	72.8	36.7	13.3	7.5
Real GNP	54.7	55.0	71.7	24.0	26.9	21.1	25.7

Sources: Land: Zenkoku Shigaichi Tochi Kakaku Shisuu (urban area index) Real Estate Institute. CPI: Management and Coordination Agency. Real GNP: Economic Planning Agency.

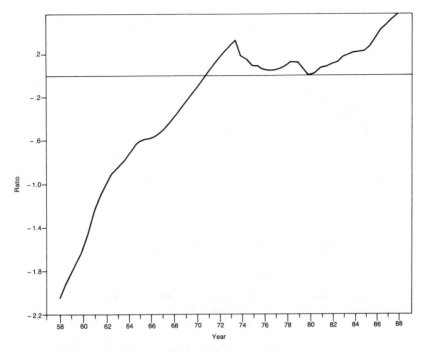

Fig. 9.1   Land prices relative to wholesale price index
Source: Land price indices published by the Real Estate Institute.

that the most recent land price increase was mainly concentrated in the large cities and pertained to commercial uses of land. In this sense, the evidence is consistent with an observation that the most recent episode of land price inflation is the "Tokyo problem," derived from the fact that Tokyo became one of the commercial (and international financial) centers of the world. It is fundamentally different from the situation in 1973–74, when the nationwide price of land rose at a rapid pace.

There have been three peaks of especially sharp real land price increases, 1961–62, 1973–74, and 1986–87. The first period was led by industrial land prices and occurred during Japan's rapid economic growth with industrialization (and a boom associated with the Tokyo Olympic Games). More generally, the high land inflation rate during the 1950s and 1960s was matched by rapid economic growth and relatively high CPI inflation rate. This is evident from a smooth trend in figure 9.1 and from table 9.2.

The second sharp acceleration appears to have been led by residential land price increases. But a sharp increase and a subsequent drop in prices for all uses suggest that presence of a bubble in 1973 and 1974.

The commercial land price increase led the third acceleration. This observation, coupled with the fact that prices in metropolitan areas outpaced prices in

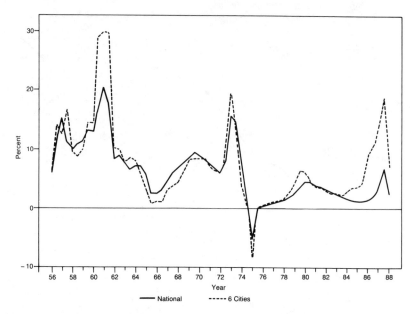

Fig. 9.2   Land inflation rates: national average versus six cities
Source: Land price indices published by the Real Estate Institute.

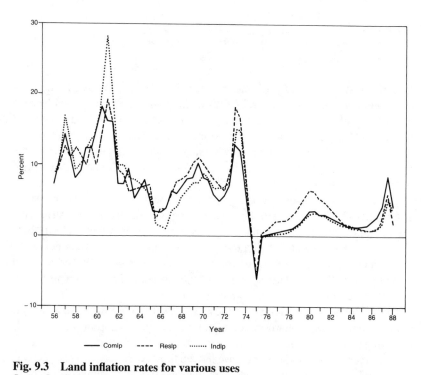

Fig. 9.3   Land inflation rates for various uses
Source: Land price indices published by the Real Estate Institute.
Notes: Comlp = commercial land price index; *Reslp* = residential land price index; *Indlp* = industrial land price index.

rural medium-sized cities, gives support to a casual observation that the 1986–87 increase was triggered, if not caused, by the internationalization and deregulation of the Tokyo financial market and by a resulting increase in demand from financial corporations for new or expanded space in the Tokyo office market.

This interpretation is based on a belief that land price movements are mostly explained by "fundamentals," with a possible episode of the forming and popping of a bubble in 1973–75. (See a theoretical model in Ito [1993] for a general-equilibrium steady state where the real land price increased at a rate of real economic growth. See also Noguchi, ch. 1 in this volume, for a view emphasizing a bubble.) However, the evidence is not clear enough to conclude one way or the other. At the least, it should be kept in mind when public policy questions are asked that not all land price increases have been bubbles.

9.2.4 Public Housing

Various government affiliated agencies build housing units for sale or for rent. At the national government level, the Housing and Urban Development Corporation, which resulted from a merger of two earlier corporations in 1981, builds apartment buildings and rents them to tenants. Local governments, that is, prefectures and municipalities, also contributed to public housing, sometimes directly operating rental apartments and sometimes setting up government-affiliated corporations.

Table 9.3 shows how the number of housing units by ownership has changed over time. Public housing was aggressively built in the 1950s and 1960s. In

Table 9.3   **Housing Units by Ownership and Landlord (in thousands)**

	Total Units (1) + (2)	Owner-Occupied (1)	Rental Total (2)	Public (2a)	Private (2b)	Employee (2c)
	17,432	12,419	5,013	614	3,233	1,166
1958	(100)	(71.2)	(28.8)	(3.5)	(18.5)	(6.7)
	20,372	13,093	7,279	944	4,904	1,433
1963	(100)	(64.3)	(35.7)	(4.6)	(24.1)	(7.0)
	24,198	14,594	9,604	1,403	6,527	1,674
1968	(100)	(60.3)	(39.7)	(5.8)	(27.0)	(6.9)
	28,731	17,007	11,724	1,995	7,889	1,839
1973	(100)	(59.2)	(40.8)	(6.9)	(27.4)	(6.4)
	32,189	19,428	12,689	2,442	8,409	1,839
1978	(100)	(60.4)	(39.4)	(7.5)	(26.1)	(5.7)
	34,705	21,650	12,951	2,645	8,487	1,819
1983	(100)	(62.4)	(37.3)	(7.6)	(24.5)	(5.2)
	37,413	22,948	14,015	2,799	9,666	1,550
1988	(100)	(61.3)	(37.5)	(7.5)	(25.8)	(4.1)

Source: Management and Coordination Agency 1986, 22, based on the housing surveys conducted every five years.

Note: Numbers in parentheses are ratio to total.

fact, the number of public housing units more than doubled from 1958 to 1968. To increase the number of housing units was a high priority. Many of the units built in those years are now considered to be too small even for the government standard.

The rate of increase has been cut by a third in recent years. It seems that the policy has shifted from just increasing public housing units to provide good quality housing and to introduce more of a market mechanism. This is a necessary change in the policy in the era of diversified needs for housing.

9.2.5 Government Guidelines

It is instructive to examine the government view of the standard quality of housing. The "minimum" and "desired" (*yudo*) standards were used, for example, by the Ministry of Construction in the fourth five-year plan installed in March 1981. The standards are defined in (1) room assignments to family members, (2) facilities, (3) environment, and (4) floor space (of rooms and of housing units) and the number of rooms. The government residential housing committee, Jutaku Takuchi Shingikai, revised the standards in 1985. In table 9.4, only the room assignments and floor space of the rooms (in tatami mats, the old standard) are used. (One tatami mat is 180 cm by 90 cm. Here it is used as a unit of floor space.) These standards are guidelines only and are not used for tax and subsidy purposes. The minimum standard, for example, means: (1) Parents exclusively occupy a bedroom of more than 6 tatami mats, with the possible exception of sharing it with a child no older than five years. (2) Children ages six to seventeen have bedrooms separate from their parents. Two children may share a bedroom of more than 6 tatami mats, or one child may occupy a bedroom of more than 4.5 tatami mats. Boys and girls age twelve and over should have separate bedrooms. (3) Any adult (age eighteen and over) should have a private bedroom with more than 4.5 tatami mats. (4) The dining-kitchen area should be separate (meaning a dining area should not be used as a bedroom at night). The desired standard has some improved conditions over the minimum: (1) Parents occupy a bedroom of more than 8 tatami mats, possi-

Table 9.4 **Housing Standards by Floor Space**

	Total (1) + (2)	Owner-Occupied (1)	Rental Total (2)	Rental Public	Rental Private	Rental Employee
Above desired standard	10,289	9,252	1,037	100	747	190
Minimum standard	23,123	13,070	10,054	1,931	6,945	1,178
Below minimum standard	3,550	626	2,924	768	1,975	182
Total	37,413	22,948	14,015	2,799	9,667	1,550

Source: 1988 Housing Survey of Japan.

Note: "Desired" and "minimum" standards are described in text.

bly sharing it with an infant age three or younger. (2) Children ages four to fourteen have bedrooms independent from parents, and two of them (under age twelve) may share a room of 8 tatami mats or larger, or each may have a room of 6 tatami mats or larger. (3) Any child age twelve and over has a separate bedroom. (4) The dining room (4.5 tatami mats for a family of three or four) and kitchen (4.5 tatami mats for a family of four or more) are separate from the bedrooms.

Some old housing units do not achieve even the minimum standard. One-fourth of public housing units fail to achieve the minimum standard, while less than 3 percent of owner-occupied housing units is below the minimum. Among the rental housing in the private market, one out of five fails the minimum standard. If public housing serves the role of safety net, the low quality may have to be endured. However, the quality of the safety net may have to be upgraded over time.

9.3   Land-Related and Housing-Related Taxes

9.3.1   Land Assessment

In the following, it is useful to distinguish the following land prices for the same piece of land: (1) the market price, or transaction price; (2) monitoring price by the Land Agency, or the government benchmark (land) prices (*koji kakaku*); (3) assessment for bequest tax purpose by the National Tax Agency, or street value (*rosen ka*); (4) assessment for the property tax, administered by the municipal government, in consultation with the central and prefectural governments; and (5) monitoring for representative places by the prefectural government. There is also the land price index of urban districts surveyed by the Japan Real Estate Institute, a nongovernment agency.

The *koji kakaku* has been tabulated by the Land Agency every January 1 since 1970. The price is determined by actual transactions in neighboring places, with some considerations to the value calculated as the sum of dis-counted future rents. Points where prices are monitored currently number about 17,000 nationwide. (The number of monitoring points was much smaller until the mid-1970s.) There are significant overlaps for monitoring points every year, although there are several substitutions. It is widely believed that the *koji kakaku* is below the market value by 20–30 percent.

How to tax real estate is a sensitive political issue, since many land and housing owners are traditional supporters of the Liberal democratic party. In the United States, various local referenda passed in the early 1980s, to limit the property tax rate in the community. In Japan, the property tax (prefectural tax) "rate" is "standardized" at 1.4 percent by law (to be explained shortly). However, assessment of real estate (mostly land) varies with prefectures: wealthy prefectures assess land far below its market value, while relatively poor prefectures assess land near its market value. Homma and Atoda (1990,

134–35) investigated the gap between the *koji kakaku* and *rosen ka* at the places of highest *rosen ka* in the capital cities of prefectures. They found that in 1988 the gap ranged from 33.5 percent (in Kyoto) to 94.1 percent (in Kōfu), with the average of 56.5 percent of *koji kakaku*.

The assessment of property for bequest taxes is based on a different assessment schedule. The *rosen ka,* for bequest, is 50–70 percent of the *koji kakaku.* This means that the *rosen ka* is about a quarter to a half of the market value.

9.3.2   Land-Related Taxes

This section summarizes all land-related taxes. Various implications are examined in section 9.4. There are four types of taxes at the time of land acquisition. (1) The property, including land and structures, is assessed at real estate tax assessment and taxed by a prefecture. The tax rate is 4 percent. Structures as well as land values are taxed. (2) Special land acquisition tax at the time of purchase is imposed by a municipality (city, town, or village). The land assessment is the actual purchase price. The tax rate is 3 percent. The real estate acquisition tax is deductible from the value. An application of this tax is very limited. (3) Registration tax is collected at the rate of 0.5 percent by the national government at the time of title transfer. Real estate tax assessment is used for valuation of land. (4) Inheritance tax is imposed on acquisition by bequest. *Rosen ka* is used for assessing the value of land. For an estate, value per beneficiary is subject to the 10–70 percent progressive marginal tax rate. (See Barthold and Ito [1992] for details.)

There are three kinds of landholding tax. (1) The property tax is imposed by a municipality on the value of land and structures assessed by real estate tax assessment. The standard rate is 1.4 percent; in limited cases, the rate is 2.1 percent. (2) City planning tax is also imposed by a municipality at the rate of 0.3 percent of the same base of real estate tax. (3) Special landholding tax may be assessed by a municipality at the rate of 1.4 percent. This is imposed on the base of the purchase price.

There are three types of capital gains tax. Individual income tax and corporate income tax is imposed by the national government. Prefectural and municipal inhabitant tax is imposed on top of the national income tax. An application of this tax is very limited.

Real Estate Tax

The assessment of real estate under the property tax is systematically below market value by as much as 50 percent. The heavy transfer tax, combined with light property tax, encourages hoarding when prices are expected to rise. As mentioned above, the standard rate for the real estate tax is nationally set at 1.4 percent. (This is legislated in the Local Tax Law, administered by the Ministry of Home Affairs [Jichisho].) However, the municipal governments tend to set the assessment below the market value (within some bound below the value of reference points in each prefecture, which is determined by the central government). One of the reasons for the proposed landholding tax is that the Ministry of Home Affairs or the Ministry of Finance has not been able to make local governments commit themselves to raise assessed land values for real estate tax purposes. Local governments are viewed as appeasing their constituents rather than popping a bubble.

Capital Gains Tax

Capital gains tax is levied when property is sold. If a property was held by an individual for more than five years, the marginal rate is 20 percent (plus local inhabitants' tax of 6 percent) for up to 40 million yen, and 25 percent (plus 7.5 percent local inhabitants' tax) for the value beyond 40 million yen. The tax schedule is higher for property held less than five years: the marginal rate is 40 percent plus inhabitants' tax of 12 percent. It is now proposed to raise the tax rate for the more-than-five year property (20 percent) to that of the less-than-five-year category (40 percent).

Another surcharge is applicable if gains were made as miscellaneous income or property business income and the land was held for less than two years. The surcharge and tax rate amounts to 50 percent plus inhabitants' tax of 15 percent. These provisions are introduced to prevent speculative (short-term) demand on land. During the periods when the land prices rose sharply, many real estate companies still made large profits by quick turnovers.

A reduction in the tax rate is applicable for an owner-occupied property where the owner lived for more than ten years. The capital gains tax rate for such a property is 10 percent (plus 4 percent inhabitants' tax) up to 4 million yen and 15 percent (plus 5 percent inhabitants' tax) beyond that.

There are several deductions in calculating taxable capital gains. One million yen is deductible for the property owned by individuals beyond five years; 30 million yen is deductible for an owner-occupied property; and 50 million yen is deductible for a property sold because of the government's forceful acquisition (eminent domain in the United States, as for construction of a road or an airport).

For corporations, the capital gains from property are treated separately. A surcharge of 30 percent of the corporate income tax is assessed for property held for less than two years, bringing the effective tax rate to 85.17 percent (surcharge of 30 percent, ordinary corporate tax of 37.5 percent, corporate inhabitants' tax of 11.67 percent, and corporate enterprise tax of 6 percent). The effective rate is reduced to 73.45 percent for property held between two and five years. The capital gains tax for property held more than five years is treated as regular corporate income tax. The capital gains tax is double-edged. On the one hand, it helps to pop a bubble and restore "equity" among people who make real estate investment in different locations. On the other hand, the capital gains tax is known to cause a lock-in effect. When a high rate of capital gains tax is applied, people are not encouraged to sell property. That is, once land is purchased and has experienced capital gains, an owner (or an investor) becomes reluctant to take capital gains realizations, even if other factors favor selling units. Other factors include a change in family size, a change in job location, a demand for liquidity of housing equities, and a desired shift of portfolio prompted by a change in various market conditions. Since property tax in Japan is generally considered lower than in the United States, this explains why some of the land in the most expensive areas in Tokyo is left without being developed. When land tends to be locked in by the tax system, it is difficult to plan large-scale housing or commercial development projects. Until 1988, the capital gains tax on residential housing was waived if the house was replaced by another house with equal or greater value (as in the U.S. system). However, in the wake of "sprawling" land price increases from the center of Tokyo to the suburbs, the Ministry of Finance suddenly suspended the provision in 1988. This has further discouraged the sale of housing in the last few years.

Economists are divided as to whether the capital gains tax should be raised or lowered. There are two major factors for the difference in judgment: whether the land price contains speculative bubbles and whether the lock-in effect is considered large. Increasing property taxes and lowering capital gains taxes on properties are advocated from the viewpoint of efficient development and usage of land by those who consider the lock-in effect to be large and the bubble component in land small. Even those who consider that land prices contain significant bubbles may favor lowering capital gains, if the tax savings can be passed on to the buyers easily, so that an imposition of capital gains would not deter speculative activities.

If land prices increases happen to have a bubble component, transaction taxes and *short-term* capital gains taxes are an effective way to curb a bubble. Increasing the capital gains tax is favored by those who think that land prices increase due to speculative activities and that an imposition of capital gains taxes would deter speculations. Those who believe that an equitable distribution of wealth has the top priority also tend to oppose lowering capital gains taxes. Lowering the current capital gains tax is *not* advocated by those who consider that the lock-in effect is small; that is, the decision to sell a property is prompted by factors other than taxes, and the current tax rate would not change the decision anyway. They also consider that, if capital gains tax relief (or deferment) is available for change of a principal residence (replacement sale), this would restore locational efficiency to some extent.

In Japan, it is currently recommended that the capital gains tax rate for a long-term property holding be increased. Since a bubble is not likely to survive five years, the new proposal is to restore "equity," or, to put it bluntly, to bash windfall gainers. However, this would make reallocation of land through the market mechanism more difficult. The trade-off is unfortunately not carefully evaluated in the tax reform discussions. The Ministry of Finance usually states that the elasticity of land supply with respect to capital gains is low. Some authors also believe that the lock-in effect is rather minor (for example,

Kanemoto, Hayashi, and Wago 1987). However, this may cause an unexpected liquidity problem.

Bequest Tax

The inheritance tax burden in Japan is much heavier than in the United States. The marginal rate goes up to 70 percent quickly, and there is no simple way to create a tax-exempt trust for one's heirs. Because the inter vivos gift is taxes at a higher tax rate (with the 600,000-yen annual deductible), most intergenerational gifts take place at the time of death. (However, annual deductibles may be used repeatedly for many years in order to lessen the taxes for intergenerational transfers.) While bonds and other securities are assessed at market value for the purpose of the inheritance tax, real estate is assessed below market value. The assessment for bequest taxes (using *rosen ka*) is about half the market value, while the liabilities for the real estate are fully deductible. (If the property is bought within three years prior to the death, the property is evaluated at the purchase price. This provision, introduced at the end of the 1980s, is to prevent "last-minute tax planning" by the family.) If and when one plans a bequest, it is preferable from the standpoint of tax savings to hold real assets rather than financial assets at the time of death. (This is analogous to "flower bonds" in the United States.) This helps explain why the elderly in Japan retain housing and other real estate until their death. The share of real estate in taxable bequests in Japan is about 60 percent, while the comparable ratio in the United States is about 25 percent. (See Barthold and Ito [1992] for details.) To the extent that real estate becomes a vehicle for bequests, land and housing prices are likely to contain a premium relating to this vehicle. Although it is not clear how significant this premium is in actual land prices, it may be quite large, given the extent of undervaluation of real estate. There is no question from the viewpoint of efficient resource allocation about the need to adjust the assessment of real properties to the market value, that is, to *increase* the effective bequest tax. However, from an equity point of view, *lowering* the bequest tax rate has been advocated. This argument emphasizes unexpected rises in land prices that jeopardize the bequest plans of ordinary citizens. If a bequest motive to hand down a family asset to the next generation should be respected, then an unexpected burden in inheritance taxes from speculative bubbles should be lightened. However, if the land price increase is within the range of expectations reflecting "fundamentals," then the increase in tax burden just reflects the increased value in resource allocations. There is no reason to reduce tax burden in this case. The value of land in the bequeathed state may be further reduced if the land, or the structure on the land, is leased or rented out. (See section 9.3.3 for details.) Moreover, the assessment of land up to two hundred square meters, in cases of owner-occupied housing and of rental business (more than ten units), is further reduced. (The provision could be applied to the sum of several lots.) For example, if the decedent owned a principal residence of two hundred square meters, then the value of land (pro-rated to two hundred square meters) is reduced by 50 percent. If the land was used for a rental business, then the land value is reduced by 60 percent.

Taxes on Agricultural Land in Cities

Agricultural land is taxed much more lightly than residential land. While some arguments, such as national security regarding food, have been made to support this approach, there is little ground for permitting preferential treatment for small agricultural lots in cities. From the viewpoint of city planning, agricultural plots in city residential areas should be taxed at the same rate as residential plots. This was what the tax law of 1982 was supposed to achieve: in the three largest metropolitan areas (Tokyo, Osaka, and Nagoya), agricultural lots in areas that city planning designates as residential or commercial and where the appraisal value is more than 30,000 yen per 3.3 square meters are supposed to be taxed at the residential rate, in order to increase land supply. However, this provision has a loophole. If a lot is more than 990 square meters and the owner farmer plans to continue farming for the coming ten years, the lot is exempted from being taxed at the residential or commercial rate. The farming rate is on average 1/37 for the three metropolitan areas and 1/57 in Tokyo. Because the definition of farming is rather arbitrary, the loophole is widely exploited. Only 15.5 percent of such agricultural lots are taxed at the residential rates (table 9.5).

Tax-Exempt Fringe Benefits

Another peculiar aspect of the Japanese housing market is the prevalence of company housing and public-servant housing, both of which are heavily subsidized in rents. Costs of operating company housing can be deducted as

Table 9.5   Agricultural Lots in the Special Residential Area

Fiscal Year	Tokyo[a] Applicable (hectares) (1)	Exempted (hectares) (2)	% (2)/(1)	Three Metropolitan Areas Applicable (hectares) (3)	Exempted (hextares) (4)	% (4)/(3)
1982	30,261	24,510	90.0	42,472	35,030	82.5
1983	29,065	24,191	83.2	40,922	34,526	84.4
1984	28,299	23,484	83.0	39,904	33,592	84.2
1985[b]	29,612	24,709	83.4	44,975	38,120	84.8
1986	28,824	23,970	83.2	43,932	37,121	84.5

Source: Namekawa 1988, 98.

[a]The Tokyo area includes Tokyo, Ibaraki, Saitama, Chiba, and Kanagawa prefectures.

[b]After an appraisal change in 1985, more land was assessed at more than 30,000 yen per 3.3 square meters.

operating expenses of the corporation, while the subsidized part of rents (fringe benefits) are not taxable in employee's income. This tax wedge is part of the reason for the prevalence of company housing. Public-servant housing is generally low quality but heavily subsidized in rents. This fringe benefit is also nontaxable in government employees' income tax. In 1983, 14 percent of rental housing units were in the form of company and public-servant housing (Management and Coordination Agency 1986).

9.3.3   Housing-Related Taxes

Owner-occupied housing enjoys some tax benefits in both Japan and the United States. The tax benefits are not readily compared. In the United States, interest payments on mortgages for owner-occupied housing (and land) may be deducted from taxable income when itemized deductions are chosen. In many cases, itemized deductions become preferable over the standard basic deduction only after one becomes an owner of a principal residence.

In Japan, a tax credit (not income deduction) for owner-occupied housing loans is calculated from the balance of loans for structures (not including loans for land) and is applicable only for six years after acquisition. This provision was introduced only in tax year 1987 (and the limit was five years until 1990). The amount of tax credit is 1 percent of the loan balance at the end of the calendar year. Because of the six-year limitation, the tax benefit for owner-occupied housing is relatively minor in Japan.

Landlords of rental housing units also benefit from favorable tax treatment. Interest payments for housing loans toward constructing rental housing units (housing and land purchases), along with maintenance costs, are fully deductible from rental income. (If interest payments and other costs exceeded rental income, deficits were deductible from other income, such as earned income. However, it has been limited to interest payments resulting from loans for structures since 1991.) Management of rental housing enjoys different kinds of tax benefits. If a landlord manages more than ten units, the rental income is considered to be a real estate business. This qualifies for broadened deductible expenses, including presumed salary payments to family members.

Holding rental housing provides additional benefits in bequest tax calculation. As mentioned above, real estate is valued at about half of the market value. However, the assessment of land and housing structures is further reduced by 30 percent if the property is rented out. (A parallel bequest tax provision is applied to leases. Leases are valued at 30 percent of the property value in the bequeathed properties of leasors. These provisions can be justified, because it is difficult to get rid of tenants, as explained in section 9.4.1.) Also, recall the special bequest tax provision: the value of land up to two hundred square meters is further reduced if the estate has rental housing of more than ten units.

In sum, tax benefits for owner-occupied housing are very limited, while there are strong tax benefits, in every year and in the case of bequests, to own properties of more than ten rental units. This is said to have contributed to a sharp increase in the supply of rental units in the second half of the 1980s.

9.4 Land-Related Legal Problems

9.4.1 Overprotection of Tenants

The law regarding the leasing of a piece of land, the Land Lease Law (Shakuchi Ho), and the law regarding the rental of a house, the Building Lease Law (Shakuya Ho), are known to protect tenants rather than landlords. The laws contain provisions to extend leases almost automatically: if land is leased indefinitely and the lessee builds a concrete building, then the lease must extend sixty years; if the structure is not concrete, for example, a wooden house, then the lease must extend thirty years. Even if the original lease expires, so long as the building is maintained in good condition, the lease is automatically extended and cannot be terminated at the will of the landlord.

In the case of house rentals, leases extend no less than one year. This is apparently not too restrictive. However, the landlord cannot terminate a lease, unless the landlord moves into the unit or under a "rightful cause," a provision that is typically interpreted, in court cases, very strictly. Raising rents in order to force tenants to move out is virtually impossible. If tenants dispute the increase in rents, they may deposit rents in an escrow account while they ask for an arbitration at the district court. Precedents in such cases allowed rents to rise at a rate near cost increases or general inflation.

In sum, it is extremely difficult for landlords to remove a tenant. One way is to pay a considerable compensation to the renter (lessee) to move out.

Several difficulties result from these laws. First, there is little large-size and/ or high-quality rental housing in Japan. Landlords are afraid of large investments that might go sour. Second, it has become common practice to require large payments from renters (equivalent to two months' rent) to initiate the lease. This constitutes a risk premium for the landlord. Third, redevelopment is impeded when it is difficult to remove a small number of remaining residents in a run-down apartment building despite large vacancies, or when a large development project covering a block contains a few renters of land.

These difficulties may also contribute to high land prices. Because the supply of land, if currently leased, is restrained by these factors, the neighborhood and relative advantage of a particular lot changes drastically.

9.4.2 Sunshine Law and Cubic Restriction

In most cases, the height and total cubic size of buildings are regulated. For example, if the area is designated as a class-one residential area, then a structure must be under ten meters high. The sunshine restriction puts limits on building a house or other structure that deprives sunlight from a neighboring house for more than certain limits (usually three hours a day during the winter time). Of course, zoning is established for a good reason, and the sunshine law is important to protect a family from negative externalities. However, a Pareto-improving solution can be prepared in most cases. If the actual development of surrounding areas, such as new subway lines and highway construction, takes a path not expected at the time of zoning, rezoning should be recommended. Moreover, if neighbors could agree, many small houses should be able to get together to build a high-rise. High-rise development may run into problems of rezoning and the tenant law mentioned above.

9.4.3   Direct Intervention (Price Monitoring)

In the wake of the sharp price increase in 1986–87, particularly in the large cities, various measures were introduced in an attempt to curb land price increases. Most of the emergency measures explained below were introduced on the implicit assumption that the price increases were mostly bubbles.

The trading of land above a certain size in a designated neighborhood of large cities became subject to a government agency's approval in 1987. Price monitoring, as a measure empowered by the Act for Planning the Use of the Land (Kokudo Riyo Keikaku Ho), was enforced in twenty-three wards and neighboring cities in Tokyo after August 1987, in suburban cities of Tokyo after 1987, in Yokohama and Kawasaki after August 1987, and in parts of Osaka after December 1987.

For example, in the twenty-three wards and some neighboring cities of Tokyo, trade involving more than one hundred square meters in commercial and residential areas (*shigaika kuiki*) has to be reviewed by the Tokyo government. If the price of land is judged to be too high, then the seller and the buyer are "advised" to lower the sale price. This price monitoring system was designed to check land price inflation and to protect innocent buyers who were uninformed of the unreasonableness of the price. In a highly publicized case, the sale of land of the Australian Embassy in Tokyo was not approved at the original terms.

Regulations invite more regulations. First, to gain information about an acceptable range, which is not made public, the realtors present insincere sale applications. In order to check these applications, regulatory authorities warn realtors that they failed to carry out preapproved trades. Second, if disapproval of a price is feared, the buyer and the seller can agree to put a higher price on structures and a lower price on land. The regulatory authority has not been prepared to evaluate the value of structures. Third, the exemption of smaller lots from price monitoring encourages subdivision. To prevent this, the threshold size had to be reduced. (In the twenty-three Tokyo wards, the threshold was reduced to one hundred from three hundreds square meters in November 1987.)

Another problem arises from the inefficient use of public lands. Auctions of unused public land have been indefinitely suspended out of concern that the high bid price would enhance a speculative bubble in the neighborhood.

These regulations are not only ineffective but counterproductive, if the real causes of land price increases are "fundamentals." Price monitoring would decrease the supply if the perceived acceptable range is too low. Moreover, if the price monitoring is viewed as a temporary measure, potential sellers may wait until it become politically unsustainable. Therefore, the supply will most likely decrease under the monitoring system, thus contributing to higher prices. Direct intervention can be unfair, too. Some individuals need to sell land to resolve immediate cash-flow problems: those who pay their bequest tax by selling a part of the bequeathed land and those who liquidate a failed company. Selling under price monitoring may mean obtaining less than fair value for their assets.

Why did these regulations come to exist, if they are ineffective, counterproductive, and unfair? One reason is that the government wanted to shift the blame for the higher price from the government, which failed to increase supply to a scapegoat, the speculators. Another reason is that the current landowners who do not plan to sell wish to keep assessment values down, by restricting sales with high prices in their neighborhood.

If the recent experience of land price increases involves an extraordinary bubble, measures to increase the land supply will pop the bubble. Direct intervention, on the other hand, would not help pop the bubble. Rather, it would make the bubble larger by restricting supply. If the land price increase is due to strong economic growth, as suggested above, then direct intervention only induces creative ways to avoid regulations. Moreover, measures to increase land supply will surely slow the price increase, even if the land price increase was caused by a demand pull.

9.5 Public Policy for Quality

The housing stock in Japan is of low quality in comparison with other Organization for Economic Cooperation and Development (OECD) countries: it is smaller and has fewer facilities and amenities. Even if the number of houses per adult in Japan rises to the U.S. level, the quality of housing in Japan is likely to remain far below that of in the United States. Although equity considerations are important, there may be better ways to help the poor while minimizing the violation of efficiency. In many ways, public policy has been targeted to increase the quantity of housing units. Only recently has attention been given to quality. Public policy for quality, if ever needed, may be quite different from that for quantity. For example, the (lowest) subsidized mortgage rate granted by the public-sector Japan Housing Loan Corporation applies only to the floor space of a purchased house below a threshold size. (See Seko, ch. 3 in this volume, for details.) Perhaps a ceiling on the yen amount of subsidized loans could be justified from the fairness point of view; however, the floor-space restriction encourages the construction of small houses and prevents development of high-quality housing in suburban areas. The government has more direct ways of contributing to improvements in the housing stock. First, many government entities maintain subsidized (rental) housing for their employees. While most of them satisfy the minimum standard of living, some are simply too old and too small. In fact, some of these units in Tokyo do not even have flush toilets. Second, much of the public rental housing is of low quality: more than 90 percent of public rental housing units fall short of the target size of housing (table 9.4).

It is extremely important to renovate or replace aging government properties with very small units, both those used by government employees and those used as rental housing. Many of those buildings are low-rises and could be replaced by high-rises with larger units. For example, the Tokyo Municipal Housing Corporation built 59,803 units between 1950 and 1985. Many units built in the 1950s and early 1960s have floor space of less than forty square meters. No buildings have been rebuilt, often because of the opposition by a small number of residents (recall the overprotection of tenants).

9.6   Efficiency versus Equity

As a philosophy (a principle beyond allocative efficiency) of public policy regarding to land and housing, protection of the underprivileged is most frequently mentioned in Japan. A close examination, however, reveals that taxes and regulations with an intention of protecting the underprivileged often have the opposite effect. For example, the Building Lease Law that overly protects the tenant discourages the supply of high-quality rental housing, so that potential tenants for that market are hurt. (There is an analogy to rent control in the United States.) Low assessments for real estate taxes and bequest taxes are often defended by the same argument. It is against the philosophy of protecting the underprivileged if market values are assessed in full when the land price is skyrocketing. It is a pity if a long-term resident has to sell a home and move due to real estate taxes. However, reducing the assessment encourages the underuse of land, while waiting for capital gains and the death of the owner. Heavy subsidies to corporate and government employee housing also work against development of high-quality housing. Hence, tax system and regulations regarding the philosophy may turn out to be counterproductive for efficient use of land. A proper balance between efficiency and equity (and not just an attempt to lower land prices) must be sought in future tax reform and regulatory changes with regard to land use.

9.7   Concluding Remarks

This paper examined important public policy related to housing in Japan. The emphasis is on analyses of effects and distortions that are implied by various land-related and housing-related taxes and regulations in Japan. The conventional wisdom is that the number of units of owner-occupied housing is enough, but household formation in Japan is discouraged, probably because of high housing costs.

From the viewpoint that more attention should be paid toward efficiency in land allocation, several problems in current taxes and regulations were critically examined. First, the land-related and housing-related taxes were examined. In particular, property taxes and the system of capital gains were discussed from the viewpoint of lock-in effects. Conventional wisdom is that the property tax is relatively low so that speculative investment in real estate is not prevented. It is often recommended to raise the real estate assessment by prefectural government and/or to create a national landholding tax. In addition, capital gains taxes are raised (especially for the short-term holding) to "prevent" a speculative demand. I cautiously advocate the use of capital gains tax for this purpose, because of its lock-in effect.

Second, the bequest tax was shown to have caused distortions. Assessment of land and structures for bequest taxes is much lower than the market value. The Japanese bequeathed assets consist mostly of real estate, in contrast to the U.S. bequeathed assets. In fact, the Japanese elderly, who plan to bequeath some assets, have strong incentive (1) to hold on to their principal residence, no matter how mismatched for their needs in retirement years, and (2) to purchase real estate with a high leverage. The latter feature is an effect tax-saving strategy, since real estate is assessed at much less than market value and liability is deducted from the estate in full. It is suspected that this tax distortion also cause a lock-in effect until the uncertain timing of death.

The paper further examined the housing-related taxes and regulations. There are two salient features on this point. First, housing loans for owner-occupied housing have only a partial tax benefit (in the form of tax credit) in Japan. This, in combination with a large down-payment burden, works to delay house purchasing in one's life cycle. In contrast, landlords of rental housing property, especially with more than ten units, enjoy various tax benefits. Second, the Land Lease and Building Lease Laws in Japan protect tenants so much that no landlords would want to put high-quality housing on the rental market. Note that the horizon of a lease is virtually indefinite, although the contract has an apparent termination date. The result is that when a family becomes large, it is necessary to purchase a house instead of relocating to larger rental housing, which is nonexistent.

Another peculiar aspect of the Japanese housing market is the prevalence of company housing and public-servant housing, both of which are heavily subsidized in rents. This seems to be at least partly due to the tax advantage that benefits both employers and employees: operating expenses of company housing are deductible in the company's profit calculation, while the subsidized part of rents (fringe benefits) are not taxable in employees' income. Public-servant housing is generally low quality but heavily subsidized in rents. This fringe benefit is also nontaxable in government employees' income tax. These distortions may partly develop high-quality housing.

Public policy regarding land and housing emphasizes protection of the underprivileged in Japan. However, taxes and regulations with an intention of protecting the underprivileged often have the opposite economic effects.

In summary, all economists in Japan recommend raising the assessments of land for property and bequest taxes in order to eliminate distortions. Those who believe that lock-in effects are large recommend a reduction in capital gains tax (at least for the long-term holding). Combined with less transactions tax, less capital gains tax would enhance the efficient allocation of land. However, these changes may be opposed by those who want to use the tax system to achieve equity instead of efficiency and to prevent bubbles from forming in the housing market. Also, economists are generally in favor of modifying the Land Lease and Building Lease Laws to allow landlords to terminate leases at the time of their expiration. These changes would increase the supply of high-quality rental housing.

References

Barthold, Thomas, and Takatoshi Ito. 1992. Bequest Taxes and Accumulation of Household Wealth: U.S.—Japan Comparison. In *The Political Economy of Tax Reforms,* ed. T. Ito and A. O. Krueger. Chicago: University of Chicago Press.

Hayashi, Fumio, Takatoshi Ito, and Joel Slemrod. 1988. Housing Finance Imperfections, Taxation, and Private Saving: A Comparative Simulation Analysis of the U.S. and Japan. *Journal of the Japanese and International Economies* 2 (3): 215–38.

Homma, Masaaki, and Masumi Atoda, eds. 1990. *Empirical Research on Tax Reform.* Tokyo: Toyo Keizai Shinpo sha.

Horioka, Charles. 1988. Saving for Housing Purchase in Japan. *Journal of the Japanese and International Economies* 2: 351–84.

Ito, Takatoshi. 1993. The Land/Housing Problem in Japan: A Macroeconomic Approach. *Journal of the Japanese and International Economies* (1): 1–31.

———. 1992. *The Japanese Economy.* Cambridge: MIT Press.

Kanemoto, Yoshitsugu, Fumio Hayashi, and Hajime Wago. 1987. An Econometric Analysis of a Capital Gains Tax on Land. *Economic Studies Quarterly* (2): 159–72.

Management and Coordination Agency. Statistics Bureau. 1986. *Housing of Japan: Summary of the Results of 1983 Housing Survey of Japan.* Tokyo: Japan Statistics Association.

Namekawa, Masashi. 1988. *Economics of Problems of Land and Its Price.* Tokyo: Toyo Keizai Shinpo sha.

10   Public Policy and Housing in the United States

James M. Poterba

10.1   Introduction

Housing accounts for one-sixth of consumption expenditure in the United States, second only to food among budget categories. It is also the expenditure category that is most directly affected by public policy. The U.S. tax code is the most important policy instrument that affects housing. The federal income tax subsidizes homeowners by not including imputed rent in the tax base, while allowing deductions for mortgage interest payments. There have also been generous subsidies to rental housing through accelerated depreciation and other tax benefits.

Public policy also affects the housing sector through a variety of programs to support borrowing for home purchase. Targeted low-interest credit initiatives, such as the Federal Housing Administration and the Veterans Administration loan program, permit certain classes of individuals to borrow at below-market interest rates. More generally, the entire housing sector has historically benefited from federal support of savings and loan institutions and from the operation of federal agencies such as the Federal National Mortgage Association, which facilitate smooth operation of a secondary mortgage market.

Finally, a number of federal and state-local programs assist low-income households in finding housing. These include community development grants, subsidies to construction of low-income housing, and direct public-sector intervention to build and operate public housing. Along with food stamps and Medicaid, these programs constitute a major source of in-kind assistance to the poverty population.

James M. Poterba is professor of economics at the Massachusetts Institute of Technology and the director of the Public Economics Program at the National Bureau of Economic Research.

The author is grateful to the National Science Foundation and the John M. Olin Foundation for research support, and to Edgar Olsen for helpful comments.

U.S. public policy toward housing has changed significantly in the last decade. The tax reforms of 1981 and 1986 reduced the value of tax-exempt imputed income for homeowners and made dramatic changes in the tax incentives for rental investment. The prospective subsidy to traditional housing finance institutions, notably thrifts, has also changed as a result of the federal rescue of thrift institutions in the late 1980s. The future therefore portends a U.S. policy stance that provides less encouragement for the housing sector than did other policies in recent history.

This paper describes each of these public policies, noting their current status and changes through time, and assesses their effects on the U.S. housing market. The paper is divided into five sections. Section 10.2 presents background information on housing markets in the United States, such as the distribution of housing expenditure, the mix of owners versus renters in different age groups, and the mortgage status of the U.S. housing stock. Section 10.3 describes the tax benefits available to homeowners and notes how these incentives have shifted through time. It also discusses the tax subsidies to rental housing, noting the controversy surrounding the links between tax subsidies to landlords and the rents ultimately charged tenants. Section 10.4 describes housing programs that operate through financial markets, both targeted mortgage subsidies and more general programs that affect the nature of mortgage markets. Section 10.5 discusses housing programs that target low-income households for direct provision of housing services. It provides information on the size of the population affected by these programs, as well as data on the level of support provided. There is a brief conclusion.

10.2   Stylized Facts about the U.S. Housing Market

This section considers the pattern of housing expenditures across different household types, the status of households as owners or renters, and the financial characteristics of both new buyers and existing homeowners.

Table 10.1 reports data on the tenure choice of households in different economic strata. The table reports tabulations from the 1986 *Consumer Expenditure Survey*. Households are divided into deciles based on their total expenditures, with higher outlays indicating better economic circumstances.[1] The table shows that most households in upper economic strata are owner-occupiers, while most lower-strata households are renters. More than 60 percent of the households in the lowest expenditure decile are renters, compared with only 15 percent of those in the highest outlay category. The bottom third of the expenditure distribution contains half of all renter households.

Table 10.2 shows the age-specific home-ownership rates for U.S. house-

---

1. Poterba (1989) argues that consumption provides a more satisfactory basis than annual income for classifying households. The results in table 10.1 are insensitive, however, to the choice of income or expenditure to define the deciles.

Table 10.1   **Housing Consumption by Expenditure Deciles, 1986**

Consumption Decile	Average ($)	Average Pretax Income ($)	Average Annual Rent (if Renters) ($)	% Renters
1	4,008	5,785	978	63.3
2	7,260	9,212	2,170	60.0
3	9,641	13,989	2,802	51.5
4	11,941	16,691	3,380	49.7
5	14,260	20,974	3,952	45.3
6	17,009	25,847	4,114	34.9
7	20,410	29,650	4,643	30.8
8	24,739	36,752	4,438	27.3
9	31,624	40,519	5,528	17.5
10	58,477	51,499	5,506	15.2

Source: Tabulations from the *Consumer Expenditure Survey,* 1986 (first-quarter expenditure data).

Table 10.2   **Age-Specific Home-ownership Rates, United States, 1988**

Age Category	% Homeowners	Age Category	% Homeowners
Under 25	15.7	50-54	77.1
25–29	35.9	55–59	79.3
30–34	53.2	60–64	79.8
35–39	63.6	65–69	80.0
40–44	70.7	70–74	77.7
45–49	74.4	Over 75	70.8

Source: Unpublished tabulations from the *Current Population Survey.*

holds in 1988. There is a sharp increase in home-ownership rates for households in their late twenties and early thirties. By age thirty-five, more than half of all households own their own homes. For those approaching retirement, the home-ownership rate exceeds 80 percent. Venti and Wise (1989) note that home equity constitutes the most important asset for many elderly households. The age-specific tenure rates provide important insight on the differential benefits of subsidies to owners and renters.

Table 10.3 presents information on changes through time in the ratio of outstanding mortgages to the value of the owner-occupied housing stock. At the end of the 1980s, housing debt accounted for nearly half of the value of owner-occupied homes. This loan-to-value ratio rose during the 1980s; it was only 36.6 percent at the end of 1980. Movements in the loan-to-value ratio are driven partly by real house price changes and partly by borrowing behavior. In the late 1970s, when real house prices rose sharply, the loan-to-value ratio declined. During the 1980s, the rise of home equity mortgages and the stability

Table 10.3   Loan-to-Value Ratios for Owner-Occupied Housing, 1960–89 (%)

Year	Loan-to-Value Ratio	Home-ownership Rate
1955	30.5	—
1960	36.8	61.9
1965	46.3	—
1970	42.0	62.9
1975	38.0	—
1980	36.6	65.6
1985	42.2	63.9
1990	51.4	64.0

Source: Board of Governors of the Federal Reserve System, *Household Net Worth*, December 1990; Current Population Survey.

of house prices coincided with an increase in loan-to-value ratios to record levels above 50 percent.

The *average* loan-to-value ratio may differ significantly from the loan-to-value ratio on newly purchased homes. Surveys by the Chicago Title Insurance Company suggest an average down payment as a fraction of sales price of 24 percent in 1988, with smaller down payments (15 percent) by first-time buyers. The deductibility provisions for mortgage interest, which now stand in sharp contrast to the nondeductibility of other types of consumer debt, are thus a critical component of the subsidy to new home buyers.

The second column in table 10.3 reports the aggregate home-ownership rate. The share of the population owning their homes grew from the Second World War until 1980. After peaking at 65.6 percent in 1980, however, the home-ownership rate *declined* during the first half of the 1980s, to below 64 percent in 1985. The tenure mix was quite stable in the late 1980s. Because the tenure mix adjusts slowly to varying economic incentives, it may still be premature to assess the effects of the decade's tax reforms on home-ownership rates.

10.3   Tax Subsidies to Housing Investments

This section describes the net tax posture toward owner-occupied and rental real estate. It contrasts the cost of housing with and without tax subsidies, and describes the important consequences of the major tax reforms in the 1980s.

10.3.1   Owner-Occupied Housing Subsidies

The single most important subsidy to housing in the United States is the federal tax code's omission of imputed housing income in defining taxable income. To calibrate the impact of tax provisions on the demand for housing, it is helpful to define the *after-tax user cost of home ownership*. This measures the marginal cost of an incremental dollar of owner-occupied housing, including the forgone return on the owner's equity. It is defined as

(1) $$c_o = [(1 - \theta)(i + \tau_p) + \delta + \alpha + m - \pi_c]P_o,$$

where i is the nominal interest rate, τ_p is the property tax rate per dollar of property value,[2] θ is the household's marginal federal income tax rate, δ is the physical decay rate for the property, α is the risk premium for housing investments, m is the cost of home maintenance as a fraction of house value, π_e is the expected rate of house price appreciation, and P_o is the real price of owner-occupied housing.[3] This expression applies only to households who itemize for federal income tax purposes. For the nearly half of all homeowners who do not, $\theta = 0$.

The user cost of home ownership varies across households. For itemizers, it is inversely related to a household's marginal tax rate. While it reflects the *marginal* cost of additional housing purchases, it may not reflect the *average* cost, which determines the most cost-effective way for a given household to obtain housing services. For homeowners who would not have itemized in the absence of the property tax and mortgage interest deduction, but do because of these items, the marginal cost of housing is given by (1) but the average cost depends on the total tax saving. This is

(2) $$\text{Tax Saving} = \theta(\tau_p + i\beta)P_o H - S,$$

where H is the quantity of housing, S is the household's standard deduction, and β is the loan-to-value ratio for the property. For homeowners who do not itemize even with their housing-related deductions, the marginal user cost is

(3) $$c_o' = \{[(1 - \beta)(1 - \theta) + \beta]i + \tau_p + \delta + m - \pi_c\}P_o.$$

Table 10.4 presents evidence on the tax status of U.S. homeowners in 1985, prior to the Tax Reform Act, which reduced the probability that homeowners would choose to itemize. The number of tax returns with itemized property tax deductions was only 57 percent of the total number of owner-occupied properties. More than 40 percent of the home-owning population therefore faced the nonitemizer user cost for housing. In part, the surprisingly small share of homeowners who itemize reflects the substantial number of properties without mortgages. Only 57.3 percent of homeowners in 1985 had mortgages; this is due to a very high rate of home ownership among elderly households, many of whom have repaid their mortgages. In 1980, the weighted-average marginal federal tax rate on mortgage interest deductions was 32 percent. By

---

2. Only the part of the property taxes that is *not* a "benefit tax," a fee for local public service provision, should actually be included in the user cost.

3. This equation assumes that all capital gains on owner-occupied dwellings are untaxed. Since each household is eligible for \$125,000 in untaxed lifetime gains, this assumption may not be unrealistic. If it were not satisfied, π_e would be replaced with $(1 - \tau_g)\pi_e$, where τ_g is the effective capital gains tax rate. A more heroic implicit assumption is that the household faces identical borrowing and lending rates. Further discussion of these assumptions and information on plausible parameter values for the components of equation (1) may be found in Poterba (1984).

Table 10.4   Itemization Status of U.S. Homeowners, 1985

	Millions	Percentage
Number of homeowners	56.2	
Number of homeowners with mortgages	32.2	57.3
Number of tax returns with mortgage deduction	28.1	50.0
Number of tax returns with real estate tax deduction	32.1	57.1

Source: Rows 1 and 2 are from U.S. Bureau of the Census, *Housing in America 1985/86*, Current Housing Report H-121, no. 19. Tax information is drawn from the *1985 Statistics of Income: Individual Income Tax Returns.*

1984, when the rate reductions of 1981 had taken full effect, this average tax rate was 28 percent.[4]

The user cost summarizes the tax code's influence on housing costs. To define the subsidy, however, it is useful to compute the user cost that would obtain if imputed income from owner-occupied housing were taxed but deductions for mortgage interest and property taxes were still allowed, *and* depreciation and maintenance expenses became deductible:

$$(4) \qquad C_o' = [i + \tau_p + \delta + m + \alpha - \pi_e]P_o.$$

Table 10.5 reports the user cost of home ownership for households at three income levels at various times during the last decade. It presents both the user cost under the prevailing tax rules and the hypothetical user cost if the tax system did not provide a subsidy. The first panel considers the user cost for a fixed pattern of interest and expected inflation rates, thereby identifying the effect of tax changes. The second panel evaluates the tax code of several selected years since 1980, using interest and expected inflation rates that prevailed at that time, thus indicating the net change in incentives for home ownership.[5] Other auxiliary parameters, such as the property tax rate and the cost of maintaining the home, are assumed constant throughout the calculations.

The results illustrate that recent reforms had their most pronounced effect on the cost of home ownership for high-income households. For a family with adjusted gross income (AGI) of $250,000 in 1988, the Tax Reform Act of 1986 lowered the marginal tax rate from .50 to .28 and raised the user cost of home ownership from .094 to .114, assuming the base case with an interest rate of 7 percent and 3 percent expected inflation rate.[6] The actual change in the user

---

4. These estimates are based on data reported in IRS (1980, 1984).

5. The first set of user cost changes reflects the effects of tax reform but in a counterfactual setting, while the second convolutes the effects of tax changes with the effects of other shocks, for example changes in monetary policy, that are unrelated to the tax system. A more complete analysis would involve general equilibrium analysis of tax policy, in particular with an endogenous real interest rate.

6. The reform would have to lower real interest rates by nearly three hundred basis points to offset the lost value of tax deductions.

Table 10.5   **User Costs of Owner-Occupied Property, 1980–88**

	1980	1982	1984	1986	1988
Case 1: Fixed parameters $i = .07$, $\pi_e = .03$					
User cost of home ownership					
1988 AGI = $25,000	.120	.122	.125	.125	.126
1988 AGI = $45,000	.110	.113	.117	.117	.114
1988 AGI = $250,000	.081	.094	.094	.094	.114
No-tax case	.129	.129	.129	.129	.129
Case 2: Prevailing interest and inflation rate					
User cost of home ownership					
1988 AGI = $25,000	.080	.094	.098	.115	.109
1988 AGI = $45,000	.064	.077	.089	.104	.095
1988 AGI = $250,000	.017	.042	.049	.074	.095
No-tax case	.141	.157	.151	.175	.156
Parameter values					
Nominal rate	.127	.151	.124	.103	.091
Expected inflation	.085	.093	.072	.037	.034

Notes: Calculations for both cases assume $\tau_p = .02$, $\delta = .014$, $\alpha = .04$, and $m = .025$. AGI = adjusted gross income.

cost of home ownership since 1986, recognizing variations in interest rates and inflationary expectations, is from .074 to .095 for this household. Assuming a price elasticity of demand of -1.0 for owner-occupied housing,[7] this tax change could have large effects on both demand and house prices.

The post-1986 change in user costs for high-income households, however, is small relative to the change from the beginning of the 1980s, when the estimated user cost was .017. The large change in the early 1980s is due to rising real interest rates, falling inflation rates, which raised the after-tax cost of borrowing because the tax system is not indexed, and declining marginal tax rates. The effect of rate reductions on home-ownership incentives for those in lower income brackets is much smaller, since the decline in tax rates in the 1986 reform was less pronounced. For the household with AGI of $25,000 in 1988, the tax reform lowered the marginal tax rate from 16 percent to 15 percent and raised the user cost (in the benchmark case) from .125 to .126. Some middle-income households, such as the $45,000 example presented here, even experienced increases in their marginal tax rates, and for them housing costs increased.

The 1986 tax reform also raised the standard deduction, reducing the fraction of the population who would itemize if they were not homeowners and raising the average cost of home ownership. For a joint filer, the standard deduction rose from $3,670 to $5,000. Higher standard deductions reduce the

---

7. Rosen (1986) and Olsen (1987) survey the voluminous housing demand literature.

incentive for a household to own, but conditional on deciding to own, they do not affect the marginal cost of additional housing services.

In both panels of table 10.5, the last row indicates the user cost of home ownership, assuming no tax distortions. For the case of a fixed inflation and interest rate, in the upper panel, the costs in all years and for all households would be .129. This implies that the tax code in 1980 reduced the user cost by 14 percent for middle-income ($45,000) households and by 12 percent for the same households in 1988. At the very high income levels, however, the subsidy is much larger. The user cost was 37 percent below the no-tax level for the $250,000 household in 1980, but only 12 percent below the no-tax cost in 1988. Again using a price elasticity of demand of -1.0 for housing services, these values imply at least a 10 percent increase in the owner-occupied housing stock as a result of the tax subsidies.[8]

10.3.2   Tax Subsidies to Rental Property

The tax system is also a critical determinant of the net incentives for rental housing investment. In analyzing the tax subsidies to rental housing, there are virtually no tax benefits to renters but substantial tax benefits directed at rental landlords. The summary statistic for policy incentives toward rental property is therefore the landlord's user cost of rental housing. This is defined as

$$(5) \qquad c_r = \{[(1 - \tau)i + \delta + \alpha - \pi_e](1 - \tau z)/(1 - \tau) + \tau_p + m\}P_r,$$

where the parameters not defined above are τ, the marginal income tax rate of the rental landlord; P_r, the real price of rental property; and z, the present value of tax depreciation allowances.[9] In equilibrium, the rent charged must equal c_r so that the landlord is willing to hold the rental property.

The tax incentives with respect to owner occupation for a given household are straightforward to measure, since they depend on that household's tax parameters. The tax subsidies to rental housing are more complex, because they depend on the tax rates of the "marginal rental landlord" whose tax parameters determine the marketwide rental rate. There is disagreement on the identity of the marginal rental landlord; this translates into uncertainty about the parameter τ in the user cost expression. Some studies, such as Titman (1982) and Scholes, Terry, and Wolfson (1989), assume that the landlord is a top-bracket individual investor. Such an investor receives maximum advantage from the depreciation allowances on rental property, since these allowances generate deductions, which reduce taxable income. If the marginal supplier of funds to the rental industry is in a lower tax bracket, however, this will reduce the value

8. Part of the tax subsidy to owner-occupied housing will be reflected in higher land values, thus blunting the subsidy effects described here.

9. Equation (5) treats the government as sharing the risk associated with rental investments, an assumption that may be incorrect. If the government is not a partner to such risk, the α term would no longer be multiplied by $(1 - \tau z)/(1 - \tau)$.

Table 10.6   **Depreciation Provisions for Residential Structures, 1969–88**

	Lifetime (years)	Depreciation Schedule
1969–81	32	150% declining balance
1981–84	15	175% declining balance
1984–85	18	175% declining balance
1985–86	19	175% declining balance
1986–	27.5	Straight line

Source: Author's compilation, based on U.S. Internal Revenue Code.

of these deductions and therefore raise equilibrium rents.[10] Particularly when the dispersion of marginal tax rates is large, as it was prior to the 1981 tax reform, assumptions about the identity of the marginal landlord significantly affect estimated user costs.

Tax depreciation benefits are a critical part of the net subsidy to rental housing. Table 10.6 shows the recent history of depreciation policy for rental property. The 1981 Economic Recovery Tax Act (ERTA) shortened the tax lifetime for residential rental property from 32 to 15 years.[11] The 1986 Tax Reform Act reversed this policy, extending the lifetime to 27.5 years and requiring straight-line depreciation rather than more accelerated 175 percent declining balance. The reduction in marginal tax rates in 1981 partly counteracted the expanded depreciation benefits in the ERTA, but in 1986 less generous depreciation rules combined with lower marginal tax rates to significantly reduce the value of depreciation benefits. Since the present value of depreciation tax benefits is a key consideration in rental investment decisions, real rents should increase because of the 1986 Tax Reform Act.[12]

The net incentive to invest in rental property is also affected by a variety of other tax code provisions, notably the capital gains tax rate and the tax rules designed to curb investment in tax shelters. A substantial fraction of the returns to property investment accrue as capital gains, so the tax reform in 1986 which *raised* the capital gains rate was unfavorable for rental housing. In addition, the Tax Reform Act of 1986 included several provisions designed to restrict

10. Gravelle (1985) argues that corporations, not individuals, are the marginal suppliers of capital to the rental housing industry. Poterba (1987) reports that corporations held only 4.5 percent of residential rental property in 1985, compared with 38.6 percent for partnerships and sole proprietorships, which are taxed at individual rates. The relative unimportance of corporate investors casts doubt on the view that they are price-setters in this market.

11. Hendershott (1987) discusses in detail the changes in depreciation provisions and their likely effects.

12. The measurement of the present discounted value of depreciation allowances is complicated because buildings may be depreciated more than once. Particularly during inflationary periods when there are substantial gains to selling a building and redepreciating its increased nominal basis, investors may "churn" their properties. This can substantially increase the present value of depreciation allowances for investors in rental property, lowering the user cost and the equilibrium rent demanded by landlords. Gordon, Hines, and Summers (1987) discuss this possibility.

Table 10.7   Rental User Costs, 1980–88

Economic Assumptions	1980	1982	1984	1986	1988
$i = .07, \pi_e = .03$	.126[a]	.116	.117	.118	.132
Actual economic conditions	.059	.096	.104	.137	.149

Note: Rental user costs assume no churning, with marginal tax rates for the rental landlord of .50 in 1980–86 and .28 in 1988. See table 10.5 for definition of "actual economic conditions."

[a]This entry is notable because it does *not* assume the highest possible marginal tax rate for the rental landlord; it assumes a 50 percent rather than a 70 percent marginal rate. At the 70 percent rate, this value would be .117.

tax shelter investments, including investments in real estate. New limitations on using tax shelter losses to offset other types of income discouraged high-leverage rental projects, because the interest deductions in these projects were no longer as valuable to their investors. In part as a result of these provisions, there was a 37 percent real decline in real estate partnership sales between 1985 and 1988.

Table 10.7 reports estimates of the user cost of rental housing at several dates during the last decade. Assuming that the marginal supplier of rental units was an individual in the top marginal tax bracket, the rental user cost rose from .137 to .149, or 9 percent, between 1986 and 1988. The increase would have been larger if the real interest rate had not declined during this period. The change in user costs in the early 1980s is smaller. If the nominal interest rate and expected inflation rate had been at their 1980 levels in 1982, rental user costs would have declined from .096 (assuming a landlord tax rate of 50 percent in 1980) to .089, or by 7.3 percent. The increase in real interest rates between 1980 and 1982, however, counteracted this effect, so the reported user costs in table 10.7 show virtually no change.[13]

The results for rental user costs during the late 1980s are sensitive to different assumptions about the "marginal investors" in rental properties. If corporations are the marginal suppliers of rental housing, for example, then the adverse effects of the 1986 Tax Reform Act on real rents would be much smaller. Corporate investors face smaller reductions in marginal tax rates and are less affected by passive loss limits, than are individual investors.

It is essential to recognize the partial-equilibrium nature of the foregoing calculations. The net incentive for investing in housing capitals depends not only on the tax treatment of housing, but on the *relative* tax burdens on housing and other assets. Housing had historically been a lightly taxed asset, and the

13. If the marginal investor in rental property in 1980 was in the 70 percent tax bracket, then the net change from 1980 to 1982 is an *increase* in rental user costs, since the reduction in the landlord's tax rate outweighs the increasingly generous depreciation provisions.

1986 reform raised the tax burden on corporate assets. Thus the present policy regime provides substantial net subsidies to housing.

10.4   Policies Affecting Financial Markets

A second set of policies that affect housing markets operates through credit markets. There are three important sets of policies in this regard. The first are mortgage guarantees, which are designed to provide housing assistance to households purchasing particular types of homes. The second are subsidies to the institutions that facilitate the secondary market for mortgages, enabling capital to flow to housing lenders. The third set of subsidies are benefits, now largely of historical interest, to the lenders such as thrift institutions who typically provided mortgage finance. This section considers each type of subsidy in turn.

10.4.1   Targeted Mortgage Assistance

There are three significant federal mortgage subsidy programs, operated by the Federal Housing Administration (FHA), the Veterans Administration (VA), and the Farmers Home Administration. The FHA is the largest program. It began in 1934, with the passage of the National Housing Act, in an effort to reduce volatility in the housing industry and to improve housing affordability. The FHA provided insurance on loans with higher loan-to-value ratios than conventional lenders, and offered longer-term loans than had been commonly available. Before the FHA, the primary mortgage on most homes had a maturity of five years or less (Wiedemer 1990, 124); the FHA popularized twenty-year level-payment mortgages.

The principal benefit of an FHA-insured mortgage, from the home buyer's perspective, is that it provides mortgage credit on more favorable terms than the private market would provide. In some cases, the FHA insurance may enable borrowers who would otherwise have been denied mortgage credit to obtain a loan. FHA provisions also enable many households to borrow with a smaller down payment than lenders typically require.

There are limits on the dollar value of the mortgages that can receive FHA assistance. In 1988, the maximum permissible loan was $101,250, compared with a median new home price of $112,500. The upper bound on the loan value as a share of the purchase price (including some costs of the housing transaction) for existing houses is 97 percent of the first $25,000, plus 95 percent of the value above $25,000. For new houses, the limit is 90 percent of the purchase price. Particularly for existing homes, the limits are higher than many commercial lenders would permit, thereby enhancing access to home ownership. Since 1982, there have been no limits on the interest rates that lenders can charge on FHA loans.

The program described above is the FHA section 203(b) program, which is the largest FHA initiative to provide mortgage financing. The VA and Farmers

Table 10.8   Volume of Guaranteed Mortgage Originations, 1978–89 (%)

Year	FHA Mortgages	VA Mortgages	Conventional Mortgages
1978	7.9	8.7	83.5
1979	11.1	10.1	78.8
1980	11.2	9.0	79.8
1981	10.7	7.7	81.6
1982	11.8	7.9	80.2
1983	14.2	9.4	76.4
1984	8.1	5.9	85.9
1985	11.7	6.4	81.9
1986	13.6	6.8	79.6
1987	11.4	4.9	83.7
1988	8.5	3.4	88.1
1989	9.8	2.9	87.1

Source: National Association of Home Builders, The Current Housing Situation, December 1990.

Home Administration programs are similar in character to those at the FHA. In the last decade, FHA has also broadened its activities to allow graduated payment mortgages and a variety of other new mortgage designs, all directed at encouraging broader participation in owner-occupied housing.

In 1989, the FHA, Farmers Home Administration, and VA insured approximately one-quarter of all new mortgages.[14] With the exception of just under 10 percent of home buyers who pay cash for their houses, the remaining mortgages are conventional loans. Table 10.8 reports the relative importance of FHA and VA mortgages as a share of all new mortgage *dollar* originations. These loans accounted for only 13 percent of the total in 1989; they are a smaller share of value than number of loans because they tend to be smaller loans than conventional financings. The table also shows that federally insured loans have become a less important part of the total mortgage pool over time. In 1980, these loans were more than 20 percent of all new mortgage debt. The decline is apparently the result of house prices rising more rapidly than FHA loan limits, making the houses that can be financed by FHA a smaller share of the total stock. This is consistent with the stated goals of housing policy in the 1980s, discussed for example in Struyk, Mayer, and Tuccillo (1983), of reducing transfer programs to the middle class.

10.4.2   Mortgage Market Support

The second component of federal support for the mortgage market operates through the securitization process, the process by which individual mortgages are repackaged into "mortgage-backed securities" and then sold to secondary

14. Data are drawn from the National Association of Homebuilders, *The Current Housing Situation*, December 1990.

market investors. Until the early 1970s, regulated thrift institutions were the principal source of funds for home mortgages lending. These financial intermediaries benefited from regulatory limits on the interest rates that could be paid at their competitor commercial banks. With a virtually assured supply of saving at low interest rates, thrifts were able to supply mortgage loans at reasonable rates. The federal insurance on deposits at thrifts was a partial compensation to depositors for the regulated rates of return. Even before the 1970s, FHA and VA loans had been sold to secondary market buyers. This was possible because these loans were relatively homogeneous, and because the presence of federal guarantees made them riskless investments, appealing to a wide range of investors.

The emergence of an active secondary market for non-FHA mortgages was the result of initiatives by the Federal National Mortgage Association (FNMA) in the early 1970s. The FNMA and Federal Home Loan Mortgage Corporation (FHLMC, a new institution created in 1970) together established industry standards with respect to documentation and credit qualification, which ultimately permitted rapid expansion of the secondary mortgage market. Neither of these organizations have federal guarantees behind their borrowing; they are quasi-governmental agencies, and while many investors expect that default is impossible because the federal government would intervene to prevent it, this is not a legal promise. Today conventional mortgages are repackaged by FNMA, FHLMC, and a variety of other financial intermediaries. Many investors who would not hold particular mortgages are active participants in the secondary mortgage markets, and funnel capital to the housing sector.

Assessing the effect of public policy on the securitization process, and ultimately on housing markets, is difficult. Hendershott and Van Order (1989) analyze the effect of integration of the non-FHA mortgage markets with broader capital markets. They conclude that the rise of pass-through securities backed by mortgages has reduced the volatility of new residential construction, but not altered the *average* level of new construction very much.

10.4.3   Federal Subsidies to the Thrift Industry

A final set of institutions, which have had important influence historically but are of shrinking importance prospectively, are government subsidies to savings and loans. These financial intermediaries benefited from federal deposit guarantees and were able to attract funds at lower rates than the riskiness of their investments should have allowed. Until 1980, federal regulation of interest rates that could be paid by the important competitors to these institutions ensured their supply of funds. Financial deregulation, combined with the high nominal interest rates of the early 1980s and the depressed real estate market in some regions in the late 1980s, removed thrifts as central actors in the housing finance process. By the late 1980s, however, the federal Resolution Trust

Corporation was closing thrifts at which the value of deposit insurance was especially large (i.e., those with very weak financial positions), and the share of mortgage financing accounted for by thrift institutions was shrinking. Nevertheless, the system of regulated deposit rates and deposit insurance undoubtedly contributed to some increase in the U.S. residential capital stock.

10.5   Targeted Housing Subsidies: Public Housing

A final dimension of public policy toward housing is the montage of income support and in-kind transfer programs designed to provide housing to low-income households. There are two types of public housing programs: those that target construction of housing units for low-income households (project-based aid), and those that provide support to households and allow them to choose their own units (household-based aid). During the last decade, federal policy has shifted toward providing household-based support.

The two most important project-based aid programs are the public housing program and the section 8 new construction program. Public housing funds support the construction of multifamily dwellings targeted at the low-income population. These projects are usually managed by the local governments, which operate the units when they are completed. These programs were sharply curtailed in the early 1980s since they did not involve market-based determination of resource allocation, a principle that the Reagan administration sought to introduce to all aspects of transfer policy. These reductions continued a trend away from project aid that began a decade earlier, with concern that public housing projects were of low quality and had some proclivity toward becoming ghettos.

Table 10.9 presents information on the importance of public housing programs at the height of their utilization, at the beginning of the 1980s. Most public housing was built in urban areas, so the table focuses on the share of the housing stock in major U.S. cities that was accounted for by public units. In many of the largest metropolitan areas, public housing accounted for more than 5 percent of all rental units. The share of public housing has declined during the subsequent decade.

Table 10.9	Share of Public Housing in Rental Housing Stock, U.S. Cities, 1980 (%)			
	New York	5.6	Washington, DC	5.9
	Chicago	5.4	San Francisco	2.4
	Los Angeles	1.1	Cleveland	8.6
	Philadelphia	9.0	Boston	8.0
	Detroit	5.0	St. Louis	5.9
	Houston	0.9	Seattle	5.4
	Baltimore	10.3	Denver	4.5
	Indianapolis	2.3	Atlanta	14.6

Source: Struyk 1980, table 2.

Table 10.10   Public Housing Starts and Other Housing Starts, 1977–88 (in
                     thousands)

	Public Housing Starts	Total starts (public + private)
1977	14.6	2001.7
1978	15.8	2036.1
1979	14.8	1760.0
1980	20.4	1312.6
1981	16.1	1100.3
1982	9.8	1072.0
1983	9.4	1712.5
1984	6.3	1755.8
1985	3.1	1745.0
1986	1.7	1807.1
1987	2.2	1622.7

Source: U.S. Department of Commerce, *Construction Review,* various issues.

Table 10.10 shows the trajectory of public housing starts during the last decade. In the late 1970s and early 1980s, public housing starts averaged between 1 and 2 percent of all new housing starts in the United States. By the second half of the 1980s, however, they had declined to a trivial flow of new construction.

The program that expanded as public housing contracted was the section 8 new construction program. In this program, a private developer who is undertaking new construction receives a federal commitment that, in return for housing low-income households, the government will insure rental payments for some period (typically twenty years). The low-income recipients of section 8 assistance may not spend more than 30 percent of their income on housing, and the federal government pays the difference between that amount and each unit's contract rent. Developers building low-income units can also avail themselves of favorable financing opportunities, for example, by financing their project with federally insured Government National Mortgage Associations (GNMA) loans. A developer who plans to significantly renovate an existing property can qualify for the same guarantee.

The second category of public housing aid programs, household-based programs, provide support for particular individuals or households and typically supplement their rental payments to avoid excessively high shares of income being spent on housing. The single most important program in this dimension is section 8 housing assistance. After a household qualifies for a section 8 certificate, it is free to select any rental unit that rents for less than the "fair market rent" specified by the section 8 program. The federal government then pays the difference between rental costs and the household's estimated rent-paying capacity. In a variation on this program, the household receives a housing voucher and faces no limits on subsequent outlays. The voucher is treated just like cash in purchasing housing services, so the household could choose to spend more than fair market rent but would bear the full marginal cost of such outlays.

To illustrate the changing composition of public housing programs in the United States, it is useful to compare the programs in 1978 and 1988. Table 10.11 provides data on the basic structure of housing assistance. In 1977, of 3.163 million households receiving assistance, 2.092 million were renters. Within this group, 1.825 million were receiving benefits that resulted from new federally supported construction (public housing), while only 268,000 received support for finding their own units in the standard market.

By 1988, the pattern had shifted radically. Of 4.296 million renter households receiving assistance, nearly one-third were receiving assistance to acquire housing units in the open market. While the number of assisted renter households rose sharply during the decade, the number of assisted homeowners remained stable at 1.082 million in 1978, and 1.059 million in 1988.

Total federal outlays for housing programs are noted in table 10.12, which shows the decline in federal commitment to this area. The table reports *budget authority,* which includes all projected outlays in multiyear building commitments. One important feature of U.S. housing policy during the 1980s has been a shift from long-term federal commitments to shorter projects, leading to smaller budget authorization for a given number of households served. The result is that average annual outlays throughout most of the 1980s remained higher than in previous decades, in spite of falling budget authority.

The 1980s witnessed an important refocusing of U.S. housing assistance policy. Programs were targeted more precisely toward low-income households, to the exclusion of lower-middle-income households who received benefits in

Table 10.11   Households Receiving Federal Housing Aid, 1977–88 (in thousands)

	Net New Commitments		Households Receiving Assistance	
	Renters	Owners	Renters	Owners
1977	375.2	112.2	2092	1071
1978	341.0	112.2	2400	1082
1979	333.8	107.9	2654	1095
1980	213.4	140.6	2895	1112
1981	178.4	74.6	3012	1127
1982	86.0	66.7	3210	1201
1983	77.9	54.6	3443	1226
1984	115.4	44.4	3700	1219
1985	128.4	45.4	3887	1193
1986	119.9	25.5	3998	1176
1987	110.0	24.1	4175	1126
1988	107.7	26.6	4296	1059

Source: U.S. House Ways and Means Committee, *Background Material and Data on Programs within the Jurisdiction of the House Ways and Means Committee* (1989), 1157–58.

Table 10.12   **Federal Appropriations for Housing Assistance, 1977–88 (in millions of 1987 dollars)**

1977	50.3	1983	11.5
1978	52.9	1984	12.7
1979	38.0	1985	12.0
1980	38.2	1986	10.3
1981	32.9	1987	9.0
1982	17.4	1988	8.8

Source: U.S. House Ways and Means Committee, *Background Material and Data on Programs within the Jurisdiction of the House Ways and Means Committee* (1989), 1157–58.

prior decades. The strategy of public provision of housing services, which had been the basis for housing policy in the 1960s and 1970s, was largely abandoned and replaced by a variety of transfer programs that take advantage of market mechanisms to deliver housing assistance. Government programs remain an important influence on the quality and affordability of housing for low-income households.

10.6 Conclusions

Public policy toward housing has undergone radical changes in the United States during the last decade. Until the early 1980s, the tax system treated housing more generously than other assets, credit institutions that supplied mortgage financing received public subsidies not available to other financial institutions, and all levels of government were active participants in building and subsidizing housing units for low-income households. The net effect of these subsidies was a strong incentive for housing capital accumulation. With these policies in place, the home-ownership rate in the United States rose for nearly four decades after World War II, and housing capital became a larger share of the nation's tangible asset stock.

A variety of policy changes during the 1980s weakened the policy bias toward housing. The net effect of the tax reforms in 1981 and 1986 was a reduction in the tax incentives for rental housing construction, and some diminution of owner-occupied housing's tax-favored status in comparison to other investments. Deregulation of financial institutions, notably removal of interest-rate restrictions on competitors to saving and loan institutions and evolving changes in deposit insurance, has reduced the supply of saving to housing-oriented institutions and integrated the housing finance market with other parts of the capital market. At the same time, federal budgetary pressures led to cutbacks in direct federal housing programs, with limited prospects for future expansion. These changes have reduced the prohousing bias of U.S. public housing policy, although they have not eliminated it.

References

Gordon, Roger H., James R. Hines, and Lawrence H. Summers. 1987. Notes on the Tax Treatment of Structures. In M. Feldstein, ed., *The Effects of Taxation on Capital Formation.* Chicago: University of Chicago Press.

Gravelle, Jane G. 1985. U.S. Tax Policy and Rental Housing: An Economic Analysis. Congressional Research Service, working paper.

Hendershott, Patric H. 1987. Tax Changes and Capital Allocation in the 1980s. In M. Feldstein, ed., *The Effects of Taxation on Capital Formation.* Chicago: University of Chicago Press.

Hendershott, Patric H., and Robert Van Order. 1989. Integration of Mortgage and Capital Markets and the Accumulation of Residential Capital. *Regional Science and Urban Economics* 19:188–210.

Olsen, Edgar O. 1987. The Demand and Supply of Housing Service: A Critical Survey of the Empirical Literature. In Edwin S. Mills, ed., *Handbook of Regional and Urban Economics,* vol. 2. Amsterdam: North-Holland.

Poterba, James M. 1984. Tax Subsidies to Owner-Occupied Housing: An Asset-Market Approach. *Quarterly Journal of Economics* 99: 729–52.

———. 1987. Tax Reform and Residential Investment Incentives. In *Proceedings of the National Tax Association-Tax Institute of America,* 112–19. May.

———. 1989. Lifetime Incidence and the Distributional Burden of Excise Taxes. *American Economic Review* 79 (May): 325–30.

Rosen, Harvey S. 1986. Housing Subsidies: Effects on Housing Decisions, Efficiency, and Equity. In M. Feldstein and A. Auerbach, eds., *Handbook of Public Economics,* 1:375–420. (Amsterdam: North-Holland).

Scholes, Myron, Eric Terry, and Mark Wolfson. 1989. Tax Policy in a Complex and Dynamic Economic Environment: Challenges and Opportunities. Mimeo. Stanford University.

Struyk, Raymond J. 1980. *A New System for Public Housing: Salvaging a National Resource.* Washington, DC: Urban Institute Press.

Struyk, Raymond J., Neil Mayer, and John Tucillo. 1983. *Rental Housing in the 1980s.* Washington, DC: Urban Institute.

Titman, Sheridan. 1982. The Effects of Anticipated Inflation on Housing Market Equilibrium. *Journal of Finance* 37:827–42.

U.S. Treasury. Internal Revenue Service. 1980. *Statistics of Income: Individual Income Tax Returns, 1980.* Washington, DC: U.S. Government Printing Office.

———. 1984. *Statistics of Income: Individual Income Tax Returns, 1984.* Washington, DC: U.S. Government Printing Office.

Venti, Steven, and David Wise. 1989. Aging, Moving, and Housing Wealth. In David Wise, ed., *The Economics of Aging.* Chicago: University of Chicago Press.

Wiedemer, John P. 1990. *Real Estate Finance.* 6th edition. Englewood Cliffs, NJ: Prentice Hall.

Contributors

Karl E. Case
Marion Butler McLean Professor
Department of Economics
Wellesley College
Wellesley, MA 02181

Tatsuo Hatta
Institute of Social and Economic
  Research
Osaka University
Ibaraki
Osaka 567, Japan

Patric H. Hendershott
Department of Finance
Hagerty Hall
Ohio State University
1775 South College Road
Columbus, Ohio 43210

Takatoshi Ito
Hitotsubashi University
Kunitachi
Tokyo 186, Japan

Yukio Noguchi
Department of Economics
Hitotsubashi University
2-1, Naka, Kunitachi-shi
Tokyo 186, Japan

Toru Ohkawara
Economic Research Center
Central Research Institute of Electric
  Power Industry
1-6-1, Otemachi, Chiyoda-ku
Tokyo 100, Japan

James M. Poterba
Department of Economics
Room E52-350
Massachusetts Institute of Technology
50 Memorial Drive
Cambridge, MA 02139

Miki Seko
College of Economics
Nihon University
1-3-2, Misaki-cho, Chiyoda-ku
Tokyo 101, Japan

Jonathan Skinner
Department of Economics
Rouss Hall
University of Virginia
Charlottesville, VA 22901

Toshiaki Tachibanaki
Institute of Economic Research
Kyoto University
Yoshida Hon-machi
Sakyo-ku
Kyoto-shi 606, Japan

Michelle J. White
Department of Economics
University of Michigan
Ann Arbor, MI 48109

Author Index

Subject Index